TEXTS IN CO

Editors
David Gries
Fred B. Schneider

Springer
New York
Berlin
Heidelberg
Hong Kong
London
Milan
Paris
Tokyo

TEXTS IN COMPUTER SCIENCE

(continued after index)

Steven S. Skiena   Miguel A. Revilla

PROGRAMMING CHALLENGES

The Programming Contest Training Manual

With 65 Illustrations

Springer

Steven S. Skiena
Department of Computer Science
SUNY Stony Brook
Stony Brook, NY 11794-4400, USA
skiena@programming-challenges.com

Miguel A. Revilla
Department of Applied Mathematics
   and Computer Science
Faculty of Sciences
University of Valladolid
Valladolid, 47011, SPAIN
revilla@programming-challenges.com

Series Editors:
David Gries
Department of Computer Science
415 Boyd Graduate Studies
   Research Center
The University of Georgia
Athens, GA 30602-7404, USA

Fred B. Schneider
Department of Computer Science
Upson Hall
Cornell University
Ithaca, NY 14853-7501, USA

Cover illustration: "Spectator," by William Rose © 2002.

Library of Congress Cataloging-in-Publication Data
Skeina, Steven S.
   Programming challenges : the programming contest training manual / Steven S. Skiena,
Miguel A. Revilla.
      p.   cm. — (Texts in computer science)
   Includes bibliographical references and index.
   ISBN 0-387-00163-8 (softcover : alk. paper)
   1. Computer programming.   I. Revilla, Miguel A.   II. Title.   III. Series.
   QA76.6.S598   2003
   005.1—dc21   2002044523

ISBN 0-387-00163-8   Printed on acid-free paper.

Printed in the United States of America.

9 8 7 6 5 4 3 2 1   SPIN 10901052

Photocomposed pages prepared by the author using Springer-Verlag's L^ATEX macros.

www.springer-ny.com

Springer-Verlag   New York Berlin Heidelberg
A member of BertelsmannSpringer Science+Business Media GmbH

To our wives, Renee and Carmela,
and children, Bonnie, Emilio, and Miguel.

The challenges in this book
are not nearly as difficult
as the challenge of making enough time
for those who we love.

Preface

There are many distinct pleasures associated with computer programming. Craftsmanship has its quiet rewards, the satisfaction that comes from building a useful object and making it work. Excitement arrives with the flash of insight that cracks a previously intractable problem. The spiritual quest for elegance can turn the hacker into an artist. There are pleasures in parsimony, in squeezing the last drop of performance out of clever algorithms and tight coding.

The games, puzzles, and challenges of problems from international programming competitions are a great way to experience these pleasures while improving your algorithmic and coding skills. This book contains over 100 problems that have appeared in previous programming contests, along with discussions of the theory and ideas necessary to attack them. Instant online grading for all of these problems is available from two WWW robot judging sites. Combining this book with a judge gives an exciting new way to challenge and improve your programming skills.

This book can be used for self-study, for teaching innovative courses in algorithms and programming, and in training for international competition.

To the Reader

The problems in this book have been selected from over 1,000 programming problems at the Universidad de Valladolid online judge, available at *http://online-judge.uva.es*. The judge has ruled on well over one million submissions from 27,000 registered users around the world to date. We have taken only the best of the best, the most fun, exciting, and interesting problems available.

We have organized these problems by topic and provided enough tutorial material (primarily in mathematics and algorithms) to give you a fair chance to solve them.

Sample programs are provided to illustrate many important concepts. By reading this book and trying the problems you will gain a concrete understanding of algorithmic techniques such as backtracking and dynamic programming, and advanced topics such as number theory and computational geometry. These subjects are well worth your attention even if you never intend to compete in programming contests.

Many of the problems are flat-out fun. They address fascinating topics in computer science and mathematics, sometimes disguised by an amusing story. These make interesting subjects for additional study, so we provide notes with further readings where appropriate.

We have found that people whose training is in the pragmatics of programming and software engineering often fail to appreciate the power of algorithmics. Similarly, the theoretically inclined typically underestimate what it takes to turn an algorithm into a program, and how clever programming can make short work of a tough problem.

For this reason, the first portion of the book focuses primarily on programming techniques, such as the proper use of data types and program libraries. This lays the foundation for the more algorithmic sections in the second part of the book. Mastery of both is required to be a complete problem solver.

To the Instructor

This book has been designed to serve as a textbook for three types of courses:

- Algorithm courses focusing on programming.

- Programming courses focusing on algorithms.

- Elective courses designed to train students to participate in competitions such as the Association for Computing Machinery (ACM) International Collegiate Programming Contest and the International Olympiad in Informatics.

Such courses can be a lot of fun for all involved. Students are easily motivated by the thrill of competition, and get positive feedback each time the judge accepts their solution. The most obvious algorithm may result in a "Time Limit Exceeded" message from the judge, thus motivating a search for efficiency. The correct insight can make for a dozen-line program instead of a huge mass of code. The best students will be inspired to try extra problems just for kicks.

Such courses are fun to teach, too. Many problems are quite clever, putting a fresh face on standard topics in programming and algorithms. Finding the best solution requires insight and inspiration. It is exciting to figure out the right way to do each of the problems, and even more exciting when the students figure it out for themselves.

Pedagogical features of this book include:

- *Complements Standard Algorithm Texts* — Although this book is self-contained, it has been written with the understanding that most students will have some prior exposure to algorithm design. This book has been designed (and priced) so it can serve as a supplementary text for traditional algorithms courses, complementing abstract descriptions with concrete implementations and theoretical analysis with hands-on experience. Further, it covers several interesting topics that are not universally included in standard algorithm texts.

- *Provides Complete Implementations of Classical Algorithms* — Many students have a difficult time going from abstract algorithm descriptions to working code. To help them, we provide carefully written implementations of all important algorithms we discuss using a subset of C designed to be easily readable by C++ and Java programmers. Several of our programming challenge problems can be solved by appropriately modifying these routines, thus providing a concrete path to get students started.

- *Integrated Course Management Environment* — We have created a special course management environment that makes it shamefully easy to administer such a course, as it will handle all testing and grading for you! Our website *http://www.programming-challenges.com* lets you assign problems to students, maintain rosters, view each student's score and programs, and even detect suspicious similarity among their solutions!

- *Help for Students at All Levels* — The challenges included in this book have been selected to span a wide range of difficulty. Many are suitable for introductory students, while others will prove challenging to those ready for international competition. Hints for most problems are provided.

  To help identify the most appropriate problems for any given student, we have annotated each problem with three distinct measures of difficulty. The *popularity* of a problem (A, B, or C) refers to how many people try it, while the *success rate* (low to high) measures how often they succeed. Finally, the *level* of a problem (1 to 4, corresponding roughly from freshman to senior) indicates how advanced a student needs to be in order to have a fair chance of solving the problem.

To the Coach or Competitor

This book has been particularly designed to serve as a training manual for programming competitions at the high school and collegiate levels. We provide a convenient summary/reference of important topics in mathematics and algorithms, along with appropriate challenges to help you master the material.

The robot judge checks the correctness of submitted programs just like the human judges of the ACM International Collegiate Programming Contest. Once you set up a personal account with the judge, you can submit solutions written in C, C++, Pascal, or Java and wait for the verdict announcing success or failure. The judge keeps statistics on how you are doing, so you can compare yourself to the thousands of other participants.

To help the competitor, we include an appendix with training secrets from finalists for the three major programming contest venues: the ACM International Collegiate Programming Contest (ICPC), the International Olympiad in Informatics (IOI), and the TopCoder Programmer Challenge. We present the history of these competitions, show how you can get involved, and help you make your best possible showing.

Roughly 80% of all finalists in the most recent ACM contest trained on the Universidad de Valladolid online judge. That the finals are held in exotic locals like Hawaii provides extra incentive to study. Good luck!

Associated Websites

This book has been designed to work hand-in-hand with two websites. Online grading for all problems is available at *http://www.programming-challenges.com*, along with lots of supporting material. In particular, we provide complete source code of all the programs that appear in the text as well as lecture notes to help integrate this material into courses.

All of the problems in this book (and many, many more) can also be graded by the Universidad de Valladolid online judge, *http://online-judge.uva.es*. In particular each programming challenge in this book has been given an ID number on both judging websites, so you can take advantage of their special features.

Acknowledgments

The existence of this book is due in great part to the generosity of all the people who let us incorporate their contest problems into the robot judge as well as in this book. No less than 17 people contributed problems to this volume, from four different continents. We are particularly indebted to Gordon Cormack and Shahriar Manzoor, problem posers on the scale of Sam Loyd and H. E. Dudeney!

A complete mapping of people to problems appears in the appendix, but we particularly thank the following contest organizers for their contributions: Gordon Cormack (38 problems), Shahriar Manzoor (28), Miguel Revilla (10), Pedro Demasi (8), Manuel Carro (4), Rujia Liu (4), Petko Minkov (4), Owen Astrakan (3), Alexander Denisjuk (3), Long Chong (2), Ralf Engels (2), Alex Gevak (1), Walter Guttmann (1), Arun Kishore (1), Erick Moreno (1), Udvranto Patik (1), and Marcin Wojciechowski (1). Several of these problems were developed by third parties, who are acknowledged in the appendix.

Tracking down the original authors of some of these problems proved almost as difficult as tracking down the author of the Bible. We have tried very hard to identify the author of each problem, and in each case received permission from someone claiming to speak for the author. We apologize in advance if there are any oversights. If so, please let us know so we can award proper credit.

The robot judge project is the work of many hands. Ciriaco García is the primary author of the robot judge software and a key supporter of the project. Fernando P. Nájera is responsible for many of the tools that help the judge in a friendly manner. Carlos M. Casas maintains the correctness of the test files, ensuring that they are both fair and demanding. José A. Caminero and Jesús Paúl help with problem curation and solution integrity. We particularly thank Miguel Revilla, Jr. for building and maintaining the *http://www.programming-challenges.com* website.

This book was partially debugged during a course taught at Stony Brook by Vinhthuy Phan and Pavel Sumazin in spring 2002. The students from our terrific programming teams this year (Larry Mak, Dan Ports, Tom Rothamel, Alexey Smirnov, Jeffrey

Versoza, and Charles Wright) helped review the manuscript and we thank them for their interest and feedback. Haowen Zhang made a significant contribution by carefully reading the manuscript, testing the programs, and tightening the code.

We thank Wayne Yuhasz, Wayne Wheeler, Frank Ganz, Lesley Poliner, and Rich Putter of Springer-Verlag for all their help turning a manuscript into a published book. We thank Gordon Cormack, Lauren Cowles, David Gries, Joe O'Rourke, Saurabh Sethia, Tom Verhoeff, Daniel Wright, and Stan Wagon for thoughtful manuscript reviews that significantly improved the final product. The Fulbright Foundation and the Department of Applied Mathematics and Computation at the Universidad de Valladolid provided essential support, enabling the two authors to work together face to face. Citigroup CIB, through the efforts of Peter Remch and Debby Z. Beckman, significantly contributed to the ACM ICPC effort at Stony Brook. Its involvement helped spark the writing of this book.

Steven S. Skiena
Stony Brook, NY

Miguel A. Revilla
Valladolid, Spain

February 2003

Contents

1
Getting Started

We kick off this book with a collection of relatively elementary programming problems, none of which require ideas more advanced than arrays and iteration.

Elementary does not necessarily mean easy, however! These problems provide a good introduction to the demanding nature of the robot judge, and the need to read carefully and understand specifications. They also provide an opportunity to discuss programming styles best suited to getting the job done.

To help you get started, we begin with a description of the robot judges and their idiosyncrasies. We follow with a discussion of basic programming style and data structures before introducing our first set of problems. As in all chapters in this book, we follow with hints for selected problems and notes for further study.

1.1   Getting Started With the Judge

This book is designed to be used in tandem with one (or both) of two robot judging websites. The Programming Challenges judge *http://www.programming-challenges.com* has been set up specifically to help you get the most from the challenges in this book. The Universidad de Valladolid judge *http://online-judge.uva.es* has a different interface as well as hundreds of additional problems available.

All the problems in the book can be judged from either website, which are both administered by Miguel Revilla. In this section, we describe how to use the two judges and explain the differences between them. Be aware that both sites are living, breathing projects, so these procedures may evolve over time. Check the current instructions at each site for clarification.

Your first task is to get an account for the judge of your choice. You will be asked to give a password governing access to your personal data, specifically your name and your email address. If you forget your password, clicking the appropriate button will get it emailed back to you.

Note that the contestant rosters of the two sites are currently kept distinct, but there is no reason why you should not register for both of them and enjoy their distinct advantages.

1.1.1   The Programming Challenges Robot Judge

The Programming Challenges website (*http://www.programming-challenges.com*) provides special features associated with each of the problems in this book. For example, a description of each challenge appearing in the book is given on site, along with down-loadable input and output files to eliminate the need for you to type this test data.

The Programming Challenges site uses a web interface for submission (the *Submit-o-Matic*) instead of the email interface of the UVa judge. This makes submission much easier and more reliable, and provides for quicker response.

Each problem in this book has two associated ID numbers, one for each judge. One advantage of the web interface is that the identifier for the Programming Challenges site (the PC ID) is not necessary for most submissions. The problem descriptions in this book have been rewritten for clarity; thus they often differ from the descriptions on the UVa judge in minor ways. However, the problems they describe are identical. Thus any solution scored as correct on one judge *should be* scored correct on the other as well.

The Programming Challenges site has a special course management interface, which permits an instructor to maintain a roster of students in each class and see their submissions and results. It also contains a program similarity tester so the instructor can verify that the solutions each student submits are indeed his or her own work. This makes it "bad karma" to hunt for solutions on the web or in your classmate's directories.

1.1.2   The Universidad de Valladolid Robot Judge

All of the problems in this book and many more appear on the Universidad de Valladolid robot judge *http://online-judge.uva.es*, the largest collection of programming problems in the world. We encourage anyone whose appetite has been whetted by our challenges to continue their studies there.

After registering on the UVa judge, you will receive email containing an ID number which will uniquely identify your programs to the judge. You will need this ID number for every solution you submit.

The UVa judge is gradually adopting a web interface but currently uses email submission. Solutions are emailed directly to *judge@uva.es* after being annotated with enough information to tell the judge which problem you are trying to solve, who the author is, and what programming language you are using.

Specifically, each submitted program must contain a line (at any location) with an @JUDGE_ID: field. Usually, this line is placed inside a comment. For example,

```
/*   @JUDGE_ID:    1000AA   100   C   "Dynamic Programming"   */
```

The argument after the @JUDGE_ID: is your user ID (1000AA in the example). This is followed by the problem number (100 in the example), and then by the language used. *Make sure you use the UVa ID number for all submissions to this judge!* Upper- and lowercase letters are indistinguishable. If you fail to specify the programming language, the judge will try to auto-detect it – but why play games? Finally, if you have used any interesting algorithm or method, you may include a note to that effect between quotes, such as Dynamic Programming in the example above.

Bracketing your program with beginning/end of source comments is a good way to make sure the judge is not confused by junk appended by your mailer.

```
/* @BEGIN_OF_SOURCE_CODE */

your program here

/* @END_OF_SOURCE_CODE */
```

Certain mysterious errors will go away when you do this.

1.1.3 Feedback From the Judge

Students should be aware that both judges are often very picky as to what denotes a correct solution. It is very important to interpret the problem specifications properly. *Never* make an assumption which is not explicitly stated in the specs. There is absolutely no reason to believe that the input is sorted, the graphs are connected, or that the integers used in a problem are positive and reasonably small unless it says so in the specification.

Just like the human judges of the ACM International Collegiate Programming Contest, the online judge provides you with very little feedback about what is wrong with your program. The judge is likely to return one of the following verdicts:

- *Accepted (AC)* — Congratulations! Your program is correct, and runs within the given time and memory limits.

- *Presentation Error (PE)* — Your program outputs are correct but are not presented in the specified format. Check for spaces, left/right justification, line feeds, etc.

- *Accepted (PE)* — Your program has a minor presentation error, but the judge is letting you off with a warning. Don't be concerned, because many problems have somewhat ambiguous output specifications. Usually your problems are something as trivial as an extra blank at the end of a line, so stop here and declare victory.

- *Wrong Answer (WA)* — This you should concern you, because your program returned an incorrect answer to one or more of the judge's secret test cases. You have some more debugging to do.

- *Compile Error (CE)* — The compiler could not figure out how to compile your program. The resulting compiler messages will be returned to you. Warning messages that do not interfere with compilation are ignored by the judge.

- *Runtime Error (RE)* — Your program failed during execution due to a segmentation fault, floating point exception, or similar problem. Its dying message will be sent back to you. Check for invalid pointer references or division by zero.

- *Time Limit Exceeded (TL)* — Your program took too much time on at least one of the test cases, so you likely have a problem with efficiency. Just because you ran out of time on one input does not mean you were correct on all the others, however!

- *Memory Limit Exceeded (ML)* — Your program tried to use more memory than the judge's default settings.

- *Output Limit Exceeded (OL)* — Your program tried to print too much output. This usually means it is trapped in a infinite loop.

- *Restricted Function (RF)* — Your source program tried to use an illegal system function such as `fork()` or `fopen()`. Behave yourself.

- *Submission Error (SE)* — You did not correctly specify one or more of the information fields, perhaps giving an incorrect user ID or problem number.

Just to reiterate: if your program is found guilty of having a wrong answer, the judge will not show you which test case it failed on, or give you any additional hints as to why it failed. This is why it is so essential to review the specifications carefully. Even when you may be *sure* that your program is correct, the judge may keep saying no. Perhaps you are overlooking a boundary case or assuming something which just ain't so. Resubmitting the program without change does you absolutely no good. Read the problem again to make sure it says what you thought it did.

The judge occasionally returns a more exotic verdict which is essentially independent of your solution. See the appropriate website for details.

1.2   Choosing Your Weapon

What programming language should you use in your battles with the judge? Most likely, the language which you know best. The judge currently accepts programs written in C, C++, Pascal, and Java, so your favorite language is probably available. One programming language may well be better than another for a specific programming task. However, these problems test general problem-solving skills far more than portability, modularity, or efficiency, which are the usual dimensions by which languages are compared.

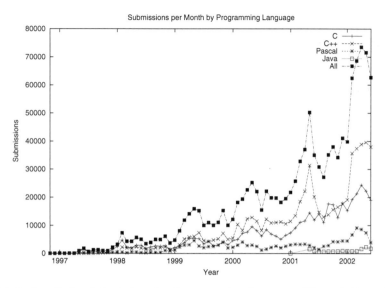

Figure 1.1. Robot Judge Submissions by Programming Language Through December 2002.

1.2.1 Programming Languages

The four languages supported by the judge were designed at different times with different goals in mind:

- *Pascal* — The most popular educational programming language of the 1980s, Pascal was designed to encourage good structured-programming habits. Its popularity has eroded almost to the point of extinction, but it retains a foothold in high schools and in Eastern Europe.

- *C* — The original language of the UNIX operating system, C was designed to provide experienced programmers with the power to do whatever needs to be done. This includes the power to hang yourself by invalid pointer references and invalid type casting. Developments in object-oriented programming during the 1990s lead to the new and improved...

- *C++* — The first commercially successful object-oriented language pulled off the neat trick of maintaining backward compatibility with C while incorporating new data abstraction and inheritance mechanisms. C++ became the primary programming language for teaching and industry during the mid-to-late 1990s, but now it looks over its shoulder at...

- *Java* — Designed as a language to support mobile programs, Java has special security mechanisms to avoid common programmer errors such as array out-of-bounds violations and illegal pointer access. It is a full-featured programming language which can do everything the others can and more.

Lang	Total	AC	PE	WA	CE	RE	TL	ML	OL	RF
C	451447	31.9%	6.7%	35.4%	8.6%	9.1%	6.2%	0.4%	1.1%	0.6%
C++	639565	28.9%	6.3%	36.8%	9.6%	9.0%	7.1%	0.6%	1.0%	0.7%
Java	16373	17.9%	3.6%	36.2%	29.8%	0.5%	8.5%	1.0%	0.5%	2.0%
Pascal	149408	27.8%	5.5%	41.8%	10.1%	6.2%	7.2%	0.4%	0.4%	0.5%
All	1256793	29.7%	6.3%	36.9%	9.6%	8.6%	6.8%	0.5%	1.0%	0.6%

Table 1.1. The Judge's Verdicts by Programming Language (Through December 2002).

Note that each of the judge's programming languages have compiler and system-specific idiosyncrasies. Thus a program which runs on your machine may not run on the judge. Read the language notes on your judge's website carefully to minimize trouble, particularly if you are using Java.

It is interesting to look at which languages people have been using. As of December 2002 over 1,250,000 program submissions have been sent to the robot judge. Almost half of them were in C++, with almost another third in C. Only a tiny fraction were written in Java, but that is not a fair test since the judge did not accept Java programs until November 2001.

These submissions are broken down by month in Figure 1.1. C proved the most popular language until late 1999, when C++ surged ahead. It is interesting to note the annual spike in demand each fall as students train for the ACM International Collegiate Programming Contest regional competitions. Every year the judge gets busier, as more and more students seek trial in its court.

It is also interesting to look at the judge's verdicts by programming language. These are tabulated in Table 1.1, according to the response codes described in Section 1.1.3. The verdicts are quite consistent across the board. However, the frequencies of certain types of errors appear to be language dependent. C++ programs run out of time and memory more often than C language programs, a sign that C++ is a relative resource hog. C has a slightly higher acceptance rate than C++, presumably reflecting its popularity at an earlier state in the judge's development. Pascal has the lowest rate of restricted function errors, reflecting its origins as a nice, safe language for students to play with. Java has had *far* more than its share of compiler errors to date, but it also crashes much less often than the other languages. Safety is indeed a virtue.

But the basic lesson is that the tools do not make the man. Your language doesn't solve the problems – you do.

1.2.2   Reading Our Programs

Several programming examples appear in this book, illustrating programming techniques and providing complete implementations of fundamental algorithms. All of this code is available at *http://www.programming-challenges.com* for you to use and experiment with. There is no finer way to debug programs than having them read by several thousand bright students, so look there for errata and revised solutions.

Our programming examples are implemented in a vanilla subset of C, which we hope will be understandable by all of our readers with relatively little effort. C itself is a subset of C++ and its syntax is quite similar to Java. We have taken care to avoid using weird C-specific constructs, pointer structures and dynamic memory allocation throughout this book, so what remain should be familiar to users of all four of the judge's programming languages.

We provide a few hints about C below which may be helpful in reading our programs:

- *Parameter Passing* — All parameters in C are passed by call-by-value, meaning that copies of all arguments are made on function calls. This would *seem* to suggest that it is impossible to write functions that have side effects. Instead, C encourages you to pass a pointer to any argument that you intend to modify within the body of the function.

  Our only use of pointers will be in parameter passing. The pointer to x is denoted by &x, while the item pointed to by p is denoted *p. Do not get confused between multiplication and pointer dereferencing!

- *Data Types* — C supports several basic data types, including int, float, and char, which should all be self-explanatory. Higher precision ints and floats are denoted long and double, respectively. All functions return a value of type int if not otherwise specified.

- *Arrays* — C array indices always range from 0 to $n - 1$, where n is the number of elements in the array. Thus if we want to start with a first index of 1 for convenience, we had better remember to allocate room for $n + 1$ elements in the array. No runtime checking is performed on the validity of array bounds, so such errors are a common cause of program crashes.

  We are not always consistent as to where the first element of each array is located. Starting from 0 is the traditional C style. However, it is sometimes clearer or easier to start at 1, and we are willing to pay one extra memory location for the privilege. Try not to be confused when reading our code.

- *Operators* — C contains a few essential operators which may be mysterious to some readers. The integer remainder or *mod* operation is denoted %. The logical-and and logical-or operations which appear in conditional statements are denoted && and ||, respectively.

1.2.3 Standard Input/Output

UNIX programmers are familiar with notions of filters and pipes–programs that take one stream of input and produce one stream of output. The output of such programs is suitable to feed to other programs as input. The paradigm is one of stringing lots of little programs together rather than producing big, complicated software systems that try to do everything.

This software tools philosophy has taken somewhat of a beating in recent years due to the popularity of graphical user interfaces. Many programmers instinctively put a point-and-click interface on every program. But such interfaces can make it very difficult to transfer data from one program to another. It is easy to manipulate text output in another program, but what can you do with an image other than look at it?

```
                                                           {$N+}
                               #include<iostream.h>        program acm;
#include<stdio.h>                                          var
                               void main()                   a, b, c : integer;
int main() {                   {                           begin
  long p,q,r;                  long long a,b,c;              while not eof do
                                                             begin
  while (scanf("%ld %ld",&p,&q)    while (cin>>a>>b) {          readln(a, b);
            !=EOF) {                 if (b>a)                   if b > a then
    if (q>p) r=q-p;                    c=b-a;                   begin
    else r=p-q;                      else                         c := b;
                                       c=a-b;                     b := a;
    printf("%ld\n",r);               cout << c << endl;           a := c
  }                              }                            end;
}                              }                              writeln(a - b);
                                                             end
                                                           end.
```

Figure 1.2. Standard Input/Output Examples in C (left), C++ (center), and Pascal (right).

The judge's I/O standards reflect the official ACM programming contest rules. Each program must read the test data from the standard input and print the results to the standard output. Programs are not allowed to open files or to execute certain system calls.

Standard input/output is fairly easy in C, C++, and Pascal. Figure 1.2 provides a simple example in each language that reads in two numbers per line and reports the absolute value of their difference. Note how your favorite language tests for the end-of-file terminating condition. Most problems make input processing even easier by specifying a count of the number of examples or describing a special termination line.

Most languages provide powerful formatted I/O functions. When used properly, single-line commands can render unnecessary certain painful parsing and formatting routines written by those who didn't read the manual.

Standard input/output is *not* easy in Java, however. A electronic template for Java I/O (35 lines long) is available from *http://www.programming-challenges.com*. Set it up once and use it for all your entries.

Java programs submitted to the judge must consist of a single source code file. They are currently compiled and run as native applications using the `gcj` compiler, although this may change in the future. Note that `java::io` use is restricted; which implies that some features are not available. Network functions and threads are also unavailable. However, methods from `math`, `util` and other common packages are authorized. All programs must begin in a static main method in a `Main` class. Do not use public classes: even `Main` must be non-public to avoid compile errors. However, you can add and instance as many classes as needed.

If you find yourself using an operating system/compiler which makes it difficult to use standard input/output, note that the judge always defines the `ONLINE_JUDGE` symbol while compiling your program. Thus, you can test for it and redirect the input/output to a file when running on your own system.

1.3 Programming Hints

It is not our purpose in this book to teach you how to program, only how to program better. We assume you are familiar with such fundamental concepts as variables, conditional statements (e.g., `if-then-else`, `case`), iteration primitives (e.g., `for-do`, `while-do`, `repeat-until`), subroutines, and functions. If you are unfamiliar with these concepts you may have picked up the wrong book, but buy it anyway for later use.

It is important to realize how much power there is in what you already know. In principle, every interesting algorithm/program can be built from what you learn in a first programming course. The powerful features of modern programming languages are not really necessary to build interesting things – only to do them in cleaner, better ways.

To put it another way, one becomes a good writer not by learning additional vocabulary words but by finding something to say. After one or two programming courses, you know all the words you need to make yourself understood. The problems in this book strive to give you something interesting to say.

We offer a few low-level coding hints that are helpful in building quality programs. The bad examples all come from actual submissions to the robot judge.

- *Write the Comments First* — Start your programs and procedures by writing a few sentences explaining what they are supposed to do. This is important because if you can't *easily* write these comments, you probably don't really understand what the program does. We find it much easier to debug our comments than our programs, and believe the additional typing is time very well spent. Of course, with the time pressure of a contest comes a tendency to get sloppy, but do so at your own risk.

- *Document Each Variable* — Write a one-line comment for each variable when you declare it so you know what it does. Again, if you can't describe it easily, you don't know why it is there. You will likely be living with the program for at least a few debug cycles, and this is a modest investment in readability which you will come to appreciate.

- *Use Symbolic Constants* — Whenever you have a constant in your program (input size, mathematical constant, data structure size, etc.) declare it to be so at the top of your program. Horribly insidious errors can result from using inconsistent constants in a program. Of course, the symbolic name helps only if you actually use it in your program whenever you need the constant...

- *Use Enumerated Types for a Reason* — Enumerated types (i.e., symbolic variables such Booleans (`true,false`)) can be terrific aids to understanding. However, they are often unnecessary in short programs. Note this example representing the suit (club, diamond, heart, spade) of a deck of cards:

```
switch(cursuit) {
    case 'C':
      newcard.suit = C;
```

```
      break;
    case 'D':
      newcard.suit = D;
      break;
    case 'H':
      newcard.suit = H;
      break;
    case 'S':
      newcard.suit = S;
 . . .
```

No additional clarity arises from using the enumerated variables (C,D,H,S) over the original character representation ('C','D','H','S'), only additional opportunities for error.

- *Use Subroutines To Avoid Redundant Code* — Read the following program fragment managing the state of a rectangular board, and think how you might shorten and simplify it:

. . .

```
    while (c != '0') {
       scanf("%c", &c);
       if (c == 'A') {
          if (row-1 >= 0) {
             temp = b[row-1][col];
             b[row-1][col] = ' ';
             b[row][col] = temp;
             row = row-1;
          }
       }
       else if (c == 'B') {
          if (row+1 <= BOARDSIZE-1) {
             temp = b[row+1][col];
             b[row+1][col] = ' ';
             b[row][col] = temp;
             row = row+1;
          }
       }
```

. . .

In the full program, there were four blocks of three lines each moving a value to a neighboring cell. Mistyping a single + or − would have lethal consequences. Much safer would be to write a single move-swap routine and call it with the proper arguments.

- *Make Your Debugging Statements Meaningful* — Learn to use the debugging environment on your system. This will enable you to stop execution at a given statement or condition, so you can see what the values of all associated variables are. This is usually faster and easier than typing in a bunch of print statements. But if you *are* going to insert debugging print statements, make them say something. Print out all relevant variables, and *label* the printed quantity with the variable name. Otherwise it is easy to get lost in your own debugging output.

Most computer science students are now well-versed in *object-oriented programming*, a software engineering philosophy designed to construct reusable software components and exploit them. Object-oriented programming is useful to build large, reusable programs. However, most of the programming challenge problems in this book are designed to be solved by short, clever programs. The basic assumption of object-oriented programming just does not apply in this domain, so defining complicated new objects (as opposed to *using* predefined objects) is likely to be a waste of time.

The trick to successful programming is not abandoning style, but using one appropriate to the scale of the job.

1.4   Elementary Data Types

Simple data structures such as arrays have an important advantage over more sophisticated data structures such as linked lists: they are simple. Many kinds of errors in pointer-based structures simply cannot happen with static arrays.

The sign of a mature professional is keeping the simple jobs simple. This is particularly challenging for those who are just learning a new subject. Medical students provide a classic example of this problem. After sitting through a few lectures on obscure tropical diseases, a young doctor worries that any patient with a sniffle and a rash might have the Ebola virus or bubonic plague, while a more experienced physician just sends them home with a bottle of aspirin.

Likewise, you may have recently learned about balanced binary search trees, exception handling, parallel processing, and various models of object inheritance. These are all useful and important subjects. But they are not necessarily the best way to get a correct program working for a simple job.

So, yes, pointer-based structures are very powerful if you do not know the maximum size of the problem in advance, or in supporting fast search and update operations. However, many of the problems you will be solving here have maximum sizes specified. Further, the robot judge typically allows several seconds for your job to complete, which is a lot of computation time when you stop to think about it. You don't get extra points for finishing faster.

So what is the simple, mature approach to data structures? First, be familiar with the basic primitive data *types* built into your programming language. In principle, you can build just about anything you want from just these:

- *Arrays* — This workhorse data type permits access to data by position, not content, just like the house numbers on a street permit access by address, not name. They are used to store sequences of single-type elements such as integers, reals, or compound objects such as records. Arrays of characters can be used to represent text strings, while arrays of text strings can be used to represent just about anything.

Sentinels can be a useful technique to simplify array-based programming. A sentinel is a guard element, implicitly checking that the program does not run beyond the bounds of the array without performing an explicit test. Consider the case of inserting element x into the proper position among n elements in a sorted array a. We can explicitly test each step to see whether we have hit the bottom of the array as on the left:

```
i = n;                              i = n;
while ((a[i]>=x) && (i>=1)) {       a[0] = - MAXINT;
        a[i] = a[i-1];              while (a[i] >= x) {
        i=i-1;                              a[i] = a[i-1];
}                                           i=i-1;
a[i+1] = x;                         }
                                    a[i+1] = x;
```

or, we can make sure that fake element a[0] is smaller than anything it will encounter as on the right. Proper use of sentinels, and making sure that your array is a little larger than it presumably needs to be, can help avoid many boundary errors.

- *Multidimensional Arrays* — Rectangular grid structures such as chessboards and images comes to mind first when thinking about two-dimensional arrays, but more generally they can be used to group together *homogeneous* data records. For example, an array of n points in the $x - y$ plane can be thought of as an $n \times 2$ array, where the second argument (0 or 1) of $A[i][j]$ dictates whether we are referring to the x or y coordinate of the point.

- *Records* — These are used to group together *heterogeneous* data records. For example, an array of people-records can lump together people's names, ID numbers, heights, and weights into a simple package. Records are important for conceptual clarity in large programs, but such fields can often be harmlessly represented using separate arrays in programs of modest size.

  Whether it is better to use records or multidimensional arrays in a problem is not always a clear-cut decision. Think of the problem of representing points in the $x - y$ plane discussed above. The obvious representation would be a record or structure such as:

```
struct point {
        int x, y;
};
```

instead of as a two-element array. A big plus for records is that the notation p.y and p.y are more akin to our natural notation for working with points. However, a disadvantage of the record representation is that you cannot loop over individual variables as you can elements in an array.

Suppose you wanted to change a geometric program to work with three-dimensional points instead of two, or even in arbitrary dimensions. Sure you can easily add extra fields to the record, but every place where you did calculations on x and y you now must replicate them for z. But by using the array representation, changing distance computations from two to three dimensions can be as simple as changing a constant:

```
typedef int point[DIMENSION];

double distance(point a, point b)
{
        int i;
        double d=0.0;

        for (i=0; i<DIMENSION; i++)
                d = d + (a[i]-b[i]) * (a[i]-b[i]);

        return( sqrt(d) );
}
```

In Chapter 2, we will review more advanced data *structures* which can be built from these basic primitives. These will let us work with higher levels of abstraction, but don't be afraid to use simple technology when it suffices for the job.

1.5 About the Problems

Each chapter of this book ends with an appropriate set of programming challenge problems. These challenges have been carefully selected from over 1,000 such problems collected at the Universidad de Valladolid website. We aimed for clear, clever problems with varying degrees of difficulty. We especially looked for that spark of insight which turns a problem into a challenge.

The description of each selected problem has been edited for correctness and readability. We have tried to preserve the local color and flavor of each original problem while making the language reasonably consistent. The identification number for each problem on both judging sites is provided. These numbers are important for successful submission. The first number for each pair is associated with *http://www.programming-challenges.com*; the second number works on *http://online-judge.uva.es*.

To give some idea as to the relative difficulty of the problems, each has been annotated in three different ways. First, each problem has been given a grade of A, B, or C, reflecting how many correct solutions the judge has seen over the years. A problems are presumably easier to solve or somehow more attractive than B problems. Second, the frequency that submitted solutions for each problem are accepted by the judge is graded as **high**, `average`, or `low`. Low percentages may indicate particularly finicky judges, or perhaps problems that require more subtlety than is initially apparent. Or they may just reflect bugs in test cases which have since been fixed. Therefore, do not obsess too much about these ratings. Finally, we give a subjective rating (from 1 to 4) of the academic level required to solve the problem. Higher numbers indicate more sophisticated problems.

Good luck, and happy hacking!

1.6 Problems

1.6.1 *The 3n + 1 Problem*

PC/UVa IDs: 110101/100, **Popularity:** A, **Success rate:** low **Level:** 1

Consider the following algorithm to generate a sequence of numbers. Start with an integer n. If n is even, divide by 2. If n is odd, multiply by 3 and add 1. Repeat this process with the new value of n, terminating when $n = 1$. For example, the following sequence of numbers will be generated for $n = 22$:

$$22\ 11\ 34\ 17\ 52\ 26\ 13\ 40\ 20\ 10\ 5\ 16\ 8\ 4\ 2\ 1$$

It is *conjectured* (but not yet proven) that this algorithm will terminate at $n = 1$ for every integer n. Still, the conjecture holds for all integers up to at least $1,000,000$.

For an input n, the *cycle-length* of n is the number of numbers generated up to and *including* the 1. In the example above, the cycle length of 22 is 16. Given any two numbers i and j, you are to determine the maximum cycle length over all numbers between i and j, *including* both endpoints.

Input

The input will consist of a series of pairs of integers i and j, one pair of integers per line. All integers will be less than 1,000,000 and greater than 0.

Output

For each pair of input integers i and j, output i, j in the same order in which they appeared in the input and then the maximum cycle length for integers between and including i and j. These three numbers should be separated by one space, with all three numbers on one line and with one line of output for each line of input.

Sample Input	Sample Output
1 10	1 10 20
100 200	100 200 125
201 210	201 210 89
900 1000	900 1000 174

1.6.2 Minesweeper

PC/UVa IDs: 110102/10189, **Popularity:** A, **Success rate:** high **Level:** 1

Have you ever played Minesweeper? This cute little game comes with a certain operating system whose name we can't remember. The goal of the game is to find where all the mines are located within a $M \times N$ field.

The game shows a number in a square which tells you how many mines there are adjacent to that square. Each square has at most eight adjacent squares. The 4×4 field on the left contains two mines, each represented by a "*" character. If we represent the same field by the hint numbers described above, we end up with the field on the right:

```
*...        *100
....        2210
.*..        1*10
....        1110
```

Input

The input will consist of an arbitrary number of fields. The first line of each field contains two integers n and m ($0 < n, m \leq 100$) which stand for the number of lines and columns of the field, respectively. Each of the next n lines contains exactly m characters, representing the field.

Safe squares are denoted by "." and mine squares by "*," both without the quotes. The first field line where $n = m = 0$ represents the end of input and should not be processed.

Output

For each field, print the message **Field #x:** on a line alone, where x stands for the number of the field starting from 1. The next n lines should contain the field with the "." characters replaced by the number of mines adjacent to that square. There must be an empty line between field outputs.

Sample Input

```
4 4
*...
....
.*..
....
3 5
**...
.....
.*...
0 0
```

Sample Output

```
Field #1:
*100
2210
1*10
1110

Field #2:
**100
33200
1*100
```

1.6.3   The Trip

PC/UVa IDs: 110103/10137, **Popularity:** B, **Success rate:** average **Level:** 1

A group of students are members of a club that travels annually to different locations. Their destinations in the past have included Indianapolis, Phoenix, Nashville, Philadelphia, San Jose, and Atlanta. This spring they are planning a trip to Eindhoven.

The group agrees in advance to share expenses equally, but it is not practical to share every expense as it occurs. Thus individuals in the group pay for particular things, such as meals, hotels, taxi rides, and plane tickets. After the trip, each student's expenses are tallied and money is exchanged so that the net cost to each is the same, to within one cent. In the past, this money exchange has been tedious and time consuming. Your job is to compute, from a list of expenses, the minimum amount of money that must change hands in order to equalize (within one cent) all the students' costs.

Input

Standard input will contain the information for several trips. Each trip consists of a line containing a positive integer n denoting the number of students on the trip. This is followed by n lines of input, each containing the amount spent by a student in dollars and cents. There are no more than 1000 students and no student spent more than $10,000.00. A single line containing 0 follows the information for the last trip.

Output

For each trip, output a line stating the total amount of money, in dollars and cents, that must be exchanged to equalize the students' costs.

Sample Input

```
3
10.00
20.00
30.00
4
15.00
15.01
3.00
3.01
0
```

Sample Output

```
$10.00
$11.99
```

1.6.4 LCD Display

PC/UVa IDs: 110104/706, **Popularity:** A, **Success rate:** average **Level:** 1

A friend of yours has just bought a new computer. Before this, the most powerful machine he ever used was a pocket calculator. He is a little disappointed because he liked the LCD display of his calculator more than the screen on his new computer! To make him happy, write a program that prints numbers in LCD display style.

Input

The input file contains several lines, one for each number to be displayed. Each line contains integers s and n, where n is the number to be displayed ($0 \leq n \leq 99,999,999$) and s is the size in which it shall be displayed ($1 \leq s \leq 10$). The input will be terminated by a line containing two zeros, which should not be processed.

Output

Print the numbers specified in the input file in an LCD display-style using s "-" signs for the horizontal segments and s "|" signs for the vertical ones. Each digit occupies exactly $s + 2$ columns and $2s + 3$ rows. Be sure to fill all the white space occupied by the digits with blanks, including the last digit. There must be exactly one column of blanks between two digits.

Output a blank line after each number. You will find an example of each digit in the sample output below.

Sample Input

```
2 12345
3 67890
0 0
```

Sample Output

```
      --   --        --
   |    |    |  |  |  |  |
   |    |    |  |  |  |  |
      --   --   --   --
   | |     |    |    |
   | |     |    |    |
      --   --        --


 ---        ---   ---   ---   ---
|             | |   | | |   | |   |
|             | |   | | |   | |   |
|             | |   | | |   | |   |
 ---              ---   ---
|        |   | |     | |   | |   |
|        |   | |     | |   | |   |
|        |   | |     | |   | |   |
 ---   ---        ---   ---   ---
```

1.6.5   Graphical Editor

PC/UVa IDs: 110105/10267, **Popularity:** B, **Success rate:** low **Level:** 1

Graphical editors such as Photoshop allow us to alter bit-mapped images in the same way that text editors allow us to modify documents. Images are represented as an $M \times N$ array of pixels, where each pixel has a given color.

Your task is to write a program which simulates a simple interactive graphical editor.

Input

The input consists of a sequence of editor commands, one per line. Each command is represented by one capital letter placed as the first character of the line. If the command needs parameters, they will be given on the same line separated by spaces.

Pixel coordinates are represented by two integers, a column number between $1 \ldots M$ and a row number between $1 \ldots N$, where $1 \leq M, N \leq 250$. The origin sits in the upper-left corner of the table. Colors are specified by capital letters.

The editor accepts the following commands:

I M N	Create a new $M \times N$ image with all pixels initially colored white (O).
C	Clear the table by setting all pixels white (O). The size remains unchanged.
L X Y C	Colors the pixel (X, Y) in color (C).
V X Y1 Y2 C	Draw a vertical segment of color (C) in column X, between the rows $Y1$ and $Y2$ inclusive.
H X1 X2 Y C	Draw a horizontal segment of color (C) in the row Y, between the columns $X1$ and $X2$ inclusive.
K X1 Y1 X2 Y2 C	Draw a filled rectangle of color C, where $(X1, Y1)$ is the upper-left and $(X2, Y2)$ the lower right corner.
F X Y C	Fill the region R with the color C, where R is defined as follows. Pixel (X, Y) belongs to R. Any other pixel which is the same color as pixel (X, Y) and shares a common side with any pixel in R also belongs to this region.
S Name	Write the file name in MSDOS 8.3 format followed by the contents of the current image.
X	Terminate the session.

Output

On every command S NAME, print the filename $NAME$ and contents of the current image. Each row is represented by the color contents of each pixel. See the sample output.

Ignore the entire line of any command defined by a character other than I, C, L, V, H, K, F, S, or X, and pass on to the next command. In case of other errors, the program behavior is unpredictable.

Sample Input

```
I 5 6
L 2 3 A
S one.bmp
G 2 3 J
F 3 3 J
V 2 3 4 W
H 3 4 2 Z
S two.bmp
X
```

Sample Output

```
one.bmp
00000
00000
0A000
00000
00000
00000
two.bmp
JJJJJ
JJZZJ
JWJJJ
JWJJJ
JJJJJ
JJJJJ
```

1.6.6 Interpreter

PC/UVa IDs: 110106/10033, **Popularity:** B, **Success rate:** low **Level:** 2

A certain computer has ten registers and 1,000 words of RAM. Each register or RAM location holds a three-digit integer between 0 and 999. Instructions are encoded as three-digit integers and stored in RAM. The encodings are as follows:

100	means *halt*
2*dn*	means *set register d to n (between 0 and 9)*
3*dn*	means *add n to register d*
4*dn*	means *multiply register d by n*
5*ds*	means *set register d to the value of register s*
6*ds*	means *add the value of register s to register d*
7*ds*	means *multiply register d by the value of register s*
8*da*	means *set register d to the value in RAM whose address is in register a*
9*sa*	means *set the value in RAM whose address is in register a to that of register s*
0*ds*	means *goto the location in register d unless register s contains 0*

All registers initially contain 000. The initial content of the RAM is read from standard input. The first instruction to be executed is at RAM address 0. All results are reduced modulo 1,000.

Input

The input begins with a single positive integer on a line by itself indicating the number of cases, each described as below. This is followed by a blank line, and there will be a blank line between each two consecutive inputs.

Each input case consists of up to 1,000 three-digit unsigned integers, representing the contents of consecutive RAM locations starting at 0. Unspecified RAM locations are initialized to 000.

Output

The output of each test case is a single integer: the number of instructions executed up to and including the *halt* instruction. You may assume that the program does halt. Separate the output of two consecutive cases by a blank line.

Sample Input

```
1

299
492
495
```

399
492
495
399
283
279
689
078
100
000
000
000

Sample Output

16

1.6.7 Check the Check

PC/UVa IDs: 110107/10196, **Popularity:** B, **Success rate:** average **Level:** 1

Your task is to write a program that reads a chessboard configuration and identifies whether a king is under attack (in check). A king is in check if it is on square which can be taken by the opponent on his next move.

White pieces will be represented by uppercase letters, and black pieces by lowercase letters. The white side will always be on the bottom of the board, with the black side always on the top.

For those unfamiliar with chess, here are the movements of each piece:

Pawn (p or P): can only move straight ahead, one square at a time. However, it takes pieces diagonally, and that is what concerns you in this problem.

Knight (n or N) : has an L-shaped movement shown below. It is the only piece that can jump over other pieces.

Bishop (b or B) : can move any number of squares diagonally, either forward or backward.

Rook (r or R) : can move any number of squares vertically or horizontally, either forward or backward.

Queen (q or Q) : can move any number of squares in any direction (diagonally, horizontally, or vertically) either forward or backward.

King (k or K) : can move one square at a time in any direction (diagonally, horizontally, or vertically) either forward or backward.

Movement examples are shown below, where "*" indicates the positions where the piece can capture another piece:

```
Pawn          Rook          Bishop        Queen         King          Knight
........      ...*....      .......*      ...*...*      ........      ........
........      ...*....      *.....*.      *..*..*.      ........      ........
........      ...*....      .*...*..      .*.*.*..      ........      ..*.*...
........      ...*....      ..*.*...      ..***...      ..***...      .*...*..
...p....      ***r****      ...b....      ***q****      ..*k*...      ...n....
..*.*...      ...*....      ..*.*...      ..***...      ..***...      .*...*..
........      ...*....      .*...*..      .*.*.*..      ........      ..*.*...
........      ...*....      *.....*.      *..*..*.      ........      ........
```

Remember that the knight is the only piece that can jump over other pieces. The pawn movement will depend on its side. If it is a black pawn, it can only move one square diagonally down the board. If it is a white pawn, it can only move one square diagonally up the board. The example above is a black pawn, described by a lowercase "p". We use *"move"* to indicate the squares where the pawn can capture another piece.

Input

There will be an arbitrary number of board configurations in the input, each consisting of eight lines of eight characters each. A "." denotes an empty square, while upper- and lowercase letters represent the pieces as defined above. There will be no invalid characters and no configurations where both kings are in check. You must read until you find an empty board consisting only of "." characters, which should not be processed. There will be an empty line between each pair of board configurations. All boards, except for the empty one, will contain exactly one white king and one black king.

Output

For each board configuration read you must output one of the following answers:
Game #*d*: white king is in check.
Game #*d*: black king is in check.
Game #*d*: no king is in check.
where *d* stands for the game number starting from 1.

Sample Input	*Sample Output*
`..k.....`	`Game #1: black king is in check.`
`PPP.PPPP`	`Game #2: white king is in check.`
`........`	
`.R...B..`	
`........`	
`........`	
`PPPPPPPP`	
`K.......`	
`rnbqk.nr`	
`ppp..ppp`	
`....p...`	
`...p....`	
`.bPP....`	
`.....N..`	
`PP..PPPP`	
`RNBQKB.R`	
`........`	
`........`	
`........`	
`........`	
`........`	
`........`	
`........`	
`........`	

1.6.8 Australian Voting

PC/UVa IDs: 110108/10142, **Popularity:** B, **Success rate:** low **Level:** 1

Australian ballots require that voters rank all the candidates in order of choice. Initially only the first choices are counted, and if one candidate receives more than 50% of the vote then that candidate is elected. However, if no candidate receives more than 50%, all candidates tied for the lowest number of votes are eliminated. Ballots ranking these candidates first are recounted in favor of their highest-ranked non-eliminated candidate. This process of eliminating the weakest candidates and counting their ballots in favor of the preferred non-eliminated candidate continues until one candidate receives more than 50% of the vote, or until all remaining candidates are tied.

Input

The input begins with a single positive integer on a line by itself indicating the number of cases following, each as described below. This line is followed by a blank line. There is also a blank line between two consecutive inputs.

The first line of each case is an integer $n \leq 20$ indicating the number of candidates. The next n lines consist of the names of the candidates in order, each up to 80 characters in length and containing any printable characters. Up to 1,000 lines follow, each containing the contents of a ballot. Each ballot contains the numbers from 1 to n in some order. The first number indicates the candidate of first choice; the second number indicates candidate of second choice, and so on.

Output

The output of each test case consists of either a single line containing the name of the winner or several lines containing the names of all candidates who are tied. The output of each two consecutive cases are separated by a blank line.

Sample Input	Sample Output
1	John Doe

```
3
John Doe
Jane Smith
Jane Austen
1 2 3
2 1 3
2 3 1
1 2 3
3 1 2
```

1.7 Hints

1.3 Who should get the extra pennies if the total does not divide evenly?

1.5 How do we best handle the fill command? Is it easier to keep separate copies of the old and new image?

1.8 Notes

1.1 The $3n + 1$ (or Collatz) problem remains open to this day. See Lagarias [Lag85] for an excellent mathematical survey. An international conference on the Collatz problem was held in 1999; see *http://www.math.grinnell.edu/~chamberl/conf.html* for the online proceedings.

1.2 The Minesweeper consistency problem takes as input an $n \times n$ rectangular grid with the squares labeled by numbers 0 to 8, mines, or left blank, and asks: is there a configuration of mines in the grid that result in the given pattern of symbols, according to the usual Minesweeper rules? The Clay Institute of Mathematics (*http://www.claymath.org/*) offers a $1,000,000 prize for an efficient algorithm which solves this problem.

But don't get too excited! The Minesweeper consistency problem has been proven NP-complete [Kay00], meaning that no efficient algorithm for it can exist without revolutionizing our understanding of computation. See [GJ79] for a thorough discussion of NP-completeness.

1.6 Software-interpreted virtual machines are the key to the portability of languages such as Java. It is an interesting project to write a simulator for the machine language of an old, obsolete, but simple computer such as the PDP-8. Today's hardware is so much faster that your virtual PDP-8 will significantly outrun the original machine!

1.7 Once you have written a legal move generator (the essence of this problem) you are not very far from building your own chess-playing program! See [New96, Sch97] for stories of how computer chess and checkers programs work and beat the human World Champions at their own games.

1.8 The mathematics of voting systems is a fascinating subject. Arrow's *impossibility theorem* states that no voting system can simultaneously satisfy all of five obviously desirable properties. See [COM94] for an interesting discussion of the mathematics of social choice.

2

Data Structures

Data structures are the heart of any sophisticated program. Selecting the right data structure can make an enormous difference in the complexity of the resulting implementation. Pick the right data representation, and your task will be easy to program. Pick the wrong representation, and you may spend enormous amounts of time and code covering up for your lousy initial decision.

In this chapter, we will review the fundamental data structures which every programmer should be familiar with. We will motivate this discussion with an example program based on a children's card game. Many classic programming problems are based on games. After all, who makes it through their introductory programming courses without moving the towers of Hanoi, taking the knight's tour, or solving the eight queens problem?

2.1 Elementary Data Structures

Here we present the abstract operations of the most important data structures: stacks, queues, dictionaries, priority queues, and sets. We also describe the simplest way to implement these structures from scratch.

Be aware, however, that modern object-oriented languages like C++ and Java come with standard libraries of fundamental data structures. These will be briefly described in Section 2.2. It is worth every programmer's time to get acquainted with your libraries instead of repeatedly reinventing the wheel. Once you do, you can read this section with an eye for what each data structure is good for instead of the details of how it should be implemented.

2.1.1 Stacks

Stacks and queues are containers where items are retrieved according to the order of insertion, independent of content. *Stacks* maintain *last-in, first-out* order. The abstract operations on a stack include –

- *Push(x,s)* — Insert item x at the top of stack s.
- *Pop(s)* — Return (and remove) the top item of stack s.
- *Initialize(s)* — Create an empty stack.
- *Full(s), Empty(s)* — Test whether the stack can accept more pushes or pops, respectively.

Note that there is no element search operation defined on standard stacks and queues.

Defining these abstract operations enables us build a stack module to use and reuse without knowing the details of the implementation. The easiest implementation uses an array with an index variable to represent the top of the stack. An alternative implementation, using linked lists, is better because it can't overflow.

Stacks naturally model piles of objects, such as dinner plates. After a new plate is washed, it is pushed on the top of the stack. When someone is hungry, a clean plate is popped off the top. A stack is an appropriate data structure for this task since the plates don't care which one is used next. Thus one important application of stacks is whenever order *doesn't* matter, because stacks are particularly simple containers to implement.

Stack order is important in processing any properly nested structure. This includes parenthesized formulas (push on a "(", pop on ")"), recursive program calls (push on a procedure entry, pop on a procedure exit), and depth-first traversals of graphs (push on discovering a vertex, pop on leaving it for the last time).

2.1.2 Queues

Queues maintain *first-in, first-out* order. This appears fairer than last-in, first-out, which is why lines at stores are organized as queues instead of stacks. Decks of playing cards can be modeled by queues, since we deal the cards off the top of the deck and add them back in at the bottom. FIFO queues will be used in implementing breadth-first search in graphs in Chapter 9.

The abstract operations on a queue include —

- *Enqueue(x,q)* — Insert item x at the back of queue q.
- *Dequeue(q)* — Return (and remove) the front item from queue q
- *Initialize(q), Full(q), Empty(q)* — Analogous to these operation on stacks.

Queues are more difficult to implement than stacks, because action happens at both ends. The *simplest* implementation uses an array, inserting new elements at one end and *moving* all remaining elements to fill the empty space created on each dequeue.

However, it is very wasteful to move all the elements on each dequeue. How can we do better? We can maintain indices to the first (head) and last (tail) elements in the array/queue and do all operations locally. There is no reason why we must explicitly clear previously used cells, although we leave a trail of garbage behind the previously dequeued items.

Circular queues let us reuse this empty space. Note that the pointer to the front of the list is always *behind* the back pointer! When the queue is full, the two indices will point to neighboring or identical elements. There are several possible ways to adjust the indices for circular queues. *All are tricky!* The easiest solution distinguishes full from empty by maintaining a count of how many elements exist in the queue:

```
typedef struct {
        int q[QUEUESIZE+1];             /* body of queue */
        int first;                      /* position of first element */
        int last;                       /* position of last element */
        int count;                      /* number of queue elements */
} queue;

init_queue(queue *q)
{
        q->first = 0;
        q->last = QUEUESIZE-1;
        q->count = 0;
}

enqueue(queue *q, int x)
{
        if (q->count >= QUEUESIZE)
                printf("Warning: queue overflow enqueue x=%d\n",x);
        else {
                q->last = (q->last+1) % QUEUESIZE;
                q->q[ q->last ] = x;
                q->count = q->count + 1;
        }
}

int dequeue(queue *q)
{
        int x;

        if (q->count <= 0) printf("Warning: empty queue dequeue.\n");
        else {
                x = q->q[ q->first ];
                q->first = (q->first+1) % QUEUESIZE;
                q->count = q->count - 1;
        }
```

```
          return(x);
}

int empty(queue *q)
{
          if (q->count <= 0) return (TRUE);
          else return (FALSE);
}
```

Queues are one of the few data structures which are easier to program using linked lists than arrays, because they eliminate the need to test for the wrap-around condition.

2.1.3 Dictionaries

Dictionaries permit content-based retrieval, unlike the position-based retrieval of stacks and queues. They support three primary operations –

- *Insert(x,d)* — Insert item x into dictionary d.

- *Delete(x,d)* — Remove item x (or the item pointed to by x) from dictionary d.

- *Search(k,d)* — Return an item with key k if one exists in dictionary d.

A data structures course may well present a dozen different ways to implement dictionaries, including sorted/unsorted linked lists, sorted/unsorted arrays, and a forest full of random, splay, AVL, and red-black trees – not to mention all the variations on hashing.

The primary issue in algorithm analysis is performance, namely, achieving the best possible trade-off between the costs of these three operations. But what we usually want in practice is the simplest way to get the job done under the given time constraints. The right answer depends on how much the contents of your dictionary change over the course of execution:

- *Static Dictionaries* — These structures get built once and never change. Thus they need to support search, but not insertion on deletion.

    The right answer for static dictionaries is typically an array. The only real question is whether to keep it sorted, in order to use binary search to provide fast membership queries. Unless you have tight time constraints, it probably isn't worth using binary search until $n > 100$ or so. You might even get away with sequential search to $n = 1,000$ or more, provided you will not be doing too many searches.

    Sorting algorithms and binary search always prove harder to debug than they should. Library sort/search routines are available for C, C++, and Java, and will be presented in Chapter 4.

- *Semi-dynamic Dictionaries* — These structures support insertion and search queries, but not deletion. If we know an upper bound on the number of elements to be inserted we can use an array, but otherwise we must use a linked structure.

Hash tables are excellent dictionary data structures, particularly if deletion need not be supported. The idea is to apply a function to the search key so we can determine *where* the item will appear in an array without looking at the other items. To make the table of reasonable size, we must allow for *collisions*, two distinct keys mapped to the same location.

The two components to hashing are (1) defining a hash function to map keys to integers in a certain range, and (2) setting up an array as big as this range, so that the hash function value can specify an index.

The basic hash function converts the key to an integer, and takes the value of this integer mod the size of the hash table. Selecting a table size to be a prime number (or at least avoiding obvious composite numbers like 1,000) is helpful to avoid trouble. Strings can be converted to integers by using the letters to form a base "alphabet-size" number system. To convert "steve" to a number, observe that e is the 5th letter of the alphabet, s is the 19th letter, t is the 20th letter, and v is the 22nd letter. Thus "steve" $\Rightarrow 26^4 \times 19 + 26^3 \times 20 + 26^2 \times 5 + 26^1 \times 22 + 26^0 \times 5 = 9,038,021$. The first, last, or middle ten characters or so will likely suffice for a good index. Tricks on how to do the modular arithmetic efficiently will be discussed in Chapter 7.

The absence of deletion makes *open addressing* a nice, easy way to resolve collisions. In open addressing, we use a simple rule to decide where to put a new item when the desired space is already occupied. Suppose we always put it in the next unoccupied cell. On searching for a given item, we go to the intended location and search sequentially. If we find an empty cell before we find the item, it does not exist anywhere in the table.

Deletion in an open addressing scheme is very ugly, since removing one element can break a chain of insertions, making some elements inaccessible. The key to efficiency is using a large-enough table that contains many holes. Don't be cheap in selecting your table size or else you will pay the price later.

- *Fully Dynamic Dictionaries* — Hash tables are great for fully dynamic dictionaries as well, provided we use *chaining* as the collision resolution mechanism. Here we associate a linked list with each table location, so insertion, deletion, and query reduce to the same problem in linked lists. If the hash function does a good job the m keys will be distributed uniformly in a table of size n, so each list will be short enough to search quickly.

2.1.4   Priority Queues

Priority queues are data structures on sets of items supporting three operations –

- *Insert(x,p)* — Insert item x into priority queue p.

- *Maximum(p)* — Return the item with the largest key in priority queue p.

- *ExtractMax(p)* — Return and remove the item with the largest key in p.

Priority queues are used to maintain schedules and calendars. They govern who goes next in simulations of airports, parking lots, and the like, whenever we need to schedule events according to a clock. In a human life simulation, it may be most convenient to determine when someone will die immediately after they are born. We can then stick this date in a priority queue so as to be reminded when to bury them.

Priority queues are used to schedule events in the sweep-line algorithms common to computational geometry. Typically, we use the priority queue to store the points we have not yet encountered, ordered by x-coordinate, and push the line forward one step at a time.

The most famous implementation of priority queues is the binary heap, which can be efficiently maintained in either a top-down or bottom-up manner. Heaps are very slick and efficient, but may be tricky to get right under time pressure. Far simpler is maintaining a sorted array, particularly if you will not be performing too many insertions.

2.1.5   Sets

Sets (or more strictly speaking *subsets*) are unordered collections of elements drawn from a given universal set U. Set data structures get distinguished from dictionaries because there is at least an implicit need to encode which elements from U are *not* in the given subset.

The basic operations on subsets are —

- *Member(x,S)* — Is an item x an element of subset S?

- *Union(A,B)* — Construct subset $A \cup B$ of all elements in subset A or in subset B.

- *Intersection(A,B)* — Construct subset $A \cap B$ of all elements in subset A and in subset B.

- *Insert(x,S), Delete(x,S)* — Insert/delete element x into/from subset S.

For sets of a large or unbounded universe, the obvious solution is representing a subset using a dictionary. Using sorted dictionaries makes union and intersection operations much easier, basically reducing the problem to merging two sorted dictionaries. An element is in the union if it appears at least once in the merged list, and in the intersection if it appears exactly twice.

For sets drawn from small, unchanging universes, bit vectors provide a convenient representation. An n-bit vector or array can represent any subset S from an n-element universe. Bit i will be 1 iff $i \in S$. Element insertion and deletion operations simply flip the appropriate bit. Intersection and union are done by "and-ing" or "or-ing" the corresponding bits together. Since only one bit is used per element, bit vectors can be space efficient for surprisingly large values of $|U|$. For example, an array of 1,000 standard four-byte integers can represent any subset on 32,000 elements.

2.2   Object Libraries

Users of modern object-oriented languages such as C++ and Java have implementations of these basic data structures available using standard library classes.

2.2.1   The C++ Standard Template Library

A C library of general-purpose data structures, like stacks and queues, cannot really exist because functions in C can't tell the type of their arguments. Thus we would have to define separate routines such as **push_int()** and **push_char()** for every possible data type. Further, such an approach couldn't generalize to construct stacks on user-defined data types.

Templates are C++'s mechanism to define abstract objects which can be parameterized by type. The C++ *Standard Template Library (STL)* provides implementations of all the data structures defined above and much more. Each data object must have the type of its elements fixed (i.e., templated) at compilation time, so

```
#include <stl.h>

  stack<int> S;
  stack<char> T;
```

declares two stacks with different element types.

Good references on STL include [MDS01] and *http://www.sgi.com/tech/stl/*. Brief descriptions of our featured data structures follow below –

- *Stack* — Methods include S.push(), S.top(), S.pop(), and S.empty(). Top returns but does not remove the element on top; while pop removes but does not return the element. Thus always top on pop [Seu63]. Linked implementations ensure the stack will never be full.

- *Queue* — Methods include Q.front(), Q.back(), Q.push(), Q.pop(), and Q.empty() and have the same idiosyncrasies as stack.

- *Dictionaries* — STL contains a wide variety of containers, including hash_map, a hashed associative container binding keys to data items. Methods include H.erase(), H.find(), and H.insert().

- *Priority Queues* — Declared priority_queue<int> Q;, methods include Q.top(), Q.push(), Q.pop(), and Q.empty().

- *Sets* — Sets are represented as sorted associative containers, declared set<key, comparison> S;. Set algorithms include set_union and set_intersection, as well as other standard set operators.

2.2.2   The Java java.util Package

Useful standard Java objects appear in the java.util package. Almost all of java.util is available on the judge, except for a few libraries which provide an unhealthy degree of power to the contestant. For details, see Sun's website *http://java.sun.com/products/jdk.*

The collection of all Java classes defines an inheritance hierarchy, which means that subclasses are built on superclasses by adding methods and variables. As you move up the inheritance hierarchy, classes become more general and more abstract. The sole purpose of an *abstract* class is to provide an appropriate superclass from which other classes may inherit its interface and/or implementation. The abstract classes can only declare objects, not instantiate them. Classes from which objects can be instantiated are called *concrete* classes.

If you want to declare a general data structure object, declare it with an interface or abstract class and instantiate it using a concrete class. For example,

```
Map myMap = new HashMap();
```

In this case, `myMap` is treated as an object of `Map` class. Otherwise, you can just declare and instantiate an object with concrete class, like

```
HashMap myMap = new HashMap();
```

Here, `myMap` is only an object of `HashMap` class.

To use `java.util` include `import java.util.*;` at the beginning of your program to import the whole package, or replace the star to import a specific class, like `import java.util.HashMap;`.

Appropriate implementations of the basic data structures include —

Data Structure	Abstract class	Concrete class	Methods
Stack	No interface	`Stack`	`pop, push, empty, peek`
Queue	`List`	`ArrayList, LinkedList`	`add, remove, clear`
Dictionaries	`Map`	`HashMap, Hashtable`	`put, get, contains`
Priority Queue	`SortedMap`	`TreeMap`	`firstKey, lastKey, headMap`
Sets	`Set`	`HashSet`	`add, remove, contains`

2.3 Program Design Example: Going to War

In the children's card game War, a standard 52-card deck is dealt to two players (1 and 2) such that each player has 26 cards. Players do not look at their cards, but keep them in a packet face down. The object of the game is to win all the cards.

Both players play by turning their top cards face up and putting them on the table. Whoever turned the higher card takes both cards and adds them (face down) to the bottom of their packet. Cards rank as usual from high to low: *A, K, Q, J, T, 9, 8, 7, 6, 5, 4, 3, 2*. Suits are ignored. Both players then turn up their next card and repeat. The game continues until one player wins by taking all the cards.

When the face up cards are of equal rank there is a war. These cards stay on the table as both players play the next card of their pile face down and then another card face up. Whoever has the higher of the new face up cards wins the war, and adds all six cards to the bottom of his or her packet. If the new face up cards are equal as well, the war continues: each player puts another card face down and one face up. The war goes on like this as long as the face up cards continue to be equal. As soon as they are different, the player with the higher face up card wins all the cards on the table.

If someone runs out of cards in the middle of a war, the other player automatically wins. The cards are added to the back of the winner's hand in the exact order they were dealt, specifically 1's first card, 2's first card, 1's second card, etc.

As anyone with a five year-old nephew knows, a game of War can take a long time to finish. But how long? Your job is to write a program to simulate the game and report the number of moves.

———————————————   Solution starts below   ———————————————

How do we read such a problem description? Keep the following in mind as you design, code, test, and debug your solutions:

- *Read the Problem Carefully* — Read each line of the problem statement carefully, and reread it when the judge complains about an error. Skim the passage first, since much of the description may be background/history that does not impact the solution. Pay particular attention to the input and output descriptions, and sample input/output, but ...

- *Don't Assume* — Reading and understanding specifications is an important part of contest (and real-life) programming. Specifications often leave unspecified traps to fall in.

  Just because certain examples exhibit some nice property does not mean that all the test data will. Be on the lookout for unspecified input orders, unbounded input numbers, long line lengths, negative numbers, etc. Any input which is not explicitly forbidden should be assumed to be permitted!

- *Not So Fast, Louie* — Efficiency is often not an important issue, unless we are using exponential algorithms for problems where polynomial algorithms suffice. Don't worry too much about efficiency unless you have seen or can predict trouble. Read the specification to learn the maximum possible input size, and decide whether the most straightforward algorithm will suffice on such inputs.

  Even though a game of war seems interminable when you are playing with your nephew (and in fact can go on forever), we see no reason to worry about efficiency with this particular problem description.

2.4   Hitting the Deck

What is the best data structure to represent a deck of cards? The answer depends upon what you are going to do with them. Are you going to shuffle them? Compare their values? Search for patterns in the deck? Your intended actions define the operations of the data structure.

The primary action we need from our deck is dealing cards out from the top and adding them to the rear of our deck. Thus it is natural to represent each player's hand using the FIFO queue we defined earlier.

But there is an even more fundamental problem. How do we represent each card? Remember that cards have both suits (clubs, diamonds, hearts, and spades) and values (ace, 2–10, jack, queen, king). We have several possible choices. We can represent each card by a pair of characters or numbers specifying the suit and value. In the war problem, we might even throw away the suit entirely – but such thinking can get us in trouble. What if we had to print the winning card, or needed strong evidence that our queue implementation was working perfectly? An alternate approach might represent each card with a distinct integer, say 0 to 51, and map in back and forth between numbers and cards as needed.

The primary operation in war is comparing cards by their face value. This is tricky to do with the first character representation, because we must compare according to the historical but arbitrary ordering of face cards. Ad hoc logic might seem necessary to deal with this problem.

Instead, we will present the mapping approach as a generally useful programming technique. Whenever we can create a numerical *ranking* function and a dual *unranking* function which hold over a particular set of items $s \in S$, we can represent any item by its integer rank. The key property is that $s = unrank(rank(s))$. Thus the ranking function can be thought of as a hash function without collisions.

How can we rank and unrank playing cards? We order the card values from lowest to highest, and note that there are four distinct cards of each value. Multiplication and division are the key to mapping them from 0 to 51:

```
#define NCARDS  52      /* number of cards */
#define NSUITS  4       /* number of suits */

char values[] = "23456789TJQKA";
char suits[] = "cdhs";

int rank_card(char value, char suit)
{
        int i,j;        /* counters */

        for (i=0; i<(NCARDS/NSUITS); i++)
                if (values[i]==value)
                        for (j=0; j<NSUITS; j++)
                                if (suits[j]==suit)
                                        return( i*NSUITS + j );

        printf("Warning: bad input value=%d, suit=%d\n",value,suit);
}

char suit(int card)
{
        return( suits[card % NSUITS] );
}
```

```
char value(int card)
{
        return( values[card/NSUITS] );
}
```

Ranking and unranking functions are easy to develop for permutations, subsets, and most combinatorial objects. They are a general programming technique which can simplify operations on many different types of data.

2.5 String Input/Output

For our war program, the input consists of pairs of lines for each input deck, the first corresponding to player 1's cards, the second to player 2's cards. Here is an example of three games' worth of cards:

```
4d Ks As 4h Jh 6h Jd Qs Qh 6s 6c 2c Kc 4s Ah 3h Qd 2h 7s 9s 3c 8h Kd 7h Th Td
8d 8c 9c 7c 5d 4c Js Qc 5s Ts Jc Ad 7d Kh Tc 3s 8s 2d 2s 5h 6d Ac 5c 9h 3d 9d
6d 9d 8c 4s Kc 7c 4d Tc Kd 3s 5h 2h Ks 5c 2s Qh 8d 7d 3d Ah Js Jd 4c Jh 6c Qc
9h Qd Qs 9s Ac 8h Td Jc 7s 2d 6s As 4h Ts 6h 2c Kh Th 7h 5s 9c 5d Ad 3h 8s 3c
Ah As 4c 3s 7d Jc 5h 8s Qc Kh Td 3h 5c 9h 8c Qs 3d Ks 4d Kd 6c 6s 7h Qh 3c Jd
2h 8h 7s 2c 5d 7c 2d Tc Jh Ac 9s 9c 5s Qd 4s Js 6d Kc 2s Th 8d 9d 4h Ad 6h Ts
```

Many problems require reading non-numerical data. Text strings will be better discussed in Chapter 3, but note that you have several choices when it comes to reading text input:

- You can repeatedly get single characters from the input stream (e.g., getchar() in C), and process them one at a time.

- You can repeatedly get formatted tokens (e.g., scanf() in C) and process them as needed.

- You can read the entire line as a single string (e.g., gets() in C), and then parse it by accessing characters/substring in the string.

- You can use modern input/output primitives such as streams if your language supports them. Of course, you are still faced with the problem of deciding whether you want characters, strings, or something else as the basic input block.

In our war implementation, we chose the first option – namely, reading characters sequentially and processing them one by one. To make the example more illustrative, we explicitly test for end of line ('\n' in C):

```
main()
{
        queue decks[2];              /* player's decks */
        char value,suit,c;           /* input characters */
        int i;                       /* deck counter */
```

```
while (TRUE) {
    for (i=0; i<=1; i++) {
        init_queue(&decks[i]);

        while ((c = getchar()) != '\n') {
            if (c == EOF) return;
            if (c != ' ') {
                value = c;
                suit = getchar();
                enqueue(&decks[i],rank_card(value,suit));
            }
        }
    }

    war(&decks[0],&decks[1]);
}
}
```

Note that we represented the two decks as an array of queues instead of as two separate queue variables. This way, we eliminate the need to duplicate all the input processing code for each deck.

2.6   Winning the War

With the proper scaffolding afforded by our data structure design, the main routine becomes fairly straightforward. Note that the order in which the conquered cards get returned to the winning deck also can be modeled as a queue, so we get to use our abstract type once again:

```
war(queue *a, queue *b)
{
    int steps=0;              /* step counter */
    int x,y;                  /* top cards */
    queue c;                  /* cards involved in the war */
    bool inwar;               /* are we involved in a war? */

    inwar = FALSE;
    init_queue(&c);

    while ((!empty(a)) && (!empty(b) && (steps < MAXSTEPS))) {
        steps = steps + 1;
        x = dequeue(a);
        y = dequeue(b);
        enqueue(&c,x);
```

```
            enqueue(&c,y);
            if (inwar) {
                    inwar = FALSE;
            } else {
                    if (value(x) > value(y))
                            clear_queue(&c,a);
                    else if  (value(x) < value(y))
                            clear_queue(&c,b);
                    else if (value(y) == value(x))
                            inwar = TRUE;
            }
    }

    if (!empty(a) && empty(b))
            printf("a wins in %d steps \n",steps);
    else if (empty(a) && !empty(b))
            printf("b wins in %d steps \n",steps);
    else if (!empty(a) && !empty(b))
            printf("game tied after %d steps, |a|=%d |b|=%d \n",
                    steps,a->count,b->count);
    else
            printf("a and b tie in %d steps \n",steps);
}

clear_queue(queue *a, queue *b)
{
    while (!empty(a)) enqueue(b,dequeue(a));
}
```

2.7 Testing and Debugging

Debugging can be particularly frustrating with the robot judge, since you never get to see the test case on which your program failed. Thus you can't fake your way around a problem – you have to do it right.

This makes it very important to test your program systematically before submission. Catching stupid errors yourself will save you time in the long run, particularly in contest situations where incorrect submissions are penalized. Several ideas go into designing good test files:

- *Test the Given Input* — Most problem specifications include sample input and output. Often (but not always) they match each other. Getting the sample input right is a necessary but not sufficient condition for correctness.

- *Test Incorrect Input* — If the problem specification tells you that your program must take action on illegal inputs, be sure to test for such problematic instances.

- *Test Boundary Conditions* — Many bugs in programs are due to "off-by-one" errors. Explicitly test your code for such conditions as empty input, one item, two items, and values which are zero.

- *Test Instances Where You Know the Correct Answer* — A critical part of developing a good test case is being sure you know what the right answer is. Your test cases should focus on simple enough instances that you can solve them by hand. It is easy to be fooled into accepting plausible-looking output without completely analyzing the desired behavior.

- *Test Big Examples Where You Don't Know the Correct Answer* — Usually only small examples are solvable by hand. This makes it difficult to validate your program on larger inputs. Try a few easily constructed large instances, such as random data or the numbers 1 to n inclusive, just to make certain the program doesn't crash or do anything stupid.

Testing is the art of revealing bugs. Debugging is the art of exterminating them. We designed this programming problem and coded it up ourselves for the purpose of this example. Yet getting it working without bugs took us significantly longer than expected. This is no surprise, for all programmers are inherent optimists. But how can you avoid falling into such traps?

- *Get To Know Your Debugger* — Any reasonable programming environment comes with a source-level debugger, which lets you stop execution at given positions or logical conditions, look at the contents of a variable, and change its value to see what happens. Source-level debuggers are well worth their weight in print statements; learn to use them. The sooner you start, the more time and frustration you will save.

- *Display Your Data Structures* — At one point in debugging our War program, we had an off-by-one error in our priority queue. This could only be revealed by displaying the contents of the priority queue to see what was missing. Write special-purpose display routines for all non-trivial data structures, as debuggers often have a hard time making sense out of them.

- *Test Invariants Rigorously* — The card ranking and unranking functions are a potential source of error whenever they are not inverses of each other. An *invariant* is a property of the program which is true regardless of the input. A simple invariant test like

```
for (i=0; i<NCARDS; i++)
    if (i != rank_card(value(i), suit(i)))
        printf("Error: rank_card(%c,%c)=%d not %d\n", value(i),
                suit(i), rank_card(value(i), suit(i)), i);
```

completely tests the correctness of the ranking and unranking functions.

- *Inspect Your Code* — Perhaps the single most powerful way to debug your program is to read it carefully. Bugs tend to infest code that is too ugly to read or too clever to understand.

- *Make Your Print Statements Mean Something* — Adding print statements to peer into the internals of your malfunctioning program is a necessary evil which can be minimized by effective use of a source-level debugger. But if you are going to add debugging print statements, make them as useful as possible. Be sure to display with the names of the variable and its position in the program as well as its value. It is easy to get lost in an enormous volume of debugging output, but the relevant lines can be quickly found by searching or greping through the output file.

  Comment out your debugging statements when you have fixed that part of the program, but don't be so fast to delete them. If you are like us, you will probably need them again.

- *Make Your Arrays a Little Larger Than Necessary* — Off-by-one errors are a particularly subtle and tricky class of bugs. Clear thinking and discipline are the right way avoid them. But thinking is hard and memory is cheap. We find it a useful crutch to define arrays one or two elements larger than *should* be necessary so as to minimize the consequences of any off-by-one error.

- *Make Sure Your Bugs are Really Bugs* — We spent some time tracking down an infinite loop in the War program, before discovering that random initial card orderings have an astonishingly high probability of creating a cycling condition where players forever alternate taking cards from each other. The culprit was the deterministic card order specified to collect the spoils of war, i.e., always interleaving player 1 and player 2's cards. In fact, there was no bug in the program at all!

  Please learn from this example. Always shuffle the pickup cards randomly to avoid having to play War with your nephew forever.

2.8 Problems

2.8.1 Jolly Jumpers

PC/UVa IDs: 110201/10038, **Popularity:** A, **Success rate:** average **Level:** 1

A sequence of $n > 0$ integers is called a *jolly jumper* if the absolute values of the differences between successive elements take on all possible values 1 through $n - 1$. For instance,

```
1 4 2 3
```

is a jolly jumper, because the absolute differences are 3, 2, and 1, respectively. The definition implies that any sequence of a single integer is a jolly jumper. Write a program to determine whether each of a number of sequences is a jolly jumper.

Input

Each line of input contains an integer $n < 3,000$ followed by n integers representing the sequence.

Output

For each line of input generate a line of output saying "`Jolly`" or "`Not jolly`".

Sample Input

```
4 1 4 2 3
5 1 4 2 -1 6
```

Sample Output

```
Jolly
Not jolly
```

2.8.2   Poker Hands

PC/UVa IDs: 110202/10315, **Popularity:** C, **Success rate:** average **Level:** 2

A poker deck contains 52 cards. Each card has a suit of either clubs, diamonds, hearts, or spades (denoted C, D, H, S in the input data). Each card also has a value of either 2 through 10, jack, queen, king, or ace (denoted 2, 3, 4, 5, 6, 7, 8, 9, T, J, Q, K, A). For scoring purposes card values are ordered as above, with 2 having the lowest and ace the highest value. The suit has no impact on value.

A poker hand consists of five cards dealt from the deck. Poker hands are ranked by the following partial order from lowest to highest.

High Card. Hands which do not fit any higher category are ranked by the value of their highest card. If the highest cards have the same value, the hands are ranked by the next highest, and so on.

Pair. Two of the five cards in the hand have the same value. Hands which both contain a pair are ranked by the value of the cards forming the pair. If these values are the same, the hands are ranked by the values of the cards not forming the pair, in decreasing order.

Two Pairs. The hand contains two different pairs. Hands which both contain two pairs are ranked by the value of their highest pair. Hands with the same highest pair are ranked by the value of their other pair. If these values are the same the hands are ranked by the value of the remaining card.

Three of a Kind. Three of the cards in the hand have the same value. Hands which both contain three of a kind are ranked by the value of the three cards.

Straight. Hand contains five cards with consecutive values. Hands which both contain a straight are ranked by their highest card.

Flush. Hand contains five cards of the same suit. Hands which are both flushes are ranked using the rules for High Card.

Full House. Three cards of the same value, with the remaining two cards forming a pair. Ranked by the value of the three cards.

Four of a Kind. Four cards with the same value. Ranked by the value of the four cards.

Straight Flush. Five cards of the same suit with consecutive values. Ranked by the highest card in the hand.

Your job is to compare several pairs of poker hands and to indicate which, if either, has a higher rank.

Input

The input file contains several lines, each containing the designation of ten cards: the first five cards are the hand for the player named "*Black*" and the next five cards are the hand for the player named "*White*".

Output

For each line of input, print a line containing one of the following:

```
Black wins.
White wins.
Tie.
```

Sample Input

```
2H 3D 5S 9C KD 2C 3H 4S 8C AH
2H 4S 4C 2D 4H 2S 8S AS QS 3S
2H 3D 5S 9C KD 2C 3H 4S 8C KH
2H 3D 5S 9C KD 2D 3H 5C 9S KH
```

Sample Output

```
White wins.
Black wins.
Black wins.
Tie.
```

2.8.3 Hartals

PC/UVa IDs: 110203/10050, **Popularity:** B, **Success rate:** high **Level:** 2

Political parties in Bangladesh show their muscle by calling for regular *hartals* (strikes), which cause considerable economic damage. For our purposes, each party may be characterized by a positive integer h called the *hartal parameter* that denotes the average number of days between two successive strikes called by the given party.

Consider three political parties. Assume $h_1 = 3$, $h_2 = 4$, and $h_3 = 8$, where h_i is the hartal parameter for party i. We can simulate the behavior of these three parties for $N = 14$ days. We always start the simulation on a Sunday. There are no hartals on either Fridays or Saturdays.

	1	2	3	4	5	6	7	8	9	10	11	12	13	14
Days	Su	Mo	Tu	We	Th	Fr	Sa	Su	Mo	Tu	We	Th	Fr	Sa
Party 1			x			x			x			x		
Party 2				x				x				x		
Party 3								x						
Hartals			1	2				3	4			5		

There will be exactly five hartals (on days 3, 4, 8, 9, and 12) over the 14 days. There is no hartal on day 6 since it falls on Friday. Hence we lose five working days in two weeks.

Given the hartal parameters for several political parties and the value of N, determine the number of working days lost in those N days.

Input

The first line of the input consists of a single integer T giving the number of test cases to follow. The first line of each test case contains an integer N ($7 \leq N \leq 3,650$), giving the number of days over which the simulation must be run. The next line contains another integer P ($1 \leq P \leq 100$) representing the number of political parties. The ith of the next P lines contains a positive integer h_i (which will never be a multiple of 7) giving the *hartal parameter* for party i ($1 \leq i \leq P$).

Output

For each test case, output the number of working days lost on a separate line.

Sample Input

```
2
14
3
3
4
```

8
100
4
12
15
25
40

Sample Output

5
15

2.8.4   Crypt Kicker

PC/UVa IDs: 110204/843, **Popularity:** B, **Success rate:** low   **Level:** 2

A common but insecure method of encrypting text is to permute the letters of the alphabet. In other words, each letter of the alphabet is consistently replaced in the text by some other letter. To ensure that the encryption is reversible, no two letters are replaced by the same letter.

Your task is to decrypt several encoded lines of text, assuming that each line uses a different set of replacements, and that all words in the decrypted text are from a dictionary of known words.

Input

The input consists of a line containing an integer n, followed by n lowercase words, one per line, in alphabetical order. These n words compose the dictionary of words which may appear in the decrypted text. Following the dictionary are several lines of input. Each line is encrypted as described above.

There are no more than 1,000 words in the dictionary. No word exceeds 16 letters. The encrypted lines contain only lower case letters and spaces and do not exceed 80 characters in length.

Output

Decrypt each line and print it to standard output. If there are multiple solutions, any one will do. If there is no solution, replace every letter of the alphabet by an asterisk.

Sample Input

```
6
and
dick
jane
puff
spot
yertle
bjvg xsb hxsn xsb qymm xsb rqat xsb pnetfn
xxxx yyy zzzz www yyyy aaa bbbb ccc dddddd
```

Sample Output

```
dick and jane and puff and spot and yertle
**** *** **** *** **** *** **** *** ******
```

2.8.5 Stack 'em Up

PC/UVa IDs: 110205/10205, **Popularity:** B, **Success rate:** average **Level:** 1

The Big City has many casinos. In one of them, the dealer cheats. She has perfected several shuffles; each shuffle rearranges the cards in exactly the same way whenever it is used. A simple example is the "bottom card" shuffle, which removes the bottom card and places it at the top. By using various combinations of these known shuffles, the crooked dealer can arrange to stack the cards in just about any particular order.

You have been retained by the security manager to track this dealer. You are given a list of all the shuffles performed by the dealer, along with visual cues that allow you to determine which shuffle she uses at any particular time. Your job is to predict the order of the cards after a sequence of shuffles.

A standard playing card deck contains 52 cards, with 13 values in each of four suits. The values are named *2, 3, 4, 5, 6, 7, 8, 9, 10, Jack, Queen, King, Ace*. The suits are named *Clubs, Diamonds, Hearts, Spades*. A particular card in the deck can be uniquely identified by its value and suit, typically denoted $< value >$ of $< suit >$. For example, "9 of Hearts" or "King of Spades." Traditionally a new deck is ordered first alphabetically by suit, then by value in the order given above.

Input

The input begins with a single positive integer on a line by itself indicating the number of test cases, followed by a blank line. There is also a blank line between two consecutive inputs.

Each case consists of an integer $n \leq 100$, the number of shuffles that the dealer knows. Then follow n sets of 52 integers, each comprising all the integers from 1 to 52 in some order. Within each set of 52 integers, i in position j means that the shuffle moves the ith card in the deck to position j.

Several lines follow, each containing an integer k between 1 and n. These indicate that you have observed the dealer applying the kth shuffle given in the input.

Output

For each test case, assume the dealer starts with a new deck ordered as described above. After all the shuffles had been performed, give the names of the cards in the deck, in the new order. The output of two consecutive cases will be separated by a blank line.

Sample Input

```
1

2
2 1 3 4 5 6 7 8 9 10 11 12 13 14 15 16 17 18 19 20 21 22 23 24 25 26
27 28 29 30 31 32 33 34 35 36 37 38 39 40 41 42 43 44 45 46 47 48 49 50 52 51
52 2 3 4 5 6 7 8 9 10 11 12 13 14 15 16 17 18 19 20 21 22 23 24 25 26
```

27 28 29 30 31 32 33 34 35 36 37 38 39 40 41 42 43 44 45 46 47 48 49 50 51 1
1
2

Sample Output

```
King of Spades
2 of Clubs
4 of Clubs
5 of Clubs
6 of Clubs
7 of Clubs
8 of Clubs
9 of Clubs
10 of Clubs
Jack of Clubs
Queen of Clubs
King of Clubs
Ace of Clubs
2 of Diamonds
3 of Diamonds
4 of Diamonds
5 of Diamonds
6 of Diamonds
7 of Diamonds
8 of Diamonds
9 of Diamonds
10 of Diamonds
Jack of Diamonds
Queen of Diamonds
King of Diamonds
Ace of Diamonds
2 of Hearts
3 of Hearts
4 of Hearts
5 of Hearts
6 of Hearts
7 of Hearts
8 of Hearts
9 of Hearts
10 of Hearts
Jack of Hearts
Queen of Hearts
King of Hearts
Ace of Hearts
2 of Spades
3 of Spades
4 of Spades
5 of Spades
6 of Spades
7 of Spades
8 of Spades
9 of Spades
10 of Spades
Jack of Spades
Queen of Spades
Ace of Spades
3 of Clubs
```

2.8.6 Erdös Numbers

PC/UVa IDs: 110206/10044, **Popularity:** B, **Success rate:** low **Level:** 2

The Hungarian Paul Erdös (1913–1996) was one of the most famous mathematicians of the 20th century. Every mathematician having the honor of being a co-author of Erdös is well respected.

Unfortunately, not everybody got the chance to write a paper with Erdös, so the best they could do was publish a paper with somebody who had published a scientific paper with Erdös. This gave rise to the so-called *Erdös numbers*. An author who has jointly published with Erdös had Erdös number 1. An author who had not published with Erdös but with somebody with Erdös number 1 obtained Erdös number 2, and so on.

Your task is to write a program which computes Erdös numbers for a given set of papers and scientists.

Input

The first line of the input contains the number of scenarios. Each scenario consists of a paper database and a list of names. It begins with the line *P N*, where *P* and *N* are natural numbers. Following this line is the paper database, with *P* lines each containing the description of one paper specified in the following way:

```
Smith, M.N., Martin, G., Erdos, P.: Newtonian forms of prime factors
```

Note that umlauts, like "ö," are simply written as "o". After the *P* papers follow *N* lines with names. Such a name line has the following format:

```
Martin, G.
```

Output

For every scenario you are to print a line containing a string "Scenario *i*" (where *i* is the number of the scenario) and the author names together with their Erdös number of all authors in the list of names. The authors should appear in the same order as they appear in the list of names. The Erdös number is based on the papers in the paper database of this scenario. Authors which do not have any relation to Erdös via the papers in the database have Erdös number "infinity."

Sample Input

```
1
4 3
Smith, M.N., Martin, G., Erdos, P.: Newtonian forms of prime factors
Erdos, P., Reisig, W.: Stuttering in petri nets
Smith, M.N., Chen, X.: First order derivates in structured programming
Jablonski, T., Hsueh, Z.: Selfstabilizing data structures
```

```
Smith, M.N.
Hsueh, Z.
Chen, X.
```

Sample Output

```
Scenario 1
Smith, M.N. 1
Hsueh, Z. infinity
Chen, X. 2
```

2.8.7   Contest Scoreboard

PC/UVa IDs: 110207/10258, **Popularity:** B, **Success rate:** average **Level:** 1

Want to compete in the ACM ICPC? Then you had better know how to keep score! Contestants are ranked first by the number of problems solved (the more the better), then by decreasing amounts of penalty time. If two or more contestants are tied in both problems solved and penalty time, they are displayed in order of increasing team numbers.

A problem is considered solved by a contestant if any of the submissions for that problem was judged correct. Penalty time is computed as the number of minutes it took until the first correct submission for a problem was received, plus 20 minutes for each incorrect submission prior to the correct solution. Unsolved problems incur no time penalties.

Input

The input begins with a single positive integer on a line by itself indicating the number of cases, each described as below. This line is followed by a blank line. There is also a blank line between two consecutive inputs.

The input consists of a snapshot of the judging queue, containing entries from some or all of contestants 1 through 100 solving problems 1 through 9. Each line of input consists of three numbers and a letter in the format *contestant problem time L*, where *L* can be C, I, R, U, or E. These stand for Correct, Incorrect, clarification Request, Unjudged, and Erroneous submission. The last three cases do not affect scoring.

The lines of input appear in the order in which the submissions were received.

Output

The output for each test case will consist of a scoreboard, sorted by the criteria described above. Each line of output will contain a contestant number, the number of problems solved by the contestant and the total time penalty accumulated by the contestant. Since not all contestants are actually participating, only display those contestants who have made a submission.

The output of two consecutive cases will be separated by a blank line.

Sample Input	Sample Output
1	1 2 66
	3 1 11
1 2 10 I	
3 1 11 C	
1 2 19 R	
1 2 21 C	
1 1 25 C	

2.8.8   Yahtzee

PC/UVa IDs: 110208/10149, **Popularity:** C, **Success rate:** average **Level:** 3

The game of Yahtzee involves five dice, which are thrown in 13 rounds. A score card contains 13 categories. Each round may be scored in a category of the player's choosing, but each category may be scored only once in the game. The 13 categories are scored as follows:

- **ones** - sum of all ones thrown

- **twos** - sum of all twos thrown

- **threes** - sum of all threes thrown

- **fours** - sum of all fours thrown

- **fives** - sum of all fives thrown

- **sixes** - sum of all sixes thrown

- **chance** - sum of all dice

- **three of a kind** - sum of all dice, provided at least three have same value

- **four of a kind** - sum of all dice, provided at least four have same value

- **five of a kind** - 50 points, provided all five dice have same value

- **short straight** - 25 points, provided four of the dice form a sequence (that is, 1,2,3,4 or 2,3,4,5 or 3,4,5,6)

- **long straight** - 35 points, provided all dice form a sequence (1,2,3,4,5 or 2,3,4,5,6)

- **full house** - 40 points, provided three of the dice are equal and the other two dice are also equal. (for example, 2,2,5,5,5)

Each of the last six categories may be scored as 0 if the criteria are not met.

The score for the game is the sum of all 13 categories plus a bonus of 35 points if the sum of the first six categories is 63 or greater.

Your job is to compute the best possible score for a sequence of rounds.

Input

Each line of input contains five integers between 1 and 6, indicating the values of the five dice thrown in each round. There are 13 such lines for each game, and there may be any number of games in the input data.

Output

Your output should consist of a single line for each game containing 15 numbers: the score in each category (in the order given), the bonus score (0 or 35), and the total score. If there is more than categorization that yields the same total score, any one will do.

Sample Input

```
1 2 3 4 5
1 2 3 4 5
1 2 3 4 5
1 2 3 4 5
1 2 3 4 5
1 2 3 4 5
1 2 3 4 5
1 2 3 4 5
1 2 3 4 5
1 2 3 4 5
1 2 3 4 5
1 2 3 4 5
1 1 1 1 1
6 6 6 6 6
6 6 6 1 1
1 1 1 2 2
1 1 1 2 3
1 2 3 4 5
1 2 3 4 6
6 1 2 6 6
1 4 5 5 5
5 5 5 5 6
4 4 4 5 6
3 1 3 6 3
2 2 2 4 6
```

Sample Output

```
1 2 3 4 5 0 15 0 0 0 25 35 0 0 90
3 6 9 12 15 30 21 20 26 50 25 35 40 35 327
```

2.9   Hints

2.2 Can we reduce the value of a poker hand to a single numerical value to make the comparison easier?

2.3 Do we need to build the actual table in order to compute the number of hartals?

2.4 Does it pay to partition the words into equivalence classes based on repeated letters and length?

2.7 What is the easiest way to sort on the multiple criteria?

2.8 Do we need to try all possible mappings of rounds to categories, or can we make certain assignments in a more straightforward way?

2.10   Notes

2.1 A jolly number is a special case of a *graceful graph* labeling. A graph is called graceful if there exists a way to label the n vertices with integers such that the absolute value of the difference between the endpoints of all m of the edges yields a distinct value between 1 and m. A jolly jumper represents a graceful labeling of an n-vertex path. The famous *graceful tree conjecture* asks whether every tree has a graceful labeling. Graceful graphs make a great topic for undergraduate student research. See Gallian's dynamic survey [Gal01] for a list of accessible open problems.

2.5 The mathematics of card shuffling is a fascinating topic. A *perfect shuffle* splits the deck in half into piles A and B, and then interleaves the cards: top of A, top of B, top of A, ... Amazingly, eight perfect shuffles take a deck back to its original state! This can be shown using either modular arithmetic or the theory of cycles in permutations. See [DGK83, Mor98] for more on perfect shuffles.

2.6 The first author of this book has an Erdös number of 2, giving the second a number of ≤ 3. Erdös was famous for posing beautiful, easy-to-understand but hard-to-solve problems in combinatorics, graph theory, and number theory. Read one of the popular biographies of his life [Hof99, Sch00] for more about this fascinating man.

3

Strings

Text strings are a fundamental data structure of growing importance. Internet search engines such as Google search billions of documents almost instantaneously. The sequencing of the human genome has given us three billion characters of text describing all the proteins we are built from. In searching this string for interesting patterns, we are literally looking for the secret of life.

The stakes in solving the programming problems in this chapter are considerably lower than that. However, they provide insight into how characters and text strings are represented in modern computers, and the clever algorithms which search and manipulate this data. We refer the interested reader to [Gus97] for a more advanced discussion of string algorithms.

3.1 Character Codes

Character codes are mappings between numbers and the symbols which make up a particular alphabet. Computers are fundamentally designed to work with numerical data. All they know about a given alphabet is which symbol is assigned to each possible number. When changing the font in a print program, all that really changes are the image bit-maps associated with each character. When changing an operating system from English to Russian all that really changes is the mapping of symbols in the character code.

It is useful to understand something about character code designs when working with text strings. The *American Standard Code for Information Interchange* (ASCII) is a

0	NUL	1	SOH	2	STX	3	ETX	4	EOT	5	ENQ	6	ACK	7	BEL
8	BS	9	HT	10	NL	11	VT	12	NP	13	CR	14	SO	15	SI
16	DLE	17	DC1	18	DC2	19	DC3	20	DC4	21	NAK	22	SYN	23	ETB
24	CAN	25	EM	26	SUB	27	ESC	28	FS	29	GS	30	RS	31	US
32	SP	33	!	34	"	35	#	36	$	37	%	38	&	39	'
40	(	41	)	42	*	43	+	44	,	45	-	46	.	47	/
48	0	49	1	50	2	51	3	52	4	53	5	54	6	55	7
56	8	57	9	58	:	59	;	60	<	61	=	62	>	63	?
64	@	65	A	66	B	67	C	68	D	69	E	70	F	71	G
72	H	73	I	74	J	75	K	76	L	77	M	78	N	79	O
80	P	81	Q	82	R	83	S	84	T	85	U	86	V	87	W
88	X	89	Y	90	Z	91	[	92	\	93	]	94	^	95	_
96	`	97	a	98	b	99	c	100	d	101	e	102	f	103	g
104	h	105	i	106	j	107	k	108	l	109	m	110	n	111	o
112	p	113	q	114	r	115	s	116	t	117	u	118	v	119	w
120	x	121	y	122	z	123	{	124	—	125	}	126	~	127	DEL

Figure 3.1. The ASCII character code.

single-byte character code where $2^7 = 128$ characters are specified.[1] Bytes are eight-bit entities; so that means the highest-order bit is left as zero.

Consider the ASCII character code table presented in Figure 3.1, where the left entry in each pair is the decimal (base-ten) value of the specification, while the right entry is the associated symbol. These symbol assignments were not done at random. Several interesting properties of the design make programming tasks easier:

- All non-printable characters have either the first three bits as zero or all seven lowest bits as one. This makes it very easy to eliminate them before displaying junk, although somehow very few programs seem to do so.

- Both the upper- and lowercase letters and the numerical digits appear sequentially. Thus we can iterate through all the letters/digits simply by looping from the value of the first symbol (say, "a") to value of the last symbol (say, "z").

- Another consequence of this sequential placement is that we can convert a character (say, "I") to its rank in the collating sequence (eighth, if "A" is the zeroth character) simply by subtracting off the first symbol ("A").

- We can convert a character (say "C") from upper- to lowercase by adding the difference of the upper and lowercase starting character ("C"-"A"+"a"). Similarly, a character x is uppercase if and only if it lies between "A" and "Z".

- Given the character code, we can predict what will happen when naively sorting text files. Which of "x" or "3" or "C" appears first in alphabetical order? Sorting alphabetically means sorting by character code. Using a different collating sequence requires more complicated comparison functions, as will be discussed in Chapter 4.

- Non-printable character codes for new-line (10) and carriage return (13) are designed to delimit the end of text lines. Inconsistent use of these codes is one of the pains in moving text files between UNIX and Windows systems.

More modern international character code designs such as *Unicode* use two or even three bytes per symbol, and can represent virtually any symbol in every language on

---

[1]Be aware that there are literally dozens of variations on ASCII. Perhaps the most important is ISO Latin-1, which is a full 8-bit code that includes European accented characters.

earth. However, good old ASCII remains alive embedded in Unicode. Whenever the high-order bits are 0, the text gets interpreted as single-byte characters instead of two-byte entities. Thus we can still use the simpler, more memory-efficient encoding while opening the door to thousands of additional symbols.

All of this makes a big difference in manipulating text in different programming languages. Older languages, like Pascal, C, and C++, view the `char` type as virtually synonymous with 8-bit entities. Thus the character data type is the choice for manipulating raw files, even for those which are not intended to be printable. Java, on the other hand, was designed to support Unicode, so characters are 16-bit entities. The upper byte is all zeros when working with ASCII/ISO Latin 1 text. Be aware of this difference when you switch between programming languages.

3.2 Representing Strings

Strings are sequences of characters, where order clearly matters. It is important to be aware of how your favorite programming language represents strings, because there are several different possibilities:

- *Null-terminated Arrays* — C/C++ treats strings as arrays of characters. The string ends the instant it hits the null character "\0", i.e., zero ASCII. Failing to end your string explicitly with a null typically extends it by a bunch of unprintable characters. In defining a string, enough array must be allocated to hold the largest possible string (plus the null) unless you want a core dump. The advantage of this array representation is that all individual characters are accessible by index as array elements.

- *Array Plus Length* — Another scheme uses the first array location to store the length of the string, thus avoiding the need for any terminating null character. Presumably this is what Java implementations do internally, even though the user's view of strings is as objects with a set of operators and methods acting on them.

- *Linked Lists of Characters* — Text strings can be represented using linked lists, but this is typically avoided because of the high space-overhead associated with having a several-byte pointer for each single byte character. Still, such a representation might be useful if you were to insert or delete substrings frequently within the body of a string.

The underlying string representation can have a big impact on which operations are easily or efficiently supported. Compare each of these three data structures with respect to the following properties:

- Which uses the least amount of space? On what sized strings?

- Which constrains the content of the strings which can possibly be represented?

- Which allow constant-time access to the ith character?

- Which allow efficient checks that the ith character is in fact within the string, thus avoiding out-of-bounds errors?

- Which allow efficient deletion or insertion of new characters at the ith position?

- Which representation is used when users are limited to strings of length at most 255, e.g., file names in Windows?

3.3   Program Design Example: Corporate Renamings

Corporate name changes are occurring with ever greater frequency, as companies merge, buy each other out, try to hide from bad publicity, or even raise their stock price – remember when adding a .com to a company's name was the secret to success!

These changes make it difficult to figure out the current name of a company when reading old documents. Your company, Digiscam (formerly Algorist Technologies), has put you to work on a program which maintains a database of corporate name changes and does the appropriate substitutions to bring old documents up to date.

Your program should take as input a file with a given number of corporate name changes, followed by a given number of lines of text for you to correct. Only *exact* matches of the string should be replaced. There will be at most 100 corporate changes, and each line of text is at most 1,000 characters long. A sample input is —

```
4
"Anderson Consulting" to "Accenture"
"Enron" to "Dynegy"
"DEC" to "Compaq"
"TWA" to "American"
5
Anderson Accounting begat Anderson Consulting, which
offered advice to Enron before it DECLARED bankruptcy,
which made Anderson
Consulting quite happy it changed its name
in the first place!
```

Which should be transformed to —

```
Anderson Accounting begat Accenture, which
offered advice to Dynegy before it CompaqLARED bankruptcy,
which made Anderson
Consulting quite happy it changed its name
in the first place!
```

The specifications do not ask you to respect word delimiters (such as blank), so transforming DECLARED to CompaqLARED is indeed the right thing to do.

——————————————   Solution starts below   ——————————————

What kind of string operations do we need to do to solve this problem? We must be able to read strings and store them, search strings for patterns, modify them, and finally print them.

Observe that the input file has been segmented into two parts. The first section, the dictionary of name changes, must be completely read and stored before starting to convert the text. To declare the relevant data structures:

```
#include <string.h>

#define MAXLEN          1001    /* longest possible string */
#define MAXCHANGES      101     /* maximum number of name changes */

typedef char string[MAXLEN];

string mergers[MAXCHANGES][2];  /* store before/after corporate names */
int nmergers;                   /* number of different name changes */
```

We represent the dictionary as a two-dimensional array of strings. We do not need to sort the keys in any particular order, since we will be scanning through each of them on each line of text.

Reading the list of company names is somewhat complicated by the fact that we must parse each input line to extract the stuff between quotes. The trick is ignoring text before the first quote, and collecting it until the second quote:

```
read_changes()
{
        int i;                  /* counter */

        scanf("%d\n",&nmergers);
        for (i=0; i<nmergers; i++) {
                read_quoted_string(&(mergers[i][0]));
                read_quoted_string(&(mergers[i][1]));
        }
}

read_quoted_string(char *s)
{
        int i=0;                /* counter */
        char c;                 /* latest character */

        while ((c=getchar()) != '\"') ;
        while ((c=getchar()) != '\"') {
                s[i] = c;
                i = i+1;
        }
        s[i] = '\0';
```

}

The more advanced operations we will need are presented in the following sections.

3.4   Searching for Patterns

The simplest algorithm to search for the presence of pattern string p in text t overlays the pattern string at every position in the text, and checks whether every pattern character matches the corresponding text character:

```
/*      Return the position of the first occurrence of the pattern p
        in the text t, and -1 if it does not occur.
*/

int findmatch(char *p, char *t)
{
        int i,j;                        /* counters */
        int plen, tlen;                 /* string lengths */

        plen = strlen(p);
        tlen = strlen(t);

        for (i=0; i<=(tlen-plen); i=i+1) {
                j=0;
                while ((j<plen) && (t[i+j]==p[j]))
                        j = j+1;
                if (j == plen) return(i);
        }

        return(-1);
}
```

Note that this routine only searches for exact pattern matches. If a letter is capitalized in the pattern but not in the text there is no match. More seriously, if a company name is split between lines (see the example input), no match will be detected. Such searches can be performed by changing the text/pattern comparison from t[i+j]==p[j] to something more interesting. The same technique can be used to allow for *wild card* characters, which match anything. A more general notion of approximate string matching is discussed in Section 11.

This naive algorithm can take as much as $O(|p||t|)$ time in the worst case. Can you construct an arbitrary-length example pattern and text where it actually takes this much time without ever matching the pattern? Usually the naive search will be much more efficient, since we advance in the text soon as we get a single mismatch. More complicated, linear-time search algorithms do exist: see [Gus97] for a complete discussion. These algorithms are likely implemented in the string library associated with your programming language.

3.5 Manipulating Strings

Manipulating strings requires knowing exactly which string representation you or your language is using. Here, we assume that strings are represented as a sequence of single-byte characters in a null-terminated array, as supported by C.

Treating strings like arrays makes many operations reasonably easy:

- *Computing the Length of a String* — Scan through the characters of the string, adding one to the count each time until we hit the null character.

- *Copying a String* — Unless your programming language supports copying entire arrays in one swoop, you must explicitly loop through each character one at a time. Remember to allocate enough memory for the new copy, and don't forget the null!

- *Reversing a String* — The easiest way to do this is to copy the string from right to left into a second array. The right endpoint is found by computing the string length. Remember to terminate the new string with a null! String reversal can also be done in place by swapping characters if you are willing to destroy the original string.

As an example, we implement a routine to replace a substring at a given position with another string. We will need it for our corporate merger program. The tricky part is moving the other characters in our string to accommodate the new text. If the replacement substring is longer than the original, we must move the suffix out of the way so it isn't stepped on. If the replacement substring is shorter, we must move the suffix in to cover up the hole:

```
/*      Replace the substring of length xlen starting at position pos in
        string s with the contents of string y.
*/

replace_x_with_y(char *s, int pos, int xlen, char *y)
{
        int i;                          /* counter */
        int slen,ylen;                  /* lengths of relevant strings */

        slen = strlen(s);
        ylen = strlen(y);

        if (xlen >= ylen)
                for (i=(pos+xlen); i<=slen; i++) s[i+(ylen-xlen)] = s[i];
        else
```

```
        for (i=slen; i>=(pos+xlen); i--) s[i+(ylen-xlen)] = s[i];

    for (i=0; i<ylen; i++) s[pos+i] = y[i];
}
```

An alternative approach would have been to assemble the new string in a temporary buffer, and then overwrite all the characters of *s* with the contents of the buffer.

3.6 Completing the Merger

With all of these supporting routines in place, the rest of the program becomes fairly simple:

```
main()
{
        string s;               /* input string */
        char c;                 /* input character */
        int nlines;             /* number of lines in text */
        int i,j;                /* counters */
        int pos;                /* position of pattern in string */

        read_changes();
        scanf("%d\n",&nlines);
        for (i=1; i<=nlines; i=i+1) {           /* read text line */
                j=0;
                while ((c=getchar()) != '\n') {
                        s[j] = c;
                        j = j+1;
                }
                s[j] = '\0';

                for (j=0; j<nmergers; j=j+1)
                        while ((pos=findmatch(mergers[j][0],s)) != -1) {
                                replace_x_with_y(s, pos,
                                        strlen(mergers[j][0]), mergers[j][1]);
                        }

                printf("%s\n",s);
        }
}
```

3.7 String Library Functions

Whether you work in C, C++, or Java, be aware of the support provided for characters and strings through libraries or classes. There is no reason to reinvent the wheel.

Strings are not a supported data type of standard Pascal, and so the details vary with the specific implementation.

C Library String Functions

C contains both character and string libraries. The C language *character* library `ctype.h` contains several simple tests and manipulations on character codes. As with all C predicates, true is defined as any non-zero quantity, and false as zero.

```
#include <ctype.h>       /* include the character library */

int isalpha(int c);      /* true if c is either upper or lower case */
int isupper(int c);      /* true if c is upper case */
int islower(int c);      /* true if c is lower case */
int isdigit(int c);      /* true if c is a numerical digit (0-9) */
int ispunct(int c);      /* true if c is a punctuation symbol */
int isxdigit(int c);     /* true if c is a hexadecimal digit (0-9,A-F) */
int isprint(int c);      /* true if c is any printable character */

int toupper(int c);      /* convert c to upper case -- no error checking */
int tolower(int c);      /* convert c to lower case -- no error checking */
```

Check the definition of each carefully before assuming it does exactly what you want.

The following functions appear in the C language *string* library `string.h`. The full library has more functions and options, so check it out.

```
#include <string.h>       /* include the string library */

char *strcat(char *dst, const char *src);     /* concatenation */
int strcmp(const char *s1, const char *s2);   /* is s1 == s2? */
char *strcpy(char *dst, const char *src);     /* copy src to dist */
size_t strlen(const char *s);                 /* length of string */
char *strstr(const char *s1, const char *s2); /* search for s2 in s1 */
char *strtok(char *s1, const char *s2);       /* iterate words in s1 */
```

C++ String Library Functions

In addition to supporting C-style strings, C++ has a string class which contains methods for these operations and more:

```
string::size()       /* string length */
string::empty()      /* is it empty */
```

```
string::c_str()          /* return a pointer to a C style string */

string::operator [](size_type i)        /* access the ith character */

string::append(s)        /* append to string */
string::erase(n,m)       /* delete a run of characters */
string::insert(size_type n, const string&s) /* insert string s at n */

string::find(s)
string::rfind(s)         /* search left or right for the given string */

string::first()
string::last()           /* get characters, also there are iterators */
```

Overloaded operators exist for concatenation and string comparison.

Java String Objects

Java strings are first-class objects deriving either from the **String** class or the **StringBuffer** class. The **String** class is for static strings which do not change, while **StringBuffer** is designed for dynamic strings. Recall that Java was designed to support Unicode, so its characters are 16-bit entities.

The **java.text** package contains more advanced operations on strings, including routines to parse dates and other structured text.

3.8   Problems

3.8.1   WERTYU

PC/UVa IDs: 110301/10082, **Popularity:** A, **Success rate:** high **Level:** 1

A common typing error is to place your hands on the keyboard one row to the right of the correct position. Then "Q" is typed as "W" and "J" is typed as "K" and so on. Your task is to decode a message typed in this manner.

Input

Input consists of several lines of text. Each line may contain digits, spaces, uppercase letters (except "Q", "A", "Z"), or punctuation shown above [except back-quote (')]. Keys labeled with words [Tab, BackSp, Control, etc.] are not represented in the input.

Output

You are to replace each letter or punctuation symbol by the one immediately to its left on the QWERTY keyboard shown above. Spaces in the input should be echoed in the output.

Sample Input

O S, GOMR YPFSU/

Sample Output

I AM FINE TODAY.

3.8.2 Where's Waldorf?

PC/UVa IDs: 110302/10010, **Popularity:** B, **Success rate:** average **Level:** 2

Given an m by n grid of letters and a list of words, find the location in the grid at which the word can be found.

A word matches a straight, uninterrupted line of letters in the grid. A word can match the letters in the grid regardless of case (i.e., upper- and lowercase letters are to be treated as the same). The matching can be done in any of the eight horizontal, vertical, or diagonal directions through the grid.

Input

The input begins with a single positive integer on a line by itself indicating the number of cases, followed by a blank line. There is also a blank line between each two consecutive cases.

Each case begins with a pair of integers m followed by n on a single line, where $1 \leq m, n \leq 50$ in decimal notation. The next m lines contain n letters each, representing the grid of letters where the words must be found. The letters in the grid may be in upper- or lowercase. Following the grid of letters, another integer k appears on a line by itself $(1 \leq k \leq 20)$. The next k lines of input contain the list of words to search for, one word per line. These words may contain upper- and lowercase letters only – no spaces, hyphens, or other non-alphabetic characters.

Output

For each word in each test case, output a pair of integers representing its location in the corresponding grid. The integers must be separated by a single space. The first integer is the line in the grid where the first letter of the given word can be found (1 represents the topmost line in the grid, and m represents the bottommost line). The second integer is the column in the grid where the first letter of the given word can be found (1 represents the leftmost column in the grid, and n represents the rightmost column in the grid). If a word can be found more than once in the grid, then output the location of the uppermost occurrence of the word (i.e., the occurrence which places the first letter of the word closest to the top of the grid). If two or more words are uppermost, output the leftmost of these occurrences. All words can be found at least once in the grid.

The output of two consecutive cases must be separated by a blank line.

Sample Input

```
1

8 11
abcDEFGhigg
hEbkWalDork
FtyAwaldORm
FtsimrLqsrc
byoArBeDeyv
Klcbqwikomk
strEBGadhrb
yUiqlxcnBjf
4
Waldorf
Bambi
Betty
Dagbert
```

Sample Output

```
2 5
2 3
1 2
7 8
```

3.8.3 Common Permutation

PC/UVa IDs: 110303/10252, **Popularity:** A, **Success rate:** average **Level:** 1

Given two strings a and b, print the longest string x of letters such that there is a permutation of x that is a subsequence of a and there is a permutation of x that is a subsequence of b.

Input

The input file contains several cases, each case consisting of two consecutive lines. This means that lines 1 and 2 are a test case, lines 3 and 4 are another test case, and so on. Each line contains one string of lowercase characters, with first line of a pair denoting a and the second denoting b. Each string consists of at most 1,000 characters.

Output

For each set of input, output a line containing x. If several x satisfy the criteria above, choose the first one in alphabetical order.

Sample Input

```
pretty
women
walking
down
the
street
```

Sample Output

```
e
nw
et
```

3.8.4   Crypt Kicker II

PC/UVa IDs: 110304/850, **Popularity:** A, **Success rate:** average   **Level:** 2

A popular but insecure method of encrypting text is to permute the letters of the alphabet. That is, in the text, each letter of the alphabet is consistently replaced by some other letter. To ensure that the encryption is reversible, no two letters are replaced by the same letter.

A powerful method of cryptanalysis is the known plain text attack. In a known plain text attack, the cryptanalyst manages to have a known phrase or sentence encrypted by the enemy, and by observing the encrypted text then deduces the method of encoding.

Your task is to decrypt several encrypted lines of text, assuming that each line uses the same set of replacements, and that one of the lines of input is the encrypted form of the plain text `the quick brown fox jumps over the lazy dog`.

Input

The input begins with a single positive integer on a line by itself indicating the number of test cases, followed by a blank line. There will also be a blank line between each two consecutive cases.

Each case consists of several lines of input, encrypted as described above. The encrypted lines contain only lowercase letters and spaces and do not exceed 80 characters in length. There are at most 100 input lines.

Output

For each test case, decrypt each line and print it to standard output. If there is more than one possible decryption, any one will do. If decryption is impossible, output

`No solution.`

The output of each two consecutive cases must be separated by a blank line.

Sample Input

```
1

vtz ud xnm xugm itr pyy jttk gmv xt otgm xt xnm puk ti xnm fprxq
xnm ceuob lrtzv ita hegfd tsmr xnm ypwq ktj
frtjrpgguvj otvxmdxd prm iev prmvx xnmq
```

Sample Output

```
now is the time for all good men to come to the aid of the party
the quick brown fox jumps over the lazy dog
programming contests are fun arent they
```

3.8.5   Automated Judge Script

PC/UVa IDs: 110305/10188, **Popularity:** B, **Success rate:** average **Level:** 1

Human programming contest judges are known to be very picky. To eliminate the need for them, write an automated judge script to judge submitted solution runs.

Your program should take a file containing the correct output as well as the output of submitted program and answer either `Accepted`, `Presentation Error`, or `Wrong Answer`, defined as follows:

Accepted: You are to report "`Accepted`" if the team's output matches the standard solution exactly. *All* characters must match and must occur in the same order.

Presentation Error: Give a "`Presentation Error`" if all *numeric* characters match in the same order, but there is at least one non-matching non-numeric character. For example, "15 0" and "150" would receive "`Presentation Error`", whereas "15 0" and "1 0" would receive "`Wrong Answer`," described below.

Wrong Answer: If the team output cannot be classified as above, then you have no alternative but to score the program a '`Wrong Answer`'.

Input

The input will consist of an arbitrary number of input sets. Each input set begins with a line containing a positive integer $n < 100$, which describes the number of lines of the correct solution. The next n lines contain the correct solution. Then comes a positive integer $m < 100$, alone on its line, which describes the number of lines of the team's submitted output. The next m lines contain this output. The input is terminated by a value of $n = 0$, which should not be processed.

No line will have more than 100 characters.

Output

For each set, output one of the following:

```
Run #x: Accepted
Run #x: Presentation Error
Run #x: Wrong Answer
```

where x stands for the number of the input set (starting from 1).

Sample Input

```
2
The answer is: 10
The answer is: 5
2
The answer is: 10
```

```
The answer is: 5
2
The answer is: 10
The answer is: 5
2
The answer is: 10
The answer is: 15
2
The answer is: 10
The answer is:  5
2
The answer is: 10
The answer is: 5
3
Input Set #1: YES
Input Set #2: NO
Input Set #3: NO
3
Input Set #0: YES
Input Set #1: NO
Input Set #2: NO
1
1 0 1 0
1
1010
1
The judges are mean!
1
The judges are good!
0
```

Sample Output

```
Run #1: Accepted
Run #2: Wrong Answer
Run #3: Presentation Error
Run #4: Wrong Answer
Run #5: Presentation Error
Run #6: Presentation Error
```

3.8.6   File Fragmentation

PC/UVa IDs: 110306/10132, **Popularity:** C, **Success rate:** average **Level:** 2

Your friend, a biochemistry major, tripped while carrying a tray of computer files through the lab. All of the files fell to the ground and broke. Your friend picked up all the file fragments and called you to ask for help putting them back together again.

Fortunately, all of the files on the tray were identical, all of them broke into exactly two fragments, and all of the file fragments were found. Unfortunately, the files didn't all break in the same place, and the fragments were completely mixed up by their fall to the floor.

The original binary fragments have been translated into strings of ASCII 1's and 0's. Your job is to write a program that determines the bit pattern the files contained.

Input

The input begins with a single positive integer on its own line indicating the number of test cases, followed by a blank line. There will also be a blank line between each two consecutive cases.

Each case will consist of a sequence of "file fragments," one per line, terminated by the end-of-file marker or a blank line. Each fragment consists of a string of ASCII 1's and 0's.

Output

For each test case, the output is a single line of ASCII 1's and 0's giving the bit pattern of the original files. If there are $2N$ fragments in the input, it should be possible to concatenate these fragments together in pairs to make N copies of the output string. If there is no unique solution, any of the possible solutions may be output.

Your friend is certain that there were no more than 144 files on the tray, and that the files were all less than 256 bytes in size.

The output from two consecutive test cases will be separated by a blank line.

Sample Input

```
1

011
0111
01110
111
0111
10111
```

Sample Output

```
01110111
```

3.8.7   Doublets

PC/UVa IDs: 110307/10150, **Popularity:** C, **Success rate:** average **Level:** 3

A *doublet* is a pair of words that differ in exactly one letter; for example, "booster" and "rooster" or "rooster" and "roaster" or "roaster" and "roasted".

You are given a dictionary of up to 25,143 lowercase words, not exceeding 16 letters each. You are then given a number of pairs of words. For each pair of words, find the shortest sequence of words that begins with the first word and ends with the second, such that each pair of adjacent words is a doublet. For example, if you were given the input pair "booster" and "roasted", a possible solution would be ("booster," "rooster," "roaster," "roasted"), provided that these words are all in the dictionary.

Input

The input file contains the dictionary followed by a number of word pairs. The dictionary consists of a number of words, one per line, and is terminated by an empty line. The pairs of input words follow; each pair of words occurs on a line separated by a space.

Output

For each input pair, print a set of lines starting with the first word and ending with the last. Each pair of adjacent lines must be a doublet.

If there are several minimal solutions, any one will do. If there is no solution, print a line: "No solution." Leave a blank line between cases.

Sample Input	*Sample Output*
booster	booster
rooster	rooster
roaster	roaster
coasted	roasted
roasted	
coastal	No solution.
postal	
booster roasted	
coastal postal	

3.8.8 Fmt

PC/UVa IDs: 110308/848, **Popularity:** C, **Success rate:** low **Level:** 2

The UNIX program *fmt* reads lines of text, combining and breaking them so as to create an output file with lines as close to 72 characters long as possible without exceeding this limit. The rules for combining and breaking lines are as follows:

- A new line may be started anywhere there is a space in the input. When a new line is started, blanks at the end of the previous line and at the beginning of the new line are eliminated.

- A line break in the input may be eliminated in the output unless (1) it is at the end of a blank or empty line, or (2) it is followed by a space or another line break. When a line break is eliminated, it is replaced by a space.

- Spaces must be removed from the end of each output line.

- Any input word containing more than 72 characters must appear on an output line by itself.

You may assume that the input text does not contain any tabbing characters.

Sample Input

```
    Unix fmt

The unix fmt program reads lines of text, combining
and breaking lines so as to create an
output file with lines as close to without exceeding
72 characters long as possible.  The rules for combining and breaking
lines are as follows.

    1.  A new line may be started anywhere there is a space in the input.
If a new line is started, there will be no trailing blanks at the
end of the previous line or at the beginning of the new line.

    2.  A line break in the input may be eliminated in the output, provided
it is not followed by a space or another line break.  If a line
break is eliminated, it is replaced by a space.
```

Sample Output

```
    Unix fmt

The unix fmt program reads lines of text, combining and breaking lines
so as to create an output file with lines as close to without exceeding
72 characters long as possible.  The rules for combining and breaking
```

lines are as follows.

1. A new line may be started anywhere there is a space in the input. If a new line is started, there will be no trailing blanks at the end of the previous line or at the beginning of the new line.

2. A line break in the input may be eliminated in the output, provided it is not followed by a space or another line break. If a line break is eliminated, it is replaced by a space.

3.9 Hints

3.1 Should you use hard-coded logic to perform the character replacement, or would a table-driven strategy of initialized arrays be easier?

3.2 Can you write a single comparison routine with arguments which can handle comparison in all eight directions when called with the right arguments? Does it pay to specify directions as pairs of integers (δ_x, δ_y) instead of by name?

3.3 Can you rearrange the letters of each word so that the common permutation becomes more apparent?

3.5 What is the easiest way to compare just the numeric characters, as required for identifying presentation errors?

3.6 Can you easily figure out which pairs of fragments go together, if not their order?

3.7 Can we model this problem as a path problem in graphs? It might pay to look ahead to Chapter 9 where we present graph data structures and traversal algorithms.

3.10 Notes

3.4 Although it has a history dating back thousands of years, cryptography has been revolutionized by computational advances and new algorithms. Read Schneier's [Sch94] and/or Stinson's [Sti02] books to learn more about this fascinating area.

3.8 The gold standard among text-formatting programs is *Latex*, the system we used to typeset this book. It is built on top of *TeX*, developed by master computer scientist Don Knuth. He is the author of the famous *Art of Computer Programming* books [Knu73a, Knu81, Knu73b], which are still fascinating and unsurpassed more than 30 years after their original publication.

4
Sorting

Sorting is the most fundamental algorithmic problem in computer science and a rich source of programming problems for two distinct reasons. First, sorting is a useful operation which efficiently solves many tasks that every programmer encounters. As soon as you recognize your job is a special case of sorting, proper use of library routines make short work of the problem.

Second, literally dozens of different sorting algorithms have been developed, each of which rests on a particular clever idea or observation. Most algorithm design paradigms lead to interesting sorting algorithms, including divide-and-conquer, randomization, incremental insertion, and advanced data structures. Many interesting programming/mathematical problems follow from properties of these algorithms.

In this chapter, we will review the primary applications of sorting, as well as the theory behind the most important algorithms. Finally, we will describe the sorting library routines provided by all modern programming languages, and show how to use them on a non-trivial problem.

4.1   Sorting Applications

The key to understanding sorting is seeing how it can be used to solve many important programming tasks:

- *Uniqueness Testing* — How can we test if the elements of a given collection of items S are all distinct? Sort them into either increasing or decreasing order so that any repeated items will fall next to each other. One pass through the elements testing if $S[i] = S[i+1]$ for any $1 \leq i < n$ then finishes the job.

- *Deleting Duplicates* — How can we remove all but one copy of any repeated elements in S? Sort and sweep again does the job. Note that the sweeping is best done by maintaining two indices — *back*, pointing to the last element in the cleaned-out prefix array, and i, pointing to the next element to be considered. If $S[back] <> S[i]$, increment *back* and copy $S[i]$ to $S[back]$.

- *Prioritizing Events* — Suppose we are given a set of jobs to do, each with its own deadline. Sorting the items according to the deadline date (or some related criteria) puts the jobs in the right order to process them. Priority queue data structures are useful for maintaining calendars or schedules when there are insertions and deletions, but sorting does the job if the set of events does not change during execution.

- *Median/Selection* — Suppose we want to find the kth largest item in set S. After sorting the items in increasing order, this fellow sits in location $S[k]$. This approach can be used to find (in a slightly inefficient manner) the smallest, largest, and median elements as special cases.

- *Frequency Counting* — Which is the most frequently occurring element in S, i.e., the mode? After sorting, a linear sweep lets us count the number of times each element occurs.

- *Reconstructing the Original Order* — How can we restore the original arrangement of a set of items after we permute them for some application? Add an extra field to the data record for the item, such that the ith record sets this field to i. Carry this field along whenever you move the record, and later sort on it when you want the initial order back.

- *Set Intersection/Union* — How can we intersect or union the elements of two containers? If both of them have been sorted, we can merge them by repeatedly taking the smaller of the two head elements, placing them into the new set if desired, and then deleting the head from the appropriate list.

- *Finding a Target Pair* — How can we test whether there are two integers $x, y \in S$ such that $x + y = z$ for some target z? Instead of testing all possible pairs, sort the numbers in increasing order and sweep. As $S[i]$ increases with i, its possible partner j such that $S[j] = z - S[i]$ decreases. Thus decreasing j appropriately as i increases gives a nice solution.

- *Efficient Searching* — How can we efficiently test whether element s is in set S? Sure, ordering a set so as to permit efficient binary search queries is perhaps the most common application of sorting. Just don't forget all the others!

4.2   Sorting Algorithms

You have quite possibly seen a dozen or more different algorithms for sorting data. Do you remember bubblesort, insertion sort, selection sort, heapsort, mergesort, quicksort, radix sort, distribution/bin sort, Shell sort, in-order tree traversal, and sorting networks? Most likely your eyes started to glaze by the time you made it halfway through the list. Who needs to know so many ways to do the same thing, especially when there already exists a sorting library function included with your favorite programming language?

The real reason to study sorting algorithms is that the *ideas* behind them reappear as the ideas behind algorithms for many other problems. Understand that heapsort is *really* about data structures, that quicksort is *really* about randomization, and that mergesort is *really* about divide-and-conquer, and you have a wide range of algorithmic tools to work with.

We review a few particularly instructive algorithms below. Be sure to note what useful properties (such as minimizing data movement) come with each algorithm.

- *Selection Sort* — This algorithm splits the input array into sorted and unsorted parts, and with each iteration finds the smallest element remaining in the unsorted region and moves it to the end of the sorted region:

```
selection_sort(int s[], int n)
{
        int i,j;                /* counters */
        int min;                /* index of minimum */

        for (i=0; i<n; i++) {
                min=i;
                for (j=i+1; j<n; j++)
                        if (s[j] < s[min]) min=j;
                swap(&s[i],&s[min]);
        }
}
```

Selection sort makes a lot of comparisons, but is quite efficient if all we count are the *number* of data moves. Only $n-1$ swaps are performed by the algorithm, which is necessary in the worst case; think about sorting a reversed permutation. It also provides an example of the power of advanced data structures. Using an efficient priority queue to maintain the unsorted portion of the array suddenly turns $O(n^2)$ selection sort into $O(n \lg n)$ heapsort!

- *Insertion Sort* — This algorithm also maintains sorted and unsorted regions of the array. In each iteration, the next unsorted element moves up to its appropriate position in the sorted region:

```
insertion_sort(int s[], int n)
{
        int i,j;                    /* counters */

        for (i=1; i<n; i++) {
                j=i;
                while ((j>0) && (s[j] < s[j-1])) {
```

```
                        swap(&s[j],&s[j-1]);
                        j = j-1;
                }
        }
}
```

Insertion sort is particularly significant as the algorithm which minimizes the *amount* of data movement. An *inversion* in a permutation p is a pair of elements which are out of order, i.e., an i, j such that $i < j$ yet $p[i] > p[j]$. Each swap in insertion sort erases exactly one inversion, and no element is otherwise moved, so the number of swaps equals the number of inversions. Since an almost-sorted permutation has few inversions, insertion sort can be very effective on such data.

• *Quicksort* — This algorithm reduces the job of sorting one big array into the job of sorting two smaller arrays by performing a *partition* step. The partition separates the array into those elements that are less than the pivot/divider element, and those which are strictly greater than this pivot/divider element. Because no element need ever move out of its region after the partition, each subarray can be sorted independently. To facilitate sorting subarrays, the arguments to quicksort include the indices of the first (1) and last (h) elements in the subarray.

```
quicksort(int s[], int l, int h)
{
        int p;                          /* index of partition */

        if ((h-l)>0) {
                p = partition(s,l,h);
                quicksort(s,l,p-1);
                quicksort(s,p+1,h);
        }
}

int partition(int s[], int l, int h)
{
        int i;                          /* counter */
        int p;                          /* pivot element index */
        int firsthigh;                  /* divider position for pivot */

        p = h;
        firsthigh = l;
        for (i=l; i<h; i++)
                if (s[i] < s[p]) {
                        swap(&s[i],&s[firsthigh]);
                        firsthigh ++;
                }
        swap(&s[p],&s[firsthigh]);
```

```
        return(firsthigh);
}
```

Quicksort is interesting for several reasons. When implemented properly, it is the fastest in-memory sorting algorithm. It is a beautiful example of the power of recursion. The **partition** algorithm is useful for many tasks in its own right. For example, how might you separate an array containing just 0's and 1's into one run of each symbol?

4.3   Program Design Example: Rating the Field

Pretty Polly has no shortage of gentlemen suitors who come a' courting. Indeed, her biggest problem is keeping track of who the best ones are. She is smart enough to realize that a program which ranks the men from most to least desirable would simplify her life. She is also persuasive enough to have talked you into writing the program.

Polly really likes to dance, and has determined the optimal partner height is 180 centimeters tall. Her first criteria is finding someone who is as close as possible to this height; whether they are a little taller or shorter doesn't matter. Among all candidates of the same height, she wants someone as close as possible to 75 kilograms without going over. If all equal-height candidates are over this limit, she will take the lightest of the bunch. If two or more people are identical by all these characteristics, sort them by last name, then by first name if it is necessary to break the tie.

Polly is only interested in seeing the candidates ranked by name, so the input file:

```
George Bush            195      110
Harry Truman           180      75
Bill Clinton           180      75
John Kennedy           180      65
Ronald Reagan          165      110
Richard Nixon          170      70
Jimmy Carter           180      77
```

yields the following output:

```
Clinton, Bill
Truman, Harry
Kennedy, John
Carter, Jimmy
Nixon, Richard
Bush, George
Reagan, Ronald
```

—————————————   Solution starts below   —————————————

The key to this problem is sorting under a fairly complex criteria defined over multiple fields. There are at least two different ways we can do this. The first makes multiple sorting passes, sorting first on the *least* important key, then the next least important key, and so on until we finally sort on the major key.

Why do we sort in this order? The minor keys are only used to break ties among the major key ordering. Provided our sorting algorithm is *stable*, meaning it preserves the relative order of equal keys, our work on the minor keys remains intact if it is relevant to the final answer.

Not all sorting algorithms are stable: indeed most fast ones are not! The `insertion_sort` and `selection_sort` functions from Section 4.2 are stable, while `quicksort` is not stable. Before you assume the stability of any sorting function, check the documentation carefully.

The other approach, which is what we opted for, rolls all the keys up into one complex comparison function. Doing it this way made it easiest to take advantage of the C library sorting routine, described in the next section.

4.4 Sorting Library Functions

Whenever possible, take advantage of the built-in sorting/searching libraries in your favorite programming language:

Sorting and Searching in C

The `stdlib.h` contains library functions for sorting and searching. For sorting, there is the function qsort:

```
#include <stdlib.h>

void qsort(void *base, size_t nel, size_t width,
           int (*compare) (const void *, const void *));
```

The key to using `qsort` is realizing what its arguments do. It sorts the first `nel` elements of an array (pointed to by `base`), where each element is `width`-bytes long. Thus we can sort arrays of 1-byte characters, 4-byte integers, or 100-byte records, all by changing the value of `width`.

The ultimate desired order is determined by the function `compare`. It takes as arguments pointers to two `width`-byte elements, and returns a negative number if the first belongs before the second in sorted order, a positive number if the second belongs before the first, or zero if they are the same.

Here is a comparison function for sorting integers in increasing order:

```
int intcompare(int *i, int *j)
{
    if (*i > *j) return (1);
    if (*i < *j) return (-1);
```

```
    return (0);
}
```

This comparison function can be used to sort an array **a**, of which the first **cnt** elements are occupied, as follows:

```
    qsort((char *) a, cnt, sizeof(int), intcompare);
```

A more sophisticated example of **qsort** in action appears in Section 4.5. The name **qsort** suggests that quicksort is the algorithm implemented in this library function, although this is usually irrelevant to the user.

Note that **qsort** destroys the contents of the original array, so if you need to restore the original order, make a copy or add an extra field to the record as described in Section 4.1.

Binary search is an amazingly tricky algorithm to implement correctly under pressure. The best solution is not to try, since the **stdlib.h** library contains an implementation called **bsearch()**. Except for the search key, the arguments are the same as for **qsort**. To search in the previously sorted array, try

```
    bsearch(key, (char *) a, cnt, sizeof(int), intcompare);
```

Sorting and Searching in C++

The C++ Standard Template Library (STL), discussed in Section 2.2.1, includes methods for sorting, searching, and more. Serious C++ users should get familiar with STL.

To sort with STL, we can either use the default comparison (e.g., $\leq$) function defined for the class, or override it with a special-purpose comparison function **op**:

```
void sort(RandomAccessIterator bg, RandomAccessIterator end)
void sort(RandomAccessIterator bg, RandomAccessIterator end,
          BinaryPredicate op)
```

STL also provides a stable sorting routine, where keys of equal value are guaranteed to remain in the same relative order. This can be useful if we are sorting by multiple criteria:

```
void stable_sort(RandomAccessIterator bg, RandomAccessIterator end)
void stable_sort(RandomAccessIterator bg, RandomAccessIterator end,
          BinaryPredicate op)
```

Other STL functions implement some of the applications of sorting described in Section 4.1, including,

- **nth_element** – Return the nth largest item in the container.

- **set_union**, **set_intersection**, **set_difference** – Construct the union, intersection, and set difference of two containers.

- **unique** – Remove all consecutive duplicates.

Sorting and Searching in Java

The `java.util.Arrays` class contains various methods for sorting and searching. In particular,

```
static void sort(Object[] a)
static void sort(Object[] a, Comparator c)
```

sorts the specified array of objects into ascending order using either the natural ordering of its elements or a specific comparator *c*. Stable sorts are also available.

Methods for searching a sorted array for a specified object using either the natural comparison function or a new comparator *c* are also provided:

```
binarySearch(Object[] a, Object key)
binarySearch(Object[] a, Object key, Comparator c)
```

4.5 Rating the Field

Our solution to Polly's dating difficulties revolved around making the multi-criteria sorting step as simple as possible. First, we had to set up the basic data structures:

```
#include <stdio.h>
#include <string.h>

#define NAMELENGTH      30                /* maximum length of name */
#define NSUITORS        100               /* maximum number of suitors */

#define BESTHEIGHT      180               /* best height in centimeters */
#define BESTWEIGHT      75                /* best weight in kilograms */

typedef struct {
        char first[NAMELENGTH];           /* suitor's first name */
        char last[NAMELENGTH];            /* suitor's last name */
        int height;                       /* suitor's height */
        int weight;                       /* suitor's weight */
} suitor;

suitor suitors[NSUITORS];                 /* database of suitors */
int nsuitors;                             /* number of suitors */
```

Then we had to read the input. Note that we did not store each fellow's actual height and weight! Polly's rating criteria for heights and weights were quite fussy, revolving around how these quantities compare to a reference height/weight instead of a usual linear order (i.e., increasing or decreasing). Instead, we altered each height and weight appropriately so the quantities were linearly ordered by desirability:

```
read_suitors()
{
        char first[NAMELENGTH], last[NAMELENGTH];
        int height, weight;

        nsuitors = 0;

        while (scanf("%s %s %d %d\n",suitors[nsuitors].first,
                suitors[nsuitors].last, &height, &weight) != EOF) {
                suitors[nsuitors].height = abs(height - BESTHEIGHT);
                if (weight > BESTWEIGHT)
                        suitors[nsuitors].weight = weight - BESTWEIGHT;
                else
                        suitors[nsuitors].weight = - weight;

                nsuitors ++;
        }
}
```

Finally, observe that we used scanf to read the first and last names as tokens, instead of character by character.

The critical comparison routine takes a pair of suitors a and b, and decides whether a is better, b is better, or they are of equal rank. To satisfy the demands of qsort, we must assign -1, 1, and 0 in these three cases, respectively. The following comparison function does the job:

```
int suitor_compare(suitor *a, suitor *b)
{
        int result;                             /* result of comparison */

        if (a->height < b->height) return(-1);
        if (a->height > b->height) return(1);

        if (a->weight < b->weight) return(-1);
        if (a->weight > b->weight) return(1);

        if ((result=strcmp(a->last,b->last)) != 0) return result;

        return(strcmp(a->first,b->first));
}
```

With the comparison function and input routines in place, all that remains is a driver program which actually calls qsort and produces the output:

```
main()
{
        int i;                                  /* counter */
```

```
    int suitor_compare();

    read_suitors();

    qsort(suitors, nsuitors, sizeof(suitor), suitor_compare);

    for (i=0; i<nsuitors; i++)
            printf("%s, %s\n",suitors[i].last, suitors[i].first);
}
```

4.6   Problems

4.6.1   Vito's Family

PC/UVa IDs: 110401/10041, **Popularity:** A, **Success rate:** high **Level:** 1

The famous gangster Vito Deadstone is moving to New York. He has a very big family there, all of them living on Lamafia Avenue. Since he will visit all his relatives very often, he wants to find a house close to them.

Indeed, Vito wants to minimize the total distance to all of his relatives and has blackmailed you to write a program that solves his problem.

Input

The input consists of several test cases. The first line contains the number of test cases.

For each test case you will be given the integer number of relatives r $(0 < r < 500)$ and the street numbers (also integers) $s_1, s_2, \ldots, s_i, \ldots, s_r$ where they live $(0 < s_i < 30,000)$. Note that several relatives might live at the same street number.

Output

For each test case, your program must write the minimal sum of distances from the optimal Vito's house to each one of his relatives. The distance between two street numbers s_i and s_j is $d_{ij} = |s_i - s_j|$.

Sample Input

```
2
2 2 4
3 2 4 6
```

Sample Output

```
2
4
```

4.6.2   Stacks of Flapjacks

PC/UVa IDs: 110402/120, **Popularity:** B, **Success rate:** high **Level:** 2

Cooking the perfect stack of pancakes on a grill is a tricky business, because no matter how hard you try all pancakes in any stack have different diameters. For neatness's sake, however, you can sort the stack by size such that each pancake is smaller than all the pancakes below it. The size of a pancake is given by its diameter.

Sorting a stack is done by a sequence of pancake "flips." A flip consists of inserting a spatula between two pancakes in a stack and flipping (reversing) *all* the pancakes on the spatula (reversing the sub-stack). A flip is specified by giving the position of the pancake on the bottom of the sub-stack to be flipped relative to the entire stack. The bottom pancake has position 1, while the top pancake on a stack of n pancakes has position n.

A stack is specified by giving the diameter of each pancake in the stack in the order in which the pancakes appear. For example, consider the three stacks of pancakes below in which pancake 8 is the top-most pancake of the left stack:

8	7	2
4	6	5
6	4	8
7	8	4
5	5	6
2	2	7

The stack on the left can be transformed to the stack in the middle via *flip(3)*. The middle stack can be transformed into the right stack via the command *flip(1)*.

Input

The input consists of a sequence of stacks of pancakes. Each stack will consist of between 1 and 30 pancakes and each pancake will have an integer diameter between 1 and 100. The input is terminated by end-of-file. Each stack is given as a single line of input with the top pancake on a stack appearing first on a line, the bottom pancake appearing last, and all pancakes separated by a space.

Output

For each stack of pancakes, your program should echo the original stack on one line, followed by a sequence of flips that results in sorting the stack of pancakes so that the largest pancake is on the bottom and the smallest on top. The sequence of flips for each stack should be terminated by a 0, indicating no more flips necessary. Once a stack is sorted, no more flips should be made.

Sample Input

```
1 2 3 4 5
5 4 3 2 1
5 1 2 3 4
```

Sample Output

```
1 2 3 4 5
0
5 4 3 2 1
1 0
5 1 2 3 4
1 2 0
```

4.6.3 Bridge

PC/UVa IDs: 110403/10037, **Popularity:** B, **Success rate:** low **Level:** 3

A group of n people wish to cross a bridge at night. At most two people may cross at any time, and each group must have a flashlight. Only one flashlight is available among the n people, so some sort of shuttle arrangement must be arranged in order to return the flashlight so that more people may cross.

Each person has a different crossing speed; the speed of a group is determined by the speed of the slower member. Your job is to determine a strategy that gets all n people across the bridge in the minimum time.

Input

The input begins with a single positive integer on a line by itself indicating the number of test cases, followed by a blank line. There is also a blank line between each two consecutive inputs.

The first line of each case contains n, followed by n lines giving the crossing times for each of the people. There are not more than 1,000 people and nobody takes more than 100 seconds to cross the bridge.

Output

For each test case, the first line of output must report the total number of seconds required for all n people to cross the bridge. Subsequent lines give a strategy for achieving this time. Each line contains either one or two integers, indicating which person or people form the next group to cross. Each person is indicated by the crossing time specified in the input. Although many people may have the same crossing time, this ambiguity is of no consequence.

Note that the crossings alternate directions, as it is necessary to return the flashlight so that more may cross. If more than one strategy yields the minimal time, any one will do.

The output of two consecutive cases must be separated by a blank line.

Sample Input	Sample Output
1	17
	1 2
4	1
1	5 10
2	2
5	1 2
10	

4.6.4 Longest Nap

PC/UVa IDs: 110404/10191, **Popularity:** B, **Success rate:** average **Level:** 1

Professors lead very busy lives with full schedules of work and appointments. Professor P likes to nap during the day, but his schedule is so busy that he doesn't have many chances to do so.

He *really* wants to take one nap every day, however. Naturally, he wants to take the longest nap possible given his schedule. Write a program to help him with the task.

Input

The input consists of an arbitrary number of test cases, where each test case represents one day.

The first line of each case contains a positive integer $s \leq 100$, representing the number of scheduled appointments for that day. The next s lines contain the appointments in the format *time1 time2 appointment*, where *time1* represents the time which the appointment starts and *time2* the time it ends. All times will be in the hh:mm format; the ending time will always be strictly after the starting time, and separated by a single space.

All times will be greater than or equal to 10:00 and less than or equal to 18:00. Thus your response must be in this interval as well; i.e., no nap can start before 10:00 and last after 18:00.

The appointment can be any sequence of characters, but will always be on the same line. You can assume that no line is be longer than 255 characters, that $10 \leq hh \leq 18$ and that $0 \leq mm < 60$. You *cannot* assume, however, that the input will be in any specific order, and must read the input until you reach the end of file.

Output

For each test case, you must print the following line:

Day #*d*: the longest nap starts at *hh* : *mm* and will last for [*H* hours and] *M* minutes. where d stands for the number of the test case (starting from 1) and $hh : mm$ is the time when the nap can start. To display the length of the nap, follow these rules:

1. If the total time X is less than 60 minutes, just print "*X* minutes."

2. If the total duration X is at least 60 minutes, print "*H* hours and *M* minutes," where

$$H = X \div 60 \quad \text{(integer division, of course) and} \quad M = X \bmod 60.$$

You don't have to worry about correct pluralization; i.e., you must print "1 minutes" or "1 hours" if that is the case.

The duration of the nap is calculated by the difference between the ending time and the beginning time. That is, if an appointment ends at 14:00 and the next one starts at 14:47, then you have 14:47 – 14:00 = 47 minutes of possible napping.

If there is more than one longest nap with the same duration, print the earliest one. You can assume the professor won't be busy all day, so there is always time for at least one possible nap.

Sample Input

```
4
10:00 12:00 Lectures
12:00 13:00 Lunch, like always.
13:00 15:00 Boring lectures...
15:30 17:45 Reading
4
10:00 12:00 Lectures
12:00 13:00 Lunch, just lunch.
13:00 15:00 Lectures, lectures... oh, no!
16:45 17:45 Reading (to be or not to be?)
4
10:00 12:00 Lectures, as everyday.
12:00 13:00 Lunch, again!!!
13:00 15:00 Lectures, more lectures!
15:30 17:15 Reading (I love reading, but should I schedule it?)
1
12:00 13:00 I love lunch! Have you ever noticed it? :)
```

Sample Output

```
Day #1: the longest nap starts at 15:00 and will last for 30 minutes.
Day #2: the longest nap starts at 15:00 and will last for 1 hours and 45 minutes.
Day #3: the longest nap starts at 17:15 and will last for 45 minutes.
Day #4: the longest nap starts at 13:00 and will last for 5 hours and 0 minutes.
```

4.6.5   Shoemaker's Problem

PC/UVa IDs: 110405/10026, **Popularity:** C, **Success rate:** average   **Level:** 2

A shoemaker has N orders from customers which he must satisfy. The shoemaker can work on only one job in each day, and jobs usually take several days. For the ith job, the integer T_i ($1 \leq T_i \leq 1,000$) denotes the number of days it takes the shoemaker to finish the job.

But popularity has its price. For each day of delay before starting to work on the ith job, the shoemaker has agreed to pay a fine of S_i ($1 \leq S_i \leq 10,000$) cents per day. Help the shoemaker by writing a program to find the sequence of jobs with minimum total fine.

Input

The input begins with a single positive integer on a line by itself indicating the number of the test cases, followed by a blank line. There is also a blank line between two consecutive cases.

The first line of each case contains an integer reporting the number of jobs N, where $1 \leq N \leq 1,000$. The ith subsequent line contains the completion time T_i and daily penalty S_i for the ith job.

Output

For each test case, your program should print the sequence of jobs with minimal fine. Each job should be represented by its position in the input. All integers should be placed on only one output line and each pair separated by one space. If multiple solutions are possible, print the first one in lexicographic order.

The output of two consecutive cases must be separated by a blank line.

Sample Input

```
1

4
3 4
1 1000
2 2
5 5
```

Sample Output

```
2 1 3 4
```

4.6.6 CDVII

PC/UVa IDs: 110406/10138, **Popularity:** C, **Success rate:** low **Level:** 2

Roman roads are famous for their sound engineering. Unfortunately, sound engineering does not come cheap, and some modern neo-Cæsars have decided to recover the costs through automated tolling.

A particular toll highway, the CDVII, has a fare structure that works as follows: travel on the road costs a certain amount per km traveled, depending on the time of day when the travel begins. Cameras at every entrance and every exit capture the license numbers of all cars entering and leaving. Every calendar month, a bill is sent to the registered owner for each km traveled (at a rate determined by the time of day), plus one dollar per trip, plus a two dollar account charge. Your job is to prepare the bill for one month, given a set of license plate photos.

Input

The input begins with an integer on a line by itself indicating the number of test cases, followed by a blank line. There will also be a blank line between each two consecutive test cases.

Each test case has two parts: the fare structure and the license photos. The fare structure consists of a line with 24 non-negative integers denoting the toll (cents/km) from 00:00 to 00:59, the toll from 01:00 to 01:59, and so on for each hour in the day. Each photo record consists of the license number of the vehicle (up to 20 alphanumeric characters), the time and date (`mm:dd:hh:mm`), the word `enter` or `exit`, and the location of the entrance or exit (in km from one end of the highway). All dates will be within a single month. Each "enter" record is paired with the chronologically next record for the same vehicle, provided it is an "exit" record. Unpaired "enter" and "exit" records are ignored. You may assume that no two records for the same vehicle have the same time. Times are recorded using a 24-hour clock. There are not more than 1,000 photo records.

Output

For each test case, print a line for each vehicle indicating the license number and the total bill in alphabetical order by license number. The output of two consecutive cases must be separated by a blank line.

Sample Input

```
1

10 10 10 10 10 10 20 20 20 15 15 15 15 15 15 15 20 30 20 15 15 10 10 10
ABCD123 01:01:06:01 enter 17
765DEF 01:01:07:00 exit 95
```

```
ABCD123 01:01:08:03 exit 95
765DEF 01:01:05:59 enter 17
```

Sample Output

```
765DEF $10.80
ABCD123 $18.60
```

4.6.7 ShellSort

PC/UVa IDs: 110407/10152, **Popularity:** B, **Success rate:** average **Level:** 2

King Yertle wishes to rearrange his turtle throne to place his highest-ranking nobles and closest advisors nearer to the top. A single operation is available to change the order of the turtles in the stack: a turtle can crawl out of its position in the stack and climb up over the other turtles to sit on the top.

Given an original ordering of a turtle stack and a required ordering for the same turtle stack, your job is to find a minimal sequence of operations that rearranges the original stack into the required stack.

Input

The first line of the input consists of a single integer K giving the number of test cases. Each test case consists of an integer n giving the number of turtles in the stack. The next n lines describe the original ordering of the turtle stack. Each of the lines contains the name of a turtle, starting with the turtle on the top of the stack and working down to the turtle at the bottom of the stack. Turtles have unique names, each of which is a string of no more than eighty characters drawn from a character set consisting of the alphanumeric characters, the space character and the period ("."). The next n lines in the input give the desired ordering of the stack, once again by naming turtles from top to bottom. Each test case consists of exactly $2n+1$ lines in total. The number of turtles (n) will be less than or equal to 200.

Output

For each test case, the output consists of a sequence of turtle names, one per line, indicating the order in which turtles are to leave their positions in the stack and crawl to the top. This sequence of operations should transform the original stack into the required stack and should be as short as possible. If more than one solution of shortest length is possible, any of the solutions may be reported.

Print a blank line after each test case.

Sample Input

```
2
3
Yertle
Duke of Earl
Sir Lancelot
Duke of Earl
Yertle
Sir Lancelot
9
```

```
Yertle
Duke of Earl
Sir Lancelot
Elizabeth Windsor
Michael Eisner
Richard M. Nixon
Mr. Rogers
Ford Perfect
Mack
Yertle
Richard M. Nixon
Sir Lancelot
Duke of Earl
Elizabeth Windsor
Michael Eisner
Mr. Rogers
Ford Perfect
Mack
```

Sample Output

```
Duke of Earl

Sir Lancelot
Richard M. Nixon
Yertle
```

4.6.8   Football (aka Soccer)

PC/UVa IDs: 110408/10194, **Popularity:** B, **Success rate:** average **Level:** 1

Football is the most popular sport in the world, even through Americans insist on calling it *"soccer."* A country such as five-time World Cup-winning Brazil has so many national and regional tournaments that is it very difficult to keep track. Your task is to write a program that receives the tournament name, team names, and games played and outputs the tournament standings so far.

A team wins a game if it scores more goals than its opponent, and loses if it scores fewer goals. Both teams tie if they score the same number of goals. A team earns 3 points for each win, 1 point for each tie, and 0 points for each loss.

Teams are ranked according to these rules (in this order):

1. Most points earned.

2. Most wins.

3. Most goal difference (i.e., goals scored – goals against)

4. Most goals scored.

5. Fewest games played.

6. Case-insensitive lexicographic order.

Input

The first line of input will be an integer N in a line alone $(0 < N < 1,000)$. Then follow N tournament descriptions, each beginning with a tournament name. These names can be any combination of at most 100 letters, digits, spaces, etc., on a single line. The next line will contain a number T $(1 < T \le 30)$, which stands for the number of teams participating on this tournament. Then follow T lines, each containing one team name. Team names consist of at most 30 characters, and may contain any character with ASCII code greater than or equal to 32 (space), except for "#" and "@" characters.

Following the team names, there will be a non-negative integer G on a single line which stands for the number of games already played on this tournament. G will be no greater than 1,000. G lines then follow with the results of games played in the format:

team_name_1#goals1@goals2#team_name_2

For instance, *Team A#3@1#Team B* means that in a game between *Team A* and *Team B*, *Team A* scored 3 goals and *Team B* scored 1. All goals will be non-negative integers less than 20. You may assume that all team names mentioned in game results will have appeared in the team names section, and that no team will play against itself.

Output

For each tournament, you must output the tournament name in a single line. In the next T lines you must output the standings, according to the rules above. Should lexicographic order be needed as a tie-breaker, it must be done in a case-insensitive manner. The output format for each line is shown below:

[a]) *Team_name* [b]p, [c]g ([d]-[e]-[f]), [g]gd ([h]-[i])

where [a] is team rank, [b] is the total points earned, [c] is the number of games played, [d] is wins, [e] is ties, [f] is losses, [g] is goal difference, [h] is goals scored, and [i] is goals against.

There must be a single blank space between fields and a single blank line between output sets. See the sample output for examples.

Sample Input

```
2
World Cup 1998 - Group A
4
Brazil
Norway
Morocco
Scotland
6
Brazil#2@1#Scotland
Norway#2@2#Morocco
Scotland#1@1#Norway
Brazil#3@0#Morocco
Morocco#3@0#Scotland
Brazil#1@2#Norway
Some strange tournament
5
Team A
Team B
Team C
Team D
Team E
5
Team A#1@1#Team B
Team A#2@2#Team C
Team A#0@0#Team D
Team E#2@1#Team C
Team E#1@2#Team D
```

Sample Output

```
World Cup 1998 - Group A
1) Brazil 6p, 3g (2-0-1), 3gd (6-3)
2) Norway 5p, 3g (1-2-0), 1gd (5-4)
3) Morocco 4p, 3g (1-1-1), 0gd (5-5)
4) Scotland 1p, 3g (0-1-2), -4gd (2-6)

Some strange tournament
1) Team D 4p, 2g (1-1-0), 1gd (2-1)
2) Team E 3p, 2g (1-0-1), 0gd (3-3)
3) Team A 3p, 3g (0-3-0), 0gd (3-3)
4) Team B 1p, 1g (0-1-0), 0gd (1-1)
5) Team C 1p, 2g (0-1-1), -1gd (3-4)
```

4.7 Hints

4.1 What is the right version of average to solve Vito's problem: mean, median, or something else?

4.3 Does sorting the people by speed help determine who should be paired up?

4.4 How does sorting help?

4.5 Does it help to sort jobs by their length, or by their penalty, or both?

4.6 Can we convert the date/time information to a single integer to make it easier to manipulate?

4.7 Under what conditions will we *not* have to move a turtle?

4.8 How can we simplify our task of writing a comparison function for such a complicated ranking system?

4.8 Notes

4.2 The problem of sorting pancakes using the minimum number of reversals is notorious as the source of the only research paper Bill Gates ever published [GP79]! Beyond the mathematical interest in the problem, it has an interesting application to reconstructing the evolutionary history between species such as human and mouse. A genome reversal event reverses a run of genes in an organism's DNA. These rare events can cause significant evolutionary impact over long periods of time, so reconstructing the order of the reversals becomes an important problem. See [Ber01, Gus97] for more on genome reversals.

5
Arithmetic and Algebra

The link between programming skills and mathematical ability has been well established. Indeed, the earliest computers were built by mathematicians to speed up their calculations. Pascal (who was a mathematician long before he became a programming language) built a gear-based mechanical adding machine in 1645. Such pioneering computer scientists as Turing and von Neumann had equal or even greater achievements in pure mathematics.

In this chapter we will explore programming challenges in arithmetic and algebra, which are ostensibly the most elementary parts of mathematics. That certain algorithms depend on advanced topics such as number theory proves that they are not as elementary as they seem.

5.1 Machine Arithmetic

Every programming language includes an integer data type supporting the four basic arithmetic operations: addition, subtraction, multiplication, and division. These operations are typically mapped almost directly to hardware-level arithmetic instructions, and so the size range of integers depends on the underlying processor.

Today's PCs are typically 32-bit machines, meaning that the standard integer data type supports integers roughly in the range $\pm 2^{31} = \pm 2{,}147{,}483{,}648$. Thus we can safely count up to a billion or so with standard integers on conventional machines.

Most programming languages support `long` or even `long long` integer data types, which often define 64-bit or occasionally even 128-bit integers. Since $2^{63} = 9{,}223{,}372{,}036{,}854{,}775{,}808$, we are talking several orders of magnitude beyond trillions.

This is a very big number, so big that just counting up to it at modern computer speeds will take far longer than you would be willing to wait. This is more than the number of pennies in the United States budget deficit, so it usually proves more than adequate except for mathematical research or programming contest challenges.

Conventional 32-bit integers are typically represented using four contiguous bytes, with 64-bit longs being arrays of eight bytes. This is inefficient when storing large numbers of not-so-very large numbers. For example, computer images are often represented as matrices of single-byte colors (i.e., 256 grey levels) for space efficiency.

Positive integers are represented as positive binary numbers. Negative numbers usually use a fancier representation such as twos-complement, which although more obscure makes it easier to do arithmetic in hardware.

Floating point numbers will be discussed in Section 5.5. The *magnitude* of numbers which can be represented as `floats` is astonishingly large, particularly when you use double-precision floating point numbers. Be aware, however, that this magnitude comes by representing the number in scientific notation, as $a \times 2^c$. Since a and c are both restricted to a given number of bits, there is still only a limited *precision*. Don't be fooled into thinking that `floats` give you the ability to count to very high numbers. Use integers and longs for such purposes.

5.1.1 Integer Libraries

Every programming language provides the basic arithmetic operators as primitives, and usually provides more advanced mathematical functions through standard libraries.

Make yourself aware of the integer functions in your math libraries. For example, the C/C++ library `stdlib.h` includes absolute value computation and random numbers, while `math.h` includes ceilings, floors, square roots, and exponentials.

The integer classes for C++ and Java are even more powerful. Indeed, the GNU g++ `Integer` class and the `java.math BigInteger` class both provide support for high-precision integers in excess of what we will develop from scratch in the next section. Use them when you can, but be aware that certain applications and special problems have attributes which require you to roll your own.

5.2 High-Precision Integers

Representing truly enormous integers requires stringing digits together. Two possible representations are —

- *Arrays of Digits* — The easiest representation for long integers is as an array of digits, where the initial element of the array represents the least significant digit. Maintaining a counter with the length of the number in digits can aid efficiency by minimizing operations which don't affect the outcome.

- *Linked Lists of Digits* — Dynamic structures are necessary if we are *really* going to do arbitrary precision arithmetic, i.e., if there is no upper bound on the length of the numbers. Note, however, that 100,000-digit integers are pretty long by any standard, yet can be represented using arrays of only 100,000 bytes each. Such space is peanuts on today's machines.

In this section, we will implement the major arithmetic operations for the array-of-digits representation. Dynamic memory allocation and linked lists provide an illusion of being able to get unlimited amounts of memory on demand. However, linked structures can be wasteful of memory, since part of each node consists of links to other nodes.

What dynamic memory *really* provides is the freedom to use space where you need it. If you wanted to create a large array of high-precision integers, a few of which were large and most of which were small, *then* you would be far better off with a list-of-digits representation, since you can't afford to allocate enormous amounts of space for all of them.

Our bignum data type is represented as follows:

```
#define MAXDIGITS        100            /* maximum length bignum */

#define PLUS             1              /* positive sign bit */
#define MINUS            -1             /* negative sign bit */

typedef struct {
        char digits[MAXDIGITS];         /* represent the number */
        int signbit;                    /* PLUS or MINUS */
        int lastdigit;                  /* index of high-order digit */
} bignum;
```

Note that each digit (0–9) is represented using a single-byte character. Although it requires a little more care to manipulate such numbers, the space savings enables us to feel less guilty about not using linked structures. Assigning 1 and -1 to be the possible values of signbit will prove convenient, because we can multiply signbits and get the right answer.

Note that there is no real reason why we have to do our computations in base-10. In fact, using higher numerical bases is more efficient, by reducing the number of digits needed to represent each number. Still, it eases the conversion to and from a nice printed representation:

```
print_bignum(bignum *n)
{
        int i;

        if (n->signbit == MINUS) printf("- ");
        for (i=n->lastdigit; i>=0; i--)
                printf("%c",'0'+ n->digits[i]);

        printf("\n");
}
```

For simplicity, our coding examples will ignore the possibility of overflow.

5.3 High-Precision Arithmetic

The first algorithms we learned in school were those for computing the four standard arithmetical operations: addition, subtraction, multiplication, and division. We learned to execute them without necessarily understanding the underlying theory.

Here we review these grade-school algorithms, with the emphasis on understanding why they work and how you can teach them to a computer. For all four operations, we interpret the arguments as $c = a \star b$, where $\star$ is $+$, $-$, $*$, or $/$.

- *Addition* — Adding two integers is done from right to left, with any overflow rippling to the next field as a carry. Allowing negative numbers complicates matters by turning addition into subtraction. This is best handled by reducing it to a special case:

```
add_bignum(bignum *a, bignum *b, bignum *c)
{
        int carry;                       /* carry digit */
        int i;                           /* counter */

        initialize_bignum(c);

        if (a->signbit == b->signbit) c->signbit = a->signbit;
        else {
                if (a->signbit == MINUS) {
                        a->signbit = PLUS;
                        subtract_bignum(b,a,c);
                        a->signbit = MINUS;
                } else {
                        b->signbit = PLUS;
                        subtract_bignum(a,b,c);
                        b->signbit = MINUS;
                }
                return;
        }

        c->lastdigit = max(a->lastdigit,b->lastdigit)+1;
        carry = 0;

        for (i=0; i<=(c->lastdigit); i++) {
                c->digits[i] = (char)
                        (carry+a->digits[i]+b->digits[i]) % 10;
                carry = (carry + a->digits[i] + b->digits[i]) / 10;
        }
```

```
        zero_justify(c);
}
```

Note a few things about the code. Manipulating the signbit is a non-trivial headache. We reduced certain cases to subtraction by negating the numbers and/or permuting the order of the operators, but took care to replace the signs first.

   The actual addition is quite simple, and made simpler by initializing all the high-order digits to 0 and treating the final carry over as a special case of digit addition. The `zero_justify` operation adjusts `lastdigit` to avoid leading zeros. It is harmless to call after every operation, particularly as it corrects for −0:

```
zero_justify(bignum *n)
{
        while ((n->lastdigit > 0) && (n->digits[ n->lastdigit ]==0))
                n->lastdigit --;

        if ((n->lastdigit == 0) && (n->digits[0] == 0))
                n->signbit = PLUS;        /* hack to avoid -0 */
}
```

- *Subtraction* — Subtraction is trickier than addition because it requires borrowing. To ensure that borrowing terminates, it is best to make sure that the larger-magnitude number is on top.

```
subtract_bignum(bignum *a, bignum *b, bignum *c)
{
        int borrow;                        /* anything borrowed? */
        int v;                             /* placeholder digit */
        int i;                             /* counter */

        if ((a->signbit == MINUS) || (b->signbit == MINUS)) {
                b->signbit = -1 * b->signbit;
                add_bignum(a,b,c);
                b->signbit = -1 * b->signbit;
                return;
        }

        if (compare_bignum(a,b) == PLUS) {
                subtract_bignum(b,a,c);
                c->signbit = MINUS;
                return;
        }

        c->lastdigit = max(a->lastdigit,b->lastdigit);
        borrow = 0;
```

```
        for (i=0; i<=(c->lastdigit); i++) {
                v = (a->digits[i] - borrow - b->digits[i]);
                if (a->digits[i] > 0)
                        borrow = 0;
                if (v < 0) {
                        v = v + 10;
                        borrow = 1;
                }

                c->digits[i] = (char) v % 10;
        }

        zero_justify(c);
}
```

- *Comparison* — Deciding which of two numbers is larger requires a comparison operation. Comparison proceeds from highest-order digit to the right, starting with the sign bit:

```
compare_bignum(bignum *a, bignum *b)
{
        int i;                          /* counter */

        if ((a->signbit==MINUS) && (b->signbit==PLUS)) return(PLUS);
        if ((a->signbit==PLUS) && (b->signbit==MINUS)) return(MINUS);

        if (b->lastdigit > a->lastdigit) return (PLUS * a->signbit);
        if (a->lastdigit > b->lastdigit) return (MINUS * a->signbit);

        for (i = a->lastdigit; i>=0; i--) {
                if (a->digits[i] > b->digits[i])
                        return(MINUS * a->signbit);
                if (b->digits[i] > a->digits[i])
                        return(PLUS * a->signbit);
        }

        return(0);
}
```

- *Multiplication* — Multiplication seems like a more advanced operation than addition or subtraction. A people as sophisticated as the Romans had a difficult time multiplying, even though their numbers look impressive on building cornerstones and Super Bowls.

    The Roman's problem was that they did not use a radix (or base) number system. Certainly multiplication can be viewed as repeated addition and thus solved in that manner, but it will be hopelessly slow. Squaring 999,999 by repeated addition requires on the order of a million operations, but is easily doable by hand using the row-by-row method we learned in school:

```
multiply_bignum(bignum *a, bignum *b, bignum *c)
{
        bignum row;                     /* represent shifted row */
        bignum tmp;                     /* placeholder bignum */
        int i,j;                        /* counters */

        initialize_bignum(c);

        row = *a;

        for (i=0; i<=b->lastdigit; i++) {
                for (j=1; j<=b->digits[i]; j++) {
                        add_bignum(c,&row,&tmp);
                        *c = tmp;
                }
                digit_shift(&row,1);
        }

        c->signbit = a->signbit * b->signbit;

        zero_justify(c);
}
```

Each operation involves shifting the first number one more place to the right and then adding the shifted first number d times to the total, where d is the appropriate digit of the second number. We might have gotten fancier than using repeated addition, but since the loop cannot spin more than nine times per digit, any possible time savings will be relatively small. Shifting a radix-number one place to the right is equivalent to multiplying it by the base of the radix, or 10 for decimal numbers:

```
digit_shift(bignum *n, int d)           /* multiply n by 10^d */
{
        int i;                          /* counter */

        if ((n->lastdigit == 0) && (n->digits[0] == 0)) return;

        for (i=n->lastdigit; i>=0; i--)
                n->digits[i+d] = n->digits[i];

        for (i=0; i<d; i++) n->digits[i] = 0;
```

```
            n->lastdigit = n->lastdigit + d;
}
```

- *Division* — Although long division is an operation feared by schoolchildren and computer architects, it too can be handled with a simpler core loop than might be imagined. Division by repeated subtraction is again far too slow to work with large numbers, but the basic repeated loop of shifting the remainder to the left, including the next digit, and subtracting off instances of the divisor is far easier to program than "guessing" each quotient digit as we were taught in school:

```
divide_bignum(bignum *a, bignum *b, bignum *c)
{
        bignum row;                          /* represent shifted row */
        bignum tmp;                          /* placeholder bignum */
        int asign, bsign;                    /* temporary signs */
        int i,j;                             /* counters */

        initialize_bignum(c);

        c->signbit = a->signbit * b->signbit;

        asign = a->signbit;
        bsign = b->signbit;

        a->signbit = PLUS;
        b->signbit = PLUS;

        initialize_bignum(&row);
        initialize_bignum(&tmp);

        c->lastdigit = a->lastdigit;

        for (i=a->lastdigit; i>=0; i--) {
                digit_shift(&row,1);
                row.digits[0] = a->digits[i];
                c->digits[i] = 0;
                while (compare_bignum(&row,b) != PLUS) {
                        c->digits[i] ++;
                        subtract_bignum(&row,b,&tmp);
                        row = tmp;
                }
        }

        zero_justify(c);

        a->signbit = asign;
```

```
        b->signbit = bsign;
}
```

This routine performs integer division and throws away the remainder. If you want to compute the remainder of $a \div b$, you can always do $a - b(a \div b)$. Slicker methods will follow when we discuss modular arithmetic in Section 7.3. The correct sign for the quotient and remainder when one or more of the operators is negative is somewhat ill-defined, so don't be surprised if the answer varies with programming language.

- *Exponentiation* — Exponentiation is repeated multiplication, and hence subject to the same performance problems as repeated addition on large numbers. The trick is to observe that

$$a^n = a^{n \div 2} \times a^{n \div 2} \times a^{n \bmod 2}$$

so it can be done using only a logarithmic number of multiplications.

5.4   Numerical Bases and Conversion

The digit representation of a given radix-number is a function of which numerical *base* is used. Particularly interesting numerical bases include:

- *Binary* — Base-2 numbers are made up of the digits 0 and 1. They provide the integer representation used within computers, because these digits map naturally to on/off or high/low states.

- *Octal* — Base-8 numbers are useful as a shorthand to make it easier to read binary numbers, since the bits can be read off from the right in groups of three. Thus $10111001_2 = 371_8 = 249_{10}$. They also play a role in the only base-conversion joke ever written. Why do programmers think Christmas is Halloween? Because 31 Oct = 25 Dec!

- *Decimal* — We use base-10 numbers because we learned to count on our ten fingers. The ancient Mayan people used a base-20 number system, presumably because they counted on both fingers and toes.

- *Hexadecimal* — Base-16 numbers are an even easier shorthand to represent binary numbers, once you get over the fact that the digits representing 10 through 15 are "A" to "F."

- *Alphanumeric* — Occasionally, one sees even higher numerical bases. Base-36 numbers are the highest you can represent using the 10 numerical digits with the 26 letters of the alphabet. Any integer can be represented in base-X provided you can display X different symbols.

There are two distinct algorithms you can use to convert base-a number x to a base-b number y —

- *Left to Right* — Here, we find the most-significant digit of y first. It is the integer d_l such that

$$(d_l + 1)b^k > x \geq d_l b^k$$

where $1 \leq d_l \leq b - 1$. In principle, this can be found by trial and error, although you must to be able to compare the magnitude of numbers in different bases. This is analogous to the long-division algorithm described above.

- *Right to Left* — Here, we find the least-significant digit of y first. This is the remainder of x divided by b. Remainders are exactly what is computed when doing modular arithmetic in Section 7.3. The cute thing is that we can compute the remainder of x on a digit-by-digit basis, making it easy to work with large integers.

Right-to-left translation is similar to how we translated conventional integers to our bignum presentation. Taking the long integer mod 10 (using the % operator) enables us to peel off the low-order digit:

```
int_to_bignum(int s, bignum *n)
{
        int i;                          /* counter */
        int t;                          /* int to work with */

        if (s >= 0) n->signbit = PLUS;
        else n->signbit = MINUS;

        for (i=0; i<MAXDIGITS; i++) n->digits[i] = (char) 0;

        n->lastdigit = -1;

        t = abs(s);

        while (t > 0) {
                n->lastdigit ++;
                n->digits[ n->lastdigit ] = (t % 10);
                t = t / 10;
        }

        if (s == 0) n->lastdigit = 0;
}
```

Using a different modulus than 10 is the key to converting numbers to alternate bases.

5.5   Real Numbers

The branches of mathematics designed to work with real numbers are real important in understanding the real world. Newton had to develop calculus before he could develop the basic laws of motion. The need to integrate or solve systems of equations occurs in every area of science. The first computers were designed as number-crunching machines, and the numbers they were designed to crunch were real numbers.

Working with real numbers on computers is very challenging because floating point arithmetic has limited precision. The most important thing to remember about real numbers is that they are not *real* real numbers:

- Much of mathematics relies on the *continuity* of the reals, the fact that there always exists a number c between a and b if $a < b$. This is not true in real numbers as they are represented in a computer.

- Many algorithms rely on an assumption of *exact* computation. This is not true of real numbers as they are represented in a computer. The associativity of addition guarantees that

$$(a + b) + c = a + (b + c)$$

Unfortunately, this is not necessarily true in computer arithmetic because of round-off errors.

There are several different types of numbers which we may well want to work with:

- *Integers* — These are the counting numbers, $-\infty, \ldots, -2, -1, 0, 1, 2, \ldots, \infty$. Subsets of the integers include the *natural* numbers (integers starting from 0) and the *positive* integers (those starting from 1), although the notation is not universal. A limiting aspect of integers is that there are gaps between them. An April Fool's Day edition of a newspaper once had a headline announcing, "Scientists Discover New Number Between 6 and 7." This is funny because while there is *always* a rational number between any two rationals x and y ($(x+y)/2$ is a good example), it would indeed be newsworthy if they found an *integer* between 6 and 7.

- *Rational Numbers* — These are the numbers which can be expressed as the ratio of two integers, i.e. c is rational if $c = a/b$ for integers a and b. Every integer can be represented by a rational, namely, $c/1$. The rational numbers are synonymous with fractions, provided we include *improper* fractions a/b where $a > b$.

- *Irrational Numbers* — There are many interesting numbers which are not rational numbers. Examples include $\pi = 3.1415926\ldots$, $\sqrt{2} = 1.41421\ldots$, and $e = 2.71828\ldots$. It can be proven that there does not exist any pair of integers x and y such that x/y equals any of these numbers.

  So how can you represent them on a computer? If you *really* need the values to arbitrary precision, they can be computed using Taylor series expansions. But for all practical purposes it suffices to approximate them using the ten digits or so.

5.5.1   Dealing With Real Numbers

The internal representation of floating point numbers varies from computer to computer, language to language, and compiler to compiler. This makes them a big pain to deal with.

There is an IEEE standard for floating point arithmetic which an increasing number of vendors adhere to, but you must always expect trouble on computations which require very high precision. Floating point numbers are represented in scientific notation, i.e., $a \times 2^c$, with a limited number of bits assigned to both the *mantissa a* and *exponent c*. Operating on two numbers with vastly different exponents often results in overflow or underflow errors, since the mantissa does not have enough bits to accommodate the answer.

Such issues are the source of many difficulties with roundoff errors. The most important problem occurs in testing for equality of real numbers, since there is usually enough garbage in the low-order bits of mantissa to render such tests meaningless. Never test whether a float is equal to zero, or any other float for that matter. Instead, test if it lies within an ϵ value plus or minus of the target.

Many problems will ask you to display an answer to a given number of digits of precision to the right of the decimal point. Here we must distinguish between *rounding* and *truncating*. Truncation is exemplified by the `floor` function, which converts a real number of an integer by chopping off the fractional part. Rounding is used to get a more accurate value for the least significant digit. To round a number X to k decimal digits, use the formula

$$\text{round}(X, k) = \text{floor}(10^k X + (1/2))/10^k$$

Use your language's formatted output function to display only the desired number of digits when so requested.

5.5.2   Fractions

Exact rational numbers x/y are best represented by pairs of integers x, y, where x is the *numerator* and y is the *denominator* of the fraction.

The basic arithmetic operations on rationals $c = x_1/y_1$ and $d = x_2/y_2$ are easy to program:

- *Addition* — We must find a common denominator before adding fractions, so

$$c + d = \frac{x_1 y_2 + x_2 y_1}{y_1 y_2}$$

- *Subtraction* — Same as addition, since $c - d = c + -1 \times d$, so

$$c - d = \frac{x_1 y_2 - x_2 y_1}{y_1 y_2}$$

- *Multiplication* — Since multiplication is repeated addition, it is easily shown that

$$c \times d = \frac{x_1 x_2}{y_1 y_2}$$

- *Division* — To divide fractions you multiply by the *reciprocal* of the denominator, so

$$c/d = \frac{x_1}{y_1} \times \frac{y_2}{x_2} = \frac{x_1 y_2}{x_2 y_1}$$

But why does this work? Because under this definition, $d(c/d) = c$, which is exactly what we want division to mean.

Blindly implementing these operations leads to a significant danger of overflows. It is important to *reduce* fractions to their simplest representation, i.e., replace 2/4 by 1/2. The secret is to cancel out the *greatest common divisor* of the numerator and the denominator, i.e., the largest integer which divides both of these integers.

Finding the greatest common divisor by trial and error or exhaustive search can be very expensive. However, the Euclidean algorithm for gcd is efficient, very simple to program, and discussed in Section 7.2.1.

5.5.3 *Decimals*

The decimal representation of real numbers is just a special case of the rational numbers. A decimal number represents the sum of two numbers; the integer part to the left of the decimal point and the fractional part to the right of the decimal. Thus the fractional representation of the first five decimal digits of π is

$$3.1415 = (3/1) + (1415/10000) = 6283/2000$$

The denominator of the fractional part is 10^{i+1} if the rightmost non-zero digit lies i places to the right of the decimal point.

Converting a rational to a decimal number is easy, in principle; just divide the numerator by the denominator. The catch is that many fractions do not have a finite decimal representation. For example, $1/3 = 0.3333333\ldots$, and $1/7 = 0.14285714285714285714\ldots$. Usually a decimal representation with the first ten or so significant digits will suffice, but sometimes we want to know the exact representation, i.e., $1/30 = 0.0\overline{3}$ or $1/7 = 0.\overline{142857}$.

What fraction goes with a given repeating decimal number? We can find it by explicitly simulating the long division. The decimal expansion of fraction $1/7$ is obtained by dividing 7 into $1.0000000\ldots$. The next digit of the quotient is obtained by multiplying the remainder by ten, adding the last digit (always zero), and finding how many times the denominator fits into this quantity. Notice that we get into an infinite loop the instant this quantity repeats. Thus the decimal digits between these positions repeats forever.

A simpler method results if we know (or guess) the length of the repeat. Suppose that the simple fraction a/b has a repeat R of length of l. Then $10^l(a/b) - (a/b) = R$, and hence $a/b = R/(10^l - 1)$. To demonstrate, suppose we want the fraction associated with $a/b = 0.0123123\ldots$. The repeat length is three digits, and $R = 12.3$ by the formula above. Thus $a/b = 12.3/999 = 123/9990$.

5.6 Algebra

In its full glory, algebra is the study of groups and rings. High-school algebra is basically limited to the study of equations, defined over the operators addition and multiplication. The most important class of formulae are the *polynomials*, such that $P(x) = c_0 + c_1 x + c_2 x^2 + \ldots$, where x is the variable and c_i is the coefficient of the ith term x^i. The degree of a polynomial is the largest i such that c_i is non-zero.

5.6.1 *Manipulating Polynomials*

The most natural representation for an nth-degree univariate (one variable) polynomial is as an array of $n + 1$ coefficients c_0 through c_n. Such a representation makes short work of the basic arithmetic operations on polynomials:

- *Evaluation* — Computing $P(x)$ for some given x can easily be done by brute force, namely, computing each term $c_i x^n$ independently and adding them together. The trouble is that this will cost $O(n^2)$ multiplications where $O(n)$ suffice. The secret is to note that $x^i = x^{i-1} x$, so if we compute the terms from smallest degree to highest degree we can keep track of the current power of x, and get away with two multiplications per term ($x^{i-1} \times x$, and then $c_i \times x^i$).

  Alternately, one can employ *Horner's rule*, an even slicker way to do the same job:

  $$a_n x^n + a_{n-1} x^{n-1} + \ldots + a_0 = ((a_n x + a_{n-1})x + \ldots)x + a_0$$

- *Addition/Subtraction* — Adding and subtracting polynomials is even easier than the same operations on long integers, since there is no borrowing or carrying. Simply add or subtract the coefficients of the ith terms for all i from zero to the maximum degree.

- *Multiplication* — The product of polynomials $P(x)$ and $Q(x)$ is the sum of the product of every pair of terms, where each term comes from a different polynomial:

  $$P(x) \times Q(x) = \sum_{i=0}^{degree(P)} \sum_{j=0}^{degree(Q)} (c_i c_j) x^{i+j}$$

Such an all-against-all operation is called a *convolution*. Other convolutions in this book include integer multiplication (all digits against all digits) and string matching (all possible positions of the pattern string against all possible text positions). There is an amazing algorithm (the fast Fourier transform, or FFT) which computes convolutions in $O(n \log n)$ time instead of $O(n^2)$, but it is well beyond the scope of this book. Still, it is nice to recognize when you are doing a convolution so you know that such tools exist.

- *Division* — Dividing polynomials is a tricky business, since the polynomials are not closed under division. Note that $1/x$ may or may not be thought of as a polynomial, since it is x^{-1}, but $2x/(x^2+1)$ certainly isn't. It is a *rational function*.

Sometimes polynomials are *sparse*, meaning that for many coefficients $c_i = 0$. Sufficiently sparse polynomials should be represented as linked lists of coefficient/degree pairs. *Multivariate polynomials* are defined over more than one variable. The bivariate polynomial $f(x, y)$ can be represented by a matrix C of coefficients, such that $C[i][j]$ is the coefficient of $x^i y^j$.

5.6.2 Root Finding

Given a polynomial $P(x)$ and a target number t, the problem of *root finding* is identifying any or all x such that $P(x) = t$.

If $P(x)$ is a first-degree polynomial, the root is simply $x = (t - a_0)/a_1$, where a_i is the coefficient of x_i in $P(x)$. If $P(x)$ is a second-degree polynomial, then the *quadratic equation* applies:

$$x = \frac{-a_1 \pm \sqrt{a_1{}^2 - 4a_2(a_0 - t)}}{2a_2}$$

There are more complicated formulae for solving third- and fourth-degree polynomials before the good times end. No closed form exists for the roots of fifth-degree (quintic) or higher-degree equations.

Beyond quadratic equations, numerical methods are typically used. Any text on numerical analysis will describe a variety of root-finding algorithms, including Newton's method and Newton-Raphson, as well as many potential traps such as numerical stability. But the basic idea is that of binary search. Suppose a function $f(x)$ is *monotonically increasing* between l and u, meaning that $f(i) \le f(j)$ for all $l \le i \le j \le u$. Now suppose we want to find the x such that $f(x) = t$. We can compare $f((l + u)/2)$ with t. If $t < f((l + u)/2)$, then the root lies between l and $(l + u)/2$; if not, it lies between $(l+u)/2$ and u. We can keep recurring until the window is narrow enough for our taste.

This method can be used to compute square roots because this is equivalent to solving $x^2 = t$ between 1 and t for all $t \ge 1$. However, a simpler method to find the ith root of t uses exponential functions and logarithms to compute $t^{1/i}$.

5.7 Logarithms

You have probably noticed the `log` and `exp` buttons on your calculator, but quite likely have never used them. You may even have forgotten why they are there. A *logarithm* is simply an inverse exponential function. Saying $b^x = y$ is equivalent to saying that $x = \log_b y$.

The b term is known as the *base* of the logarithm. Two bases are of particular importance for mathematical and historical reasons. The *natural log*, usually denoted $\ln x$, is a base $e = 2.71828\ldots$ logarithm. The inverse of $\ln x$ is the exponential function $\exp x = e^x$. Thus by composing these functions we get

$$\exp(\ln x) = x$$

Less common today is the base-10 or *common logarithm*, usually denoted $\log x$. Common logarithms were particularly important in the days before pocket calculators.[1] Logarithms provided the easiest way to multiply big numbers by hand, either implicitly using a slide rule or explicitly by using a book of logarithms.

Logarithms are still useful for multiplication, particularly for exponentiation. Recall that $\log_a xy = \log_a x + \log_a y$; i.e., the log of a product is the sum of the logs. A direct consequence of this is that

$$\log_a n^b = b \cdot \log_a n$$

So how can we compute a^b for any a and b using the $\exp(x)$ and $\ln(x)$ functions? We know

$$a^b = \exp(\ln(a^b)) = \exp(b \ln a)$$

so the problem is reduced to one multiplication plus one call of each of these functions.

We can use this method to compute square roots since $\sqrt{x} = x^{1/2}$, and for any other fractional power as well. Such applications are one reason why the mathematics library of any reasonable programming language includes the ln and exp functions. Be aware that these are complicated numerical functions (computed using Taylor-series expansions) which have inherent computational uncertainty, so do not expect that $\exp(0.5 \ln 4)$ will give you exactly 2.

The other important fact to remember about logarithms is that it is easy to convert the logarithm from one base to another, as a consequence of the following formula:

$$\log_a b = \frac{\log_c b}{\log_c a}$$

Thus changing the base of $\log b$ from base-a to base-c simply involves dividing by $\log_c a$. Thus it is easy to write a common log function from a natural log function, and vice versa.

5.8 Real Mathematical Libraries

Math Libraries in C/C++

The standard C/C++ math library has several useful functions for working with real numbers:

---

[1] The authors of this book are old enough to remember this pre-1972 era.

```
#include <math.h>              /* include the math library */

double floor(double x);    /* chop off fractional part of x */
double ceil (double x);    /* raise x to next largest integer */
double fabs(double x);     /* compute the absolute value of x */

double sqrt(double x);     /* compute square roots */
double exp(double x);      /* compute e^x */
double log(double x);      /* compute the base-e logarithm */
double log10(double x);    /* compute the base-10 logarithm */
double pow(double x, double y);   /* compute x^y */
```

Math Libraries in Java

The java class *java.lang.Math* has all of these functions and a few more, most obviously a **round** function to take a real to the nearest integer.

5.9 Problems

5.9.1 Primary Arithmetic

PC/UVa IDs: 110501/10035, **Popularity:** A, **Success rate:** average **Level:** 1

Children are taught to add multi-digit numbers from right to left, one digit at a time. Many find the "carry" operation, where a 1 is carried from one digit position to the next, to be a significant challenge. Your job is to count the number of carry operations for each of a set of addition problems so that educators may assess their difficulty.

Input

Each line of input contains two unsigned integers less than 10 digits. The last line of input contains "0 0".

Output

For each line of input except the last, compute the number of carry operations that result from adding the two numbers and print them in the format shown below.

Sample Input

```
123 456
555 555
123 594
0 0
```

Sample Output

```
No carry operation.
3 carry operations.
1 carry operation.
```

5.9.2   Reverse and Add

PC/UVa IDs: 110502/10018, **Popularity:** A, **Success rate:** low **Level:** 1

The *reverse and add* function starts with a number, reverses its digits, and adds the reverse to the original. If the sum is not a palindrome (meaning it does not give the same number read from left to right and right to left), we repeat this procedure until it does.

For example, if we start with 195 as the initial number, we get 9,339 as the resulting palindrome after the fourth addition:

195	786	1,473	5,214
591	687	3,741	4,125
+ ──	+ ──	+ ──	+ ──
786	1,473	5,214	9,339

This method leads to palindromes in a few steps for almost all of the integers. But there are interesting exceptions. 196 is the first number for which no palindrome has been found. It has never been proven, however, that no such palindrome exists.

You must write a program that takes a given number and gives the resulting palindrome (if one exists) and the number of iterations/additions it took to find it.

You may assume that all the numbers used as test data will terminate in an answer with less than 1,000 iterations (additions), and yield a palindrome that is not greater than 4,294,967,295.

Input

The first line will contain an integer N ($0 < N \leq 100$), giving the number of test cases, while the next N lines each contain a single integer P whose palindrome you are to compute.

Output

For each of the N integers, print a line giving the minimum number of iterations to find the palindrome, a single space, and then the resulting palindrome itself.

Sample Input	*Sample Output*
3	4 9339
195	5 45254
265	3 6666
750	

5.9.3   The Archeologist's Dilemma

PC/UVa IDs: 110503/701, **Popularity:** A, **Success rate:** low **Level:** 1

An archaeologist, seeking proof of the presence of extraterrestrials in the Earth's past, has stumbled upon a partially destroyed wall containing strange chains of numbers. The left-hand part of these lines of digits is always intact, but unfortunately the right-hand one is often lost because of erosion of the stone. However, she notices that all the numbers with all its digits intact are powers of 2, so that the hypothesis that all of them are powers of 2 is obvious. To reinforce her belief, she selects a list of numbers on which it is apparent that the number of legible digits is strictly smaller than the number of lost ones, and asks you to find the smallest power of 2 (if any) whose first digits coincide with those of the list.

Thus you must write a program that, given an integer, determines the smallest exponent E (if it exists) such that the first digits of 2^E coincide with the integer (remember that more than half of the digits are missing).

Input

Each line contains a positive integer N not bigger than 2,147,483,648.

Output

For every one of these integers, print a line containing the smallest positive integer E such that the first digits of 2^E are precisely the digits of N, or, if there isn't one, the sentence "no power of 2".

Sample Input

```
1
2
10
```

Sample Output

```
7
8
20
```

5.9.4   Ones

PC/UVa IDs: 110504/10127, **Popularity:** A, **Success rate:** high **Level:** 2

Given any integer $0 \leq n \leq 10,000$ not divisible by 2 or 5, some multiple of n is a number which in decimal notation is a sequence of 1's. How many digits are in the smallest such multiple of n?

Input

A file of integers at one integer per line.

Output

Each output line gives the smallest integer $x > 0$ such that $p = \sum_{i=0}^{x-1} 1 \times 10^i$, where a is the corresponding input integer, $p = a \times b$, and b is an integer greater than zero.

Sample Input

```
3
7
9901
```

Sample Output

```
3
6
12
```

5.9.5 A Multiplication Game

PC/UVa IDs: 110505/847, **Popularity:** A, **Success rate:** high **Level:** 3

Stan and Ollie play the game of multiplication by multiplying an integer p by one of the numbers 2 to 9. Stan always starts with $p = 1$, does his multiplication, then Ollie multiplies the number, then Stan, and so on. Before a game starts, they draw an integer $1 < n < 4,294,967,295$ and the winner is whoever reaches $p \geq n$ first.

Input

Each input line contains a single integer n.

Output

For each line of input, output one line – either

```
Stan wins.
```

or

```
Ollie wins.
```

assuming that both of them play perfectly.

Sample Input

```
162
17
34012226
```

Sample Output

```
Stan wins.
Ollie wins.
Stan wins.
```

5.9.6   Polynomial Coefficients

PC/UVa IDs: 110506/10105, **Popularity:** B, **Success rate:** high **Level:** 1

This problem seeks the coefficients resulting from the expansion of the polynomial

$$P = (x_1 + x_2 + \ldots + x_k)^n$$

Input

The input will consist of a set of pairs of lines. The first line of the pair consists of two integers n and k separated with space ($0 < k, n < 13$). These integers define the power of the polynomial and the number of variables. The second line in each pair consists of k non-negative integers $n_1, \ldots, n_k$, where $n_1 + \ldots + n_k = n$.

Output

For each input pair of lines the output line should consist of one integer, the coefficient of the monomial $x_1^{n_1} x_2^{n_2} \ldots x_k^{n_k}$ in expansion of the polynomial $(x_1 + x_2 + \ldots + x_k)^n$.

Sample Input

```
2 2
1 1
2 12
1 0 0 0 0 0 0 0 0 0 1 0
```

Sample Output

```
2
2
```

5.9.7   The Stern-Brocot Number System

PC/UVa IDs: 110507/10077, **Popularity:** C, **Success rate:** high **Level:** 1

The *Stern-Brocot tree* is a beautiful way for constructing the set of all non-negative fractions $\frac{m}{n}$ where m and n are relatively prime. The idea is to start with two fractions $\left(\frac{0}{1}, \frac{1}{0}\right)$ and then repeat the following operation as many times as desired:

Insert $\frac{m+m'}{n+n'}$ between two adjacent fractions $\frac{m}{n}$ and $\frac{m'}{n'}$.

For example, the first step gives us one new entry between $\frac{0}{1}$ and $\frac{1}{0}$,

$$\frac{0}{1}, \frac{1}{1}, \frac{1}{0}$$

and the next gives two more:

$$\frac{0}{1}, \frac{1}{2}, \frac{1}{1}, \frac{2}{1}, \frac{1}{0}$$

The next gives four more:

$$\frac{0}{1}, \frac{1}{3}, \frac{1}{2}, \frac{2}{3}, \frac{1}{1}, \frac{3}{2}, \frac{2}{1}, \frac{3}{1}, \frac{1}{0}$$

The entire array can be regarded as an infinite binary tree structure whose top levels look like this–

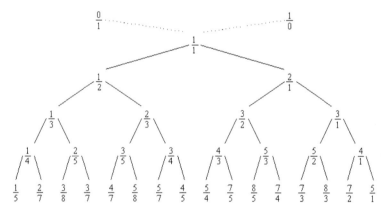

This construction preserves order, and thus we cannot possibly get the same fraction in two different places.

We can, in fact, regard the *Stern-Brocot tree* as a *number system* for representing rational numbers, because each positive, reduced fraction occurs exactly once. Let us use the letters "L" and "R" to stand for going down the left or right branch as we proceed from the root of the tree to a particular fraction; then a string of L's and R's uniquely identifies a place in the tree. For example, LRRL means that we go left from $\frac{1}{1}$ down to $\frac{1}{2}$, then right to $\frac{2}{3}$, then right to $\frac{3}{4}$, then left to $\frac{5}{7}$. We can consider LRRL to be a representation of $\frac{5}{7}$. Every positive fraction gets represented in this way as a unique string of L's and R's.

Well, almost every fraction. The fraction $\frac{1}{1}$ corresponds to the empty string. We will denote it by I, since that looks something like 1 and stands for "identity."

In this problem, given a positive rational fraction, represent it in the *Stern-Brocot number system*.

Input

The input file contains multiple test cases. Each test case consists of a line containing two positive integers m and n, where m and n are relatively prime. The input terminates with a test case containing two 1's for m and n, and this case must not be processed.

Output

For each test case in the input file, output a line containing the representation of the given fraction in the *Stern-Brocot number system*.

Sample Input

```
5 7
878 323
1 1
```

Sample Output

```
LRRL
RRLRRLRLLLLRLRRR
```

5.9.8   Pairsumonious Numbers

PC/UVa IDs: 110508/10202, **Popularity:** B, **Success rate:** high   **Level:** 4

Any set of n integers form $n(n-1)/2$ sums by adding every possible pair. Your task is to find the n integers given the set of sums.

Input

Each line of input contains n followed by $n(n-1)/2$ integer numbers separated by a space, where $2 < n < 10$.

Output

For each line of input, output one line containing n integers in non-descending order such that the input numbers are pairwise sums of the n numbers. If there is more than one solution, any one will do. If there is no solution, print "`Impossible`"...

Sample Input

```
3 1269 1160 1663
3 1 1 1
5 226 223 225 224 227 229 228 226 225 227
5 216 210 204 212 220 214 222 208 216 210
5 -1 0 -1 -2 1 0 -1 1 0 -1
5 79950 79936 79942 79962 79954 79972 79960 79968 79924 79932
```

Sample Output

```
383 777 886
Impossible
111 112 113 114 115
101 103 107 109 113
-1 -1 0 0 1
39953 39971 39979 39983 39989
```

5.10 Hints

5.1 Do we need to implement complete high-precision addition for this problem, or can we extract the number of carry operations using a simpler method?

5.3 Do we need to implement complete high-precision multiplication for this problem, or does the fact that we are looking for a power of 2 simplify matters?

5.4 Do we actually have to compute the number in order to find the number of digits it contains?

5.5 Might it be easier to solve a more general problem – who wins if they start with number x and end on number n?

5.6 Do we need to compute the resulting polynomial, or is there an easier way to calculate the resulting coefficient? Does the binomial theorem help?

5.8 Is an exhaustive search of the possibilities necessary? If so, look ahead to backtracking in Chapter 8.

5.11 Notes

5.2 A three-year computer search for an addition palindrome from 196 went up to 2 million digits without ever finding such a palindrome. It becomes progressively less likely that a palindrome exists the longer we search. See *http://www.fourmilab.ch/documents/threeyears/threeyears.html* for details.

6

Combinatorics

Combinatorics is the mathematics of counting. There are several basic counting problems that occur repeatedly throughout computer science and programming.

Combinatorics problems are notorious for their reliance on cleverness and insight. Once you look at the problem in the right way, the answer suddenly becomes obvious. This *aha!* phenomenon makes them ideal for programming contests, because the right observation can replace the need to write a complicated program that generates and counts all solutions with one call to a simple formula. It sometimes leads to "off-line" contest solutions. If the resulting computations are tractable only on small integers or are in fact the same for all input, one might be able to compute all possible solutions using (say) a pocket calculator and then write a program to print out the answers on demand. Remember, the judge can't look into your heart or your program to see your intentions – it only checks the results.

6.1   Basic Counting Techniques

Here we review certain basic counting rules and formulas you may have seen but possibly forgotten. In particular, there are three basic counting rules from which many counting formulae are generated. It is important to see which rule applies for your particular problem:

- *Product Rule* —   The *product rule* states that if there are $|A|$ possibilities from set A and $|B|$ possibilities from set B, then there are $|A| \times |B|$ ways to combine one from A and one from B. For example, suppose you own 5 shirts and 4 pants. Then there are $5 \times 4 = 20$ different ways you can get dressed tomorrow.

- *Sum Rule* — The *sum rule* states that if there are $|A|$ possibilities from set A and $|B|$ possibilities from set B, then there are $|A| + |B|$ ways for either A *or* B to occur – assuming the elements of A and B are distinct. For example, given that you own 5 shirts and 4 pants and the laundry ruined one of them, there are 9 possible ruined items.[1]

- *Inclusion-Exclusion Formula* — The sum rule is a special case of a more general formula when the two sets can overlap, namely,

$$|A \cup B| = |A| + |B| - |A \cap B|$$

  For example, let A represent the set of colors of my shirts and B the colors of my pants. Via inclusion-exclusion, I can calculate the total number of colors given the number of color-matched garments or vice versa. The reason this works is that summing the sets double counts certain possibilities, namely, those occurring in both sets. The inclusion-exclusion formula generalizes to three sets and beyond in a natural way:

$$|A \cup B \cup C| = |A| + |B| + |C| - |A \cap B| - |A \cap C| - |B \cap C| + |A \cap B \cap C|$$

Double counting is a slippery aspect of combinatorics, which can make it difficult to solve problems via inclusion-exclusion. Another powerful technique is establishing a bijection. A *bijection* is a one-to-one mapping between the elements of one set and the elements of another. Whenever you have such a mapping, counting the size of one of the sets automatically gives you the size of the other set.

For example, if we count the number of pants currently being worn in a given class, and can assume that all students wears pants, then this tells us the number of people in the class. It works because there is a one-to-one mapping between pants and people, and would break if we exchanged pants for socks or removed the dress code and allowed people to wear skirts instead.

Exploiting bijections requires us to have a repertoire of sets which we know how to count, so we can map other objects to them. Basic combinatorial objects you should be familiar with include the following. It is useful to have a feeling for how fast the number of objects grows, to know when exhaustive search breaks down as a possible technique:

- *Permutations* — A *permutation* is an arrangement of n items, where every item appears exactly once. There are $n! = \prod_{i=1}^{n} i$ different permutations. The $3! = 6$ permutations of three items are 123, 132, 213, 231, 312, and 321. For $n = 10$, $n! = 3,628,800$, so we start to approach the limits of exhaustive search.

- *Subsets* — A *subset* is a selection of elements from n possible items. There are 2^n distinct subsets of n things. Thus there are $2^3 = 8$ subsets of three items, namely, 1, 2, 3, 12, 13, 23, 123, and the empty set: never forget the empty set. For $n = 20$, $2^n = 1,048,576$, so we start to approach the limits of exhaustive search.

- *Strings* — A *string* is a sequence of items which are drawn *with repetition*. There are m^n distinct sequences of n items drawn from m items. The 27 length-3 strings

---

[1]This is not true in practice, because the ruined item is certain to be your favorite of the bunch.

on 123 are 111, 112, 113, 121, 122, 123, 131, 132, 133, 211, 212, 213, 221, 222, 223, 231, 232, 233, 311, 312, 313, 321, 322, 323, 331, 332, and 333. The number of binary strings of length n is identical to the number of subsets of n items (why?), and the number of possibilities increases even more rapidly with larger m.

6.2 Recurrence Relations

Recurrence relations make it easy to count a variety of recursively defined structures. Recursively defined structures include trees, lists, well-formed formulae, and divide-and-conquer algorithms – so they lurk wherever computer scientists do.

What is a recurrence relation? It is an equation which is defined in terms of itself. Why are they good things? Because many natural functions are easily expressed as recurrences! Any polynomial can be represented by a recurrence, including the linear function:

$$a_n = a_{n-1} + 1, a_1 = 1 \longrightarrow a_n = n$$

Any exponential can be represented by a recurrence:

$$a_n = 2a_{n-1}, a_1 = 2 \longrightarrow a_n = 2^n$$

Finally, certain weird but interesting functions which are not easily represented using conventional notation can be described by recurrences:

$$a_n = na_{n-1}, a_1 = 1 \longrightarrow a_n = n!$$

Thus recurrence relations are a very versatile way to represent functions. It is often easy to find a recurrence as the answer to a counting problem. *Solving* the recurrence to get a nice closed form can be somewhat of an art, but as we shall see, computer programs can easily evaluate the value of a given recurrence even without the existence of a nice closed form.

6.3 Binomial Coefficients

The most important class of counting numbers are the *binomial coefficients*, where $\binom{n}{k}$ counts the number of ways to choose k things out of n possibilities. What do they count?

- *Committees* — How many ways are there to form a k-member committee from n people? By definition, $\binom{n}{k}$ is the answer.

- *Paths Across a Grid* — How many ways are there to travel from the upper-left corner of an $n \times m$ grid to the lower-right corner by walking only down and to the right? Every path must consist of $n + m$ steps, n downward and m to the right. Every path with a different set of downward moves is distinct, so there are $\binom{n+m}{n}$ such sets/paths.

- *Coefficients of $(a + b)^n$* — Observe that

$$(a + b)^3 = 1a^3 + 3a^2b + 3ab^2 + 1b^3$$

What is the coefficient of the term $a^k b^{n-k}$? Clearly $\binom{n}{k}$, because it counts the number of ways we can choose the k a-terms out of n possibilities.

- *Pascal's Triangle* — No doubt you played with this arrangement of numbers in high school. Each number is the sum of the two numbers directly above it:

```
            1
          1   1
        1   2   1
      1   3   3   1
    1   4   6   4   1
  1   5  10  10   5   1
```

Why did you or Pascal care? Because this table constructs the binomial coefficients! The $(n + 1)$st row of the table gives the values $\binom{n}{i}$ for $0 \le i \le n$. The neat thing about the triangle is how it reveals certain interesting identities, such that the sum of the entries on the $(n + 1)$st row equals 2^n.

How do you compute the binomial coefficients? First, $\binom{n}{k} = n!/((n - k)!k!)$, so in principle you can compute them straight from factorials. However, this method has a serious drawback. Intermediate calculations can easily cause arithmetic overflow even when the final coefficient fits comfortably within an integer.

A more stable way to compute binomial coefficients is using the recurrence relation implicit in the construction of Pascal's triangle, namely, that

$$\binom{n}{k} = \binom{n-1}{k-1} + \binom{n-1}{k}$$

Why does this work? Consider whether the nth element appears in one of the $\binom{n}{k}$ subsets of k elements. If so, we can complete the subset by picking $k - 1$ other items from the other $n - 1$. If not, we must pick all k items from the remaining $n - 1$. There is no overlap between these cases, and all possibilities are included, so the sum counts all k-subsets.

No recurrence is complete without basis cases. What binomial coefficient values do we know without computing them? The left term of the sum eventually drives us down to $\binom{n-k}{0}$. How many ways are there to choose 0 things from a set? Exactly one, the empty set. If this is not convincing, then it is equally good to accept that $\binom{m}{1} = m$. The right term of the sum drives us up to $\binom{k}{k}$. How many ways are there to choose k things from a k-element set? Exactly one, the complete set. Together with the recurrence these basis cases define the binomial coefficients on all interesting values.

The best way to evaluate such a recurrence is to build a table of all possible values, at least up to the size that you are interested in. Study the function below to see how we did it.

```
#define MAXN      100              /* largest n or m */

long binomial_coefficient(n,m)
int n,m;                           /* computer n choose m */
{
        int i,j;                   /* counters */
        long bc[MAXN][MAXN];       /* table of binomial coefficients */

        for (i=0; i<=n; i++) bc[i][0] = 1;

        for (j=0; j<=n; j++) bc[j][j] = 1;

        for (i=1; i<=n; i++)
                for (j=1; j<i; j++)
                        bc[i][j] = bc[i-1][j-1] + bc[i-1][j];

        return( bc[n][m] );
}
```

Such programs to evaluate recurrences are the foundation for dynamic programming, an algorithmic technique we will study in Chapter 11.

6.4   Other Counting Sequences

There are several other counting sequences which repeatedly emerge in applications, and which are easily computed using recurrence relations. The wise combinatorialist keeps them in mind whenever they count:

- *Fibonacci numbers* — Defined by the recurrence $F_n = F_{n-1} + F_{n-2}$ and the initial values $F_0 = 0$ and $F_1 = 1$, they emerge repeatedly because this is perhaps the simplest interesting recurrence relation. The first several values are 0, 1, 1, 2, 3, 5, 8, 13, 21, 34, 55, ... The Fibonacci numbers lend themselves to an amazing variety of mathematical identities, and are just fun to play with. They have the following hard-to-guess but simple-to-derive closed form:

$$F_n = \frac{1}{\sqrt{5}} \left(\left(\frac{1 + \sqrt{5}}{2} \right)^n - \left(\frac{1 - \sqrt{5}}{2} \right)^n \right)$$

This closed form has certain important implications. Since $(1 - \sqrt{5})/2$ is between 0 and 1, raising it to any power leaves a number in this range. Thus the first term, ϕ^n where $\phi = (1 + \sqrt{5})/2$ is the driving quantity, and can be used to estimate F_n to within plus or minus 1.

- *Catalan Numbers* — The recurrence and associated closed form

$$C_n = \sum_{k=0}^{n-1} C_k C_{n-1-k} = \frac{1}{n+1} \binom{2n}{n}$$

defines the *Catalan numbers*, which occur in a surprising number of problems in combinatorics. The first several terms are $2, 5, 14, 42, 132, 429, 1430, \ldots$ when $C_0 = 1$.

How many ways are there to build a balanced formula from n sets of left and right parentheses? For example, there are five ways to do it for $n = 3$: $((()))$, $()(())$, $(())()$, $(()())$, and $()()()$. The leftmost parenthesis l matches some right parenthesis r, which must partition the formula into two balanced pieces, the part between l and r, and the part to the right of r. If the left part contains k pairs, the right part must contain $n - k - 1$ pairs, since l, r represent one pair. Both of these subformulas must be well formed, which leads to the recurrence:

$$C_n = \sum_{k=0}^{n-1} C_k C_{n-1-k}$$

and we have the Catalan numbers.

The exact same reasoning arises in counting the number of triangulations of a convex polygon, counting the number of rooted binary trees on $n+1$ leaves, and counting the number of paths across a lattice which do not rise above the main diagonal. The Catalan numbers have the nice closed form $C_n = \frac{1}{n+1} \binom{2n}{n}$.

- *Eulerian Numbers* — The *Eulerian* numbers $\left\langle {n \atop k} \right\rangle$ count the number of permutations of length n with exactly k ascending sequences or *runs*. A recurrence can be formulated by considering each permutation p of $1, \ldots, n-1$. There are n places to insert element n, and each either splits an existing run of p or occurs immediately after the last element of an existing run, thus preserving the run count. Thus $\left\langle {n \atop k} \right\rangle = k \left\langle {n-1 \atop k} \right\rangle + (n - k + 1) \left\langle {n-1 \atop k-1} \right\rangle$. Can you construct the eleven permutations of length four with exactly two runs?

- *Stirling Numbers* — There are two different types of Stirling numbers. The first, $\left[{n \atop k} \right]$, counts the number of permutations on n elements with exactly k cycles. To formulate the recurrence, observe the nth element either forms a singleton cycle or it doesn't. If it does, there are $\left[{n-1 \atop k-1} \right]$ ways to arrange the rest of the elements to form $k - 1$ cycles. If not, the nth element can be inserted in every possible position of every cycle of the $\left[{n-1 \atop k} \right]$ ways to make k cycles out of $n - 1$ elements. Thus

$$\left[{n \atop k} \right] = \left[{n-1 \atop k-1} \right] + (n - 1) \left[{n-1 \atop k} \right]$$

There are 11 permutations of four elements with exactly two cycles.

- *Set Partitions* — The second kind of Stirling number $\{{n \atop k}\}$ counts the number of ways to partition n items into k sets. For example, there are seven ways to partition four items into exactly two subsets: $(1)(234)$, $(12)(34)$, $(13)(24)$, $(14)(23)$, $(123)(4)$, $(124)(3)$ and $(134)(2)$. The nth item can be inserted into any of the k subsets of an $n-1$-part partition or it forms a singleton set. Thus by a similar argument to that of the other Stirling numbers they are defined by the recurrence $\{{n \atop k}\} = k\{{n-1 \atop k}\} + \{{n-1 \atop k}\}$. The special case of $\{{n \atop 2}\} = 2^{n-1} - 1$, since any proper subset of the elements 2 to n can be unioned with (1) to define the set partition. The second part of the partition consists of exactly the elements not in this first part.

- *Integer Partitions* — An integer partition of n is an unordered set of positive integers which add up to n. For example, there are seven partitions of 5, namely, (5), $(4, 1)$, $(3, 2)$, $(3, 1, 1)$, $(2, 2, 1)$, $(2, 1, 1, 1)$, and $(1, 1, 1, 1, 1)$. The easiest way to count them is to define a function $f(n, k)$ giving the number of integer partitions of n with largest part at most k. In any acceptable partition the largest part either does or does not reach with limit, so $f(n, k) = f(n - k, k) + f(n, k - 1)$. The basis cases are $f(1, 1) = 1$ and $f(n, k) = 0$ whenever $k > n$.

The interested student should read [GKP89] for more on these and other interesting counting sequences. It is also worth visiting Sloane's *Handbook of Integer Sequences* on the web at *http://www.research.att.com/~njas/sequences/* to help identify virtually any interesting sequence of integers.

6.5   Recursion and Induction

Mathematical induction provides a useful tool to solve recurrences. When we first learned about mathematical induction in high school it seemed like complete magic. You proved the formula for some basis case like 1 or 2, then *assumed* it was true all the way to $n - 1$ before proving it was true for general n using the assumption. That was a proof? Ridiculous!

When we first learned the programming technique of recursion in college it also seemed like complete magic. Your program tested whether the input argument was some basis case like 1 or 2. If not, you solved the bigger case by breaking it up into pieces and *calling the subprogram itself* to solve these pieces. That was a program? Ridiculous!

The reason both seemed like magic is because recursion *is* mathematical induction! In both, we have general and boundary conditions, with the general condition breaking the problem into smaller and smaller pieces. The *initial* or boundary condition terminates the recursion. Once you understand either recursion or induction, you should be able to turn it around to see why the other one also works.

A powerful way to solve recurrence relations is to guess a solution and then prove it by induction. When trying to guess a solution, it pays to tabulate small values of the function and stare at them until you see a pattern.

For example, consider the following recurrence relation:

$$T_n = 2T_{n-1} + 1, T_0 = 0$$

Building a table of values yields the following:

n	0	1	2	3	4	5	6	7
T_n	0	1	3	7	15	31	63	127

Can you guess what the solution is? You should notice that things look like they are doubling each time, no surprise considering the formula. But it is not quite 2^n. By playing around with variations of this function, you should be able to stumble on the conjecture that $T_n = 2^n - 1$. To finish the job, we must prove this conjecture, using the three steps of induction:

1. Show that the basis is true: $T_0 = 2^0 - 1 = 0$.

2. Now assume it is true for T_{n-1}.

3. Use this assumption to complete the argument:

$$T_n = 2T_{n-1} + 1 = 2(2^{n-1} - 1) + 1 = 2^n - 1$$

Guessing the solution is usually the hard part of the job, and where the art and experience comes in. The key is playing around with small values for insight, and having some feel for what kind of closed form the answer will be.

6.6 Problems

6.6.1 How Many Fibs?

PC/UVa IDs: 110601/10183, **Popularity:** B, **Success rate:** average **Level:** 1

Recall the definition of the Fibonacci numbers:

$$
\begin{aligned}
f_1 &:= 1 \\
f_2 &:= 2 \\
f_n &:= f_{n-1} + f_{n-2} \qquad (n \geq 3)
\end{aligned}
$$

Given two numbers a and b, calculate how many Fibonacci numbers are in the range $[a, b]$.

Input

The input contains several test cases. Each test case consists of two non-negative integer numbers a and b. Input is terminated by $a = b = 0$. Otherwise, $a \leq b \leq 10^{100}$. The numbers a and b are given with no superfluous leading zeros.

Output

For each test case output on a single line the number of Fibonacci numbers f_i with $a \leq f_i \leq b$.

Sample Input

```
10 100
1234567890 9876543210
0 0
```

Sample Output

```
5
4
```

6.6.2 How Many Pieces of Land?

PC/UVa IDs: 110602/10213, **Popularity:** B, **Success rate:** average **Level:** 2

You are given an elliptical-shaped land and you are asked to choose n arbitrary points on its boundary. Then you connect each point with every other point using straight lines, forming $n(n-1)/2$ connections. What is the maximum number of pieces of land you will get by choosing the points on the boundary carefully?

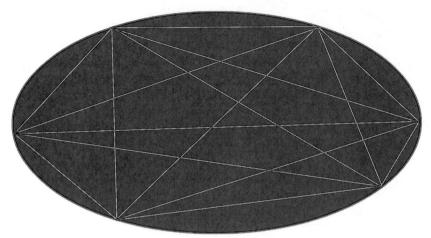

Dividing the land when $n = 6$.

Input

The first line of the input file contains one integer s $(0 < s < 3,500)$, which indicates how many input instances there are. The next s lines describe s input instances, each consisting of exactly one integer n $(0 \leq n < 2^{31})$.

Output

For each input instance output the maximum possible number pieces of land defined by n points, each printed on its own line.

Sample Input	Sample Output
4	1
1	2
2	4
3	8
4	

6.6.3 Counting

PC/UVa IDs: 110603/10198, **Popularity:** B, **Success rate:** high **Level:** 2

Gustavo knows how to count, but he is just now learning how to write numbers. He has already learned the digits 1, 2, 3, and 4. But he does not yet realize that 4 is different than 1, so he thinks that 4 is just another way to write 1.

He is having fun with a little game he created: he makes numbers with the four digits that he knows and sums their values. For example:

```
132 = 1 + 3 + 2 = 6
112314 = 1 + 1 + 2 + 3 + 1 + 1 = 9 (remember that Gustavo thinks that 4 = 1)
```

Gustavo now wants to know how many such numbers he can create whose sum is a number n. For $n = 2$, he can make 5 numbers: 11, 14, 41, 44, and 2. (He knows how to count up beyond five, just not how to write it.) However, he can't figure out this sum for n greater than 2, and asks for your help.

Input

Input will consist of an arbitrary number of integers n such that $1 \leq n \leq 1,000$. You must read until you reach the end of file.

Output

For each integer read, output an single integer on a line stating how many numbers Gustavo can make such that the sum of their digits is equal to n.

Sample Input

```
2
3
```

Sample Output

```
5
13
```

6.6.4   Expressions

PC/UVa IDs: 110604/10157, **Popularity:** C, **Success rate:** average **Level:** 2

Let X be the set of *correctly built parenthesis expressions*. The elements of X are strings consisting only of the characters "(" and ")", defined as follows:

- The empty string belongs to X.

- If A belongs to X, then (A) belongs to X.

- If both A and B belong to X, then the concatenation AB belongs to X.

For example, the strings ()(())() and (()(())) are correctly built parenthesis expressions, and therefore belong to the set X. The expressions (()))(() and ())(() are not correctly built parenthesis expressions and are thus not in X.

The *length* of a correctly built parenthesis expression E is the number of single parenthesis (characters) in E. The *depth* $D(E)$ of E is defined as follows:

$$D(E) = \begin{cases} 0 & \text{if } E \text{ is empty} \\ D(A) + 1 & \text{if } E = (A), \text{ and } A \text{ is in X} \\ \max(D(A), D(B)) & \text{if } E = AB, \text{ and } A, B \text{ are in X} \end{cases}$$

For example, ()(())() has length 8 and depth 2. Write a program which reads in n and d and computes the number of correctly built parenthesis expressions of length n and depth d.

Input

The input consists of pairs of integers n and d, with at most one pair per line and $2 \leq n \leq 300$, $1 \leq d \leq 150$. The input may contain empty lines, which you don't need to consider.

Output

For every pair of integers in the input, output a single integer on one line – the number of correctly built parenthesis expressions of length n and depth d.

Sample Input	Sample Output
6 2	3
300 150	1

Note: The three correctly built parenthesis expressions of length 6 and depth 2 are (())(), ()(()), and (()()).

6.6.5 Complete Tree Labeling

PC/UVa IDs: 110605/10247, **Popularity:** C, **Success rate:** average **Level:** 2

A complete k-ary tree is a k-ary tree in which all leaves have same depth and all internal nodes have degree or (equivalently) branching factor k. It is easy to determine the number of nodes of such a tree.

Given the depth and branching factor of such a tree, you must determine in how many different ways you can number the nodes of the tree so that the label of each node is less that that of its descendants. This is the property which defines the binary heap priority queue data structure for $k = 2$. In numbering a tree with N nodes, assume you have the labels $(1, 2, 3, \ldots, N - 1, N)$ available.

Input

The input file will contain several lines of input. Each line will contain two integers k and d. Here $k > 0$ is the branching factor of the complete k-ary tree and $d > 0$ is the depth of the complete k-ary tree. Your program must work for all pairs such that $k \times d \leq 21$.

Output

For each line of input, produce one line of output containing an integer counting the number of ways the k-ary tree can be labeled, maintaining the constraints described above.

Sample Input

```
2 2
10 1
```

Sample Output

```
80
3628800
```

6.6.6 The Priest Mathematician

PC/UVa IDs: 110606/10254, **Popularity:** C, **Success rate:** high **Level:** 2

The ancient folklore behind the *"Towers of Hanoi"* puzzle is quite well known. A more recent legend tells us that once the Brahmin monks discovered how long it would take to finish transferring the 64 discs from the needle which they were on to one of the other needles, they decided to find a faster strategy and be done with it.

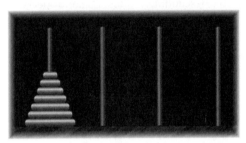

The Four Needle (Peg) Tower of Hanoi

One of the priests at the temple informed his colleagues that they could achieve the transfer in single afternoon at a one disc-per-second rhythm by using an additional needle. He proposed the following strategy:

- First move the topmost discs (say the top k discs) to one of the spare needles.

- Then use the standard three needles strategy to move the remaining $n - k$ discs (for a general case with n discs) to their destination.

- Finally, move the top k discs into their final destination using the four needles.

He calculated the value of k which minimized the number of movements and found that 18,433 transfers would suffice. Thus they could spend just 5 hours, 7 minutes, and 13 seconds with this scheme versus over $500,000$ million years without the additional needle!

Try to follow the clever priest's strategy and calculate the number of transfers using four needles, where the priest can move only one disc at a time and must place each disc on a needle such that there is no smaller disc below it. Calculate the k that minimizes the number of transfers under this strategy.

Input

The input file contains several lines of input. Each line contains a single integer $0 \leq N \leq 10,000$ giving the number of disks to be transferred. Input is terminated by end of file.

Output

For each line of input produce one line of output which indicates the number of movements required to transfer the N disks to the final needle.

Sample Input

1
2
28
64

Sample Output

1
3
769
18433

6.6.7 Self-describing Sequence

PC/UVa IDs: 110607/10049, **Popularity:** C, **Success rate:** high **Level:** 2

Solomon Golomb's *self-describing sequence* $\langle f(1), f(2), f(3), \ldots \rangle$ is the only non-decreasing sequence of positive integers with the property that it contains exactly $f(k)$ occurrences of k for each k. A few moment's thought reveals that the sequence must begin as follows:

n	1	2	3	4	5	6	7	8	9	10	11	12
$f(n)$	1	2	2	3	3	4	4	4	5	5	5	6

In this problem you are expected to write a program that calculates the value of $f(n)$ given the value of n.

Input

The input may contain multiple test cases. Each test case occupies a separate line and contains an integer n ($1 \le n \le 2,000,000,000$). The input terminates with a test case containing a value 0 for n and this case must not be processed.

Output

For each test case in the input, output the value of $f(n)$ on a separate line.

Sample Input

```
100
9999
123456
1000000000
0
```

Sample Output

```
21
356
1684
438744
```

6.6.8 Steps

PC/UVa IDs: 110608/846, **Popularity:** A, **Success rate:** high **Level:** 2

Consider the process of stepping from integer x to integer y along integer points of the straight line. The length of each step must be non-negative and can be one bigger than, equal to, or one smaller than the length of the previous step.

What is the minimum number of steps in order to get from x to y? The length of both the first and the last step must be 1.

Input

The input begins with a line containing n, the number of test cases. Each test case that follows consists of a line with two integers: $0 \leq x \leq y < 2^{31}$.

Output

For each test case, print a line giving the minimum number of steps to get from x to y.

Sample Input

```
3
45 48
45 49
45 50
```

Sample Output

```
3
3
4
```

6.7   Hints

6.1 Can the closed form for F_n be used to minimize the need for arbitrary-precision arithmetic?

6.2 Can you find a recurrence for the desired quantity?

6.3 Can you find a recurrence for the desired sum?

6.4 Can you formulate a recurrence, maybe a two-parameter version of the Catalan numbers?

6.5 Can you find a recurrence for the desired quantity?

6.7 Can you explicitly build the sequence, or must you do something more clever because of limited memory?

6.8 What kind of step sequences are defined by optimal solutions?

6.8   Notes

6.6 Although the problem asks for a fast way to solve the four-peg Tower of Hanoi problem under this strategy, it is not known that this strategy is in fact optimal! See [GKP89] for more discussion.

7
Number Theory

Number theory is perhaps the most interesting and beautiful area of mathematics. Euclid's proof that there are an infinite number of primes remains just as clear and elegant today as it was more than two thousand years ago. Innocent-looking questions like whether the equation $a^n + b^n = c^n$ has solutions for integer values of a, b, c, and $n > 2$ often turn out not to be so innocent. Indeed, this is the statement of Fermat's last theorem!

Number theory is great training in formal, rigorous reasoning, because number-theoretic proofs are clear and decisive. Studying the integers is interesting because they are such concrete and important objects. Discovering new properties of the integers is discovering something exciting about the natural world.

Computers have long been used in number theoretic research. Performing interesting number-theoretic computations on large integers requires great efficiency. Fortunately there are many clever algorithms to help us out.

7.1   Prime Numbers

A *prime number* is an integer $p > 1$ which is only divisible by 1 and itself. Said another way, if p is a prime number, then $p = a \cdot b$ for integers $a \leq b$ implies that $a = 1$ and $b = p$. The first ten prime numbers are 2, 3, 5, 7, 11, 13, 17, 19, 23, and 27.

Prime numbers are important because of the *fundamental theorem of arithmetic.* Despite the impressive title, all it states is that every integer can be expressed in only one way as the product of primes. For example, 105 is uniquely expressed as $3 \times 5 \times 7$, while 32 is uniquely expressed as $2 \times 2 \times 2 \times 2 \times 2$. This unique set of numbers multiplying to n is called the *prime factorization* of n. Order doesn't matter in a prime factorization, so we can canonically list the numbers in sorted order. But multiplicity does; it is what distinguishes the prime factorization of 4 from 8.

We say a prime number p is a *factor* of x if it appears in its prime factorization. Any number which is not prime is said to be *composite*.

7.1.1 Finding Primes

The easiest way to test if a given number x is prime uses repeated division. Start from the smallest candidate divisor, and then try all possible divisors up from there. Since 2 is the only even prime, once we verify that x isn't even we only need try the odd numbers as candidate factors. Further, we can bless n as prime the instant we have shown that it has no non-trivial prime factors below $\sqrt{n}$. Why? Suppose not – i.e., x is composite but has a smallest non-trivial prime factor p which is greater than $\sqrt{n}$. Then x/p must also divide x, and must be larger than p, or else we would have seen it earlier. But the product of two numbers greater than $\sqrt{n}$ must be larger than n, a contradiction.

Computing the prime factorization involves not only finding the first prime factor, but stripping off all occurrences of this factor and recurring on the remaining product:

```
prime_factorization(long x)
{
        long i;                 /* counter */
        long c;                 /* remaining product to factor */

        c = x;
        while ((c % 2) == 0) {
                printf("%ld\n",2);
                c = c / 2;
        }

        i = 3;
        while (i <= (sqrt(c)+1)) {
                if ((c % i) == 0) {
                        printf("%ld\n",i);
                        c = c / i;
                }
                else
                        i = i + 2;
        }

        if (c > 1) printf("%ld\n",c);
}
```

Testing the terminating condition $i > \sqrt{c}$ is somewhat problematic, because `sqrt()` is a numerical function with imperfect precision. Just to be safe, we let i run an extra iteration. Another approach would be to avoid floating point computation altogether and terminate when `i*i > c`. However, the multiplication might cause overflow when working on very large integers. Multiplication can be avoided by observing that $(i+1)^2 = i^2 + 2i + 1$, so adding $i + i + 1$ to i^2 yields $(i + 1)^2$.

For higher performance, we could move the `sqrt(c)` computation outside the main loop and only update it when `c` changes value. However, this program responds instantly on my computer for the prime 2,147,483,647. There exist fascinating randomized algorithms which are more efficient for testing primality on very large integers, but these are not something for us to worry about at this scale – except as the source of interesting contest problems themselves.

7.1.2 Counting Primes

How many primes are there? It makes sense that primes become rarer and rarer as we consider larger and larger numbers, but do they ever vanish? The answer is no, as shown by Euclid's proof that there are an infinite number of primes. It uses an elegant *proof by contradiction.* Knowing this proof is not strictly necessary to compete in programming contests, but it is one sign of being an educated person. Thus there is no shame in reviewing it here.

Let us assume the converse, that there are only a finite number of primes, $p_1, p_2, \ldots, p_n$. Let $m = 1 + \prod_{i=1}^{n} p_i$, i.e., the product of all of these primes, plus one. Since this is bigger than any of the primes on our list, m must be composite. Therefore some prime must divide it.

But which prime? We know that m is not divisible by p_1, because it leaves a remainder of 1. Further, m is not divisible by p_2, because it also leaves a remainder of 1. In fact, m leaves a remainder of 1 when divided by any prime p_i, for $1 \leq i \leq n$. Thus $p_1, p_2, \ldots, p_n$ cannot be the complete list of primes, because if so m must also be prime.

Since this contradicts the assumption it means there cannot exist such a complete list of primes; therefore the number of primes must be infinite! QED! [1]

Not only are there an infinite number of primes, but in fact the primes are relatively common. There are roughly $x/\ln x$ primes less than or equal to x, or put another way, roughly one out of every $\ln x$ numbers is prime.

7.2 Divisibility

Number theory is the study of integer divisibility. We say b *divides* a (denoted $b|a$) if $a = bk$ for some integer k. Equivalently, we say that b is a *divisor of* a or a is a *multiple of* b if $b|a$.

---

[1] Now a little puzzle to test your understanding of the proof. Suppose we take the first n primes, multiply them together, and add one. Does this number have to be prime? Give a proof or a counterexample.

As a consequence of this definition, the smallest natural divisor of every non-zero integer is 1. Why? It should be clear that there is in general no integer k such that $a = 0 \cdot k$.

How do we find all divisors of a given integer? From the prime number theorem, we know that x is uniquely represented by the product of its prime factors. Every divisor is the product of some subset of these prime factors. Such subsets can be constructed using backtracking techniques as discussed in Chapter 8, but we must be careful about duplicate prime factors. For example, the prime factorization of 12 has three terms (2, 2, and 3) but 12 has only 6 divisors (1, 2, 3, 4, 6, 12).

7.2.1   Greatest Common Divisor

Since 1 divides every integer, the least common divisor of every pair of integers a, b is 1. Far more interesting is the *greatest common divisor*, or *gcd*, the *largest* divisor shared by a given pair of integers. Consider a fraction x/y, say, 24/36. The reduced form of this fraction comes after we divide both the numerator and denominator by $gcd(x, y)$, in this case 12. We say two integers are *relatively prime* if their greatest common divisor is 1.

Euclid's algorithm for finding the greatest common divisor of two integers has been called history's first interesting algorithm. The naive way to compute gcd would be to test all divisors of the first integer explicitly on the second, or perhaps to find the prime factorization of both integers and take the product of all factors in common. But both approaches involve computationally intensive operations.

Euclid's algorithm rests on two observations. First,

If $b|a$, then $gcd(a, b) = b$.

This should be pretty clear. If b divides a, then $a = bk$ for some integer k, and thus $gcd(bk, b) = b$. Second,

If $a = bt + r$ for integers t and r, then $gcd(a, b) = gcd(b, r)$.

Why? By definition, $gcd(a, b) = gcd(bt + r, b)$. Any common divisor of a and b must rest totally with r, because bt clearly must be divisible by any divisor of b.

Euclid's algorithm is recursive, repeated replacing the bigger integer by its remainder mod the smaller integer. This typically cuts one of the arguments down by about half, and so after a logarithmic number of iterations gets down to the base case. Consider the following example. Let $a = 34398$ and $b = 2132$.

$$\begin{aligned} gcd(34398, 2132) &= gcd(34398 \bmod 2132, 2132) = gcd(2132, 286) \\ gcd(2132, 286) &= gcd(2132 \bmod 286, 286) = gcd(286, 130) \\ gcd(286, 130) &= gcd(286 \bmod 130, 130) = gcd(130, 26) \\ gcd(130, 26) &= gcd(130 \bmod 26, 26) = gcd(26, 0) \end{aligned}$$

Therefore, $gcd(34398, 2132) = 26$.

However, Euclid's algorithm can give us more than just the $gcd(a, b)$. It can also find integers x and y such that

$$a \cdot x + b \cdot y = gcd(a, b)$$

which will prove quite useful in solving linear congruences. We know that $gcd(a, b) = gcd(b, a')$, where $a' = a - b\lfloor a/b \rfloor$. Further, assume we know integers x' and y' such that

$$b \cdot x' + a' \cdot y' = gcd(a, b)$$

by recursion. Substituting our formula for a' into the above expression gives us

$$b \cdot x' + (a - b\lfloor a/b \rfloor) \cdot y' = gcd(a, b)$$

and rearranging the terms will give us our desired x and y. We need a basis case to complete our algorithm, but that is easy since $a \cdot 1 + 0 \cdot 0 = gcd(a, 0)$.

For the previous example, we get that $34398 \times 15 + 2132 \times -242 = 26$. An implementation of this algorithm follows below:

```
/*      Find the gcd(p,q) and x,y such that p*x + q*y = gcd(p,q)      */

long gcd(long p, long q, long *x, long *y)
{
        long x1,y1;                     /* previous coefficients */
        long g;                         /* value of gcd(p,q) */

        if (q > p) return(gcd(q,p,y,x));

        if (q == 0) {
                *x = 1;
                *y = 0;
                return(p);
        }

        g = gcd(q, p%q, &x1, &y1);

        *x = y1;
        *y = (x1 - floor(p/q)*y1);

        return(g);
}
```

7.2.2   Least Common Multiple

Another useful function on two integers is the *least common multiple* (lcm), the *smallest* integer which is divided by both of a given pair of integers. For example, the least common multiple of 24 and 36 is 72.

Least common multiple arises when we want to compute the simultaneous periodicity of two distinct periodic events. When is the next year (after 2000) that the presidential election (which happens every 4 years) will coincide with census (which happens every 10 years)? The events coincide every twenty years, because $lcm(4, 10) = 20$.

It is self-evident that $lcm(x, y) \geq \max(x, y)$. Similarly, since $x \cdot y$ is a multiple of both x and y, $lcm(x, y) \leq xy$. The only way that there can be a smaller common multiple is if there is some non-trivial factor shared between x and y.

This observation, coupled with Euclid's algorithm, gives an efficient way to compute least common multiple, namely, $lcm(x, y) = xy/gcd(x, y)$. A slicker algorithm appears in [Dij76], which avoids the multiplication and hence possibility of overflow.

7.3 Modular Arithmetic

In Chapter 5, we reviewed the basic arithmetic algorithms for integers, such as addition and multiplication. We are not always interested in the full answers, however. Sometimes the remainder suffices for our purposes. For example, suppose your birthday this year falls on a Wednesday. What day of the week will it it will fall on next year? All you need to know is the remainder of the number of days between now and then (either 365 or 366) when dividing by the 7 days of the week. Thus it will fall on Wednesday plus one (365 mod 7) or two (366 mod 7) days, i.e., Thursday or Friday depending upon whether it is affected by a leap year.

The key to such efficient computations is *modular arithmetic*. Of course, we can in principle explicitly compute the entire number and then find the remainder. But for large enough integers, it can be much easier to just work with remainders via modular arithmetic.

The number we are dividing by is called the *modulus*, and the remainder left over is called the *residue*. The key to efficient modular arithmetic is understanding how the basic operations of addition, subtraction, and multiplication work over a given modulus:

- *Addition* — What is $(x + y) \bmod n$? We can simplify this to

$$((x \bmod n) + (y \bmod n)) \bmod n$$

  to avoid adding big numbers. How much small change will I have if given \$123.45 by my mother and \$94.67 by my father?

$$(12{,}345 \bmod 100) + (9{,}467 \bmod 100) = (45 + 67) \bmod 100 = 12 \bmod 100$$

- *Subtraction* — Subtraction is just addition with negative values. How much small change will I have after spending \$52.53?

$$(12 \bmod 100) - (53 \bmod 100) = -41 \bmod 100 = 59 \bmod 100$$

  Notice how we can convert a negative number mod n to a positive number by adding a multiple of n to it. Further, this answer makes sense in this change example. It is usually best to keep the residue between 0 and $n - 1$ to ensure we are working with the smallest-magnitude numbers possible.

- *Multiplication* — Since multiplication is just repeated addition,

$$xy \bmod n = (x \bmod n)(y \bmod n) \bmod n$$

How much change will you have if you earn \$17.28 per hour for 2,143 hours?

$$(1,728 \times 2,143) \bmod 100 = (28 \bmod 100) \times (43 \bmod 100) = 4 \bmod 100$$

Further, since exponentiation is just repeated multiplication,

$$x^y \bmod n = (x \bmod n)^y \bmod n$$

Since exponentiation is the quickest way to produce really large integers, this is where modular arithmetic really proves its worth.

- *Division* — Division proves considerably more complicated to deal with, and will be discussed in Section 7.4.

Modular arithmetic has many interesting applications, including:

- *Finding the Last Digit* — What is the last digit of 2^{100}? Sure we can use infinite precision arithmetic and look at the last digit, but why? We can do this computation by hand. What we really want to know is what $2^{100} \bmod 10$ is. By doing repeated squaring, and taking the remainder mod 10 at each step we make progress very quickly:

$$
\begin{aligned}
2^3 \bmod 10 &= 8 \\
2^6 \bmod 10 &= 8 \times 8 \bmod 10 \to 4 \\
2^{12} \bmod 10 &= 4 \times 4 \bmod 10 \to 6 \\
2^{24} \bmod 10 &= 6 \times 6 \bmod 10 \to 6 \\
2^{48} \bmod 10 &= 6 \times 6 \bmod 10 \to 6 \\
2^{96} \bmod 10 &= 6 \times 6 \bmod 10 \to 6 \\
2^{100} \bmod 10 &= 2^{96} \times 2^3 \times 2^1 \bmod 10 \to 6
\end{aligned}
$$

- *RSA Encryption Algorithm* — A classic application of modular arithmetic on large integers arises in public-key cryptography, namely, the RSA algorithm. Here, our message is encrypted by coding it as an integer m, raising it to a power k, where k is the so-called public-key or encryption key, and taking the results mod n. Since m, n, and k are all huge integers, computing $m^k \bmod n$ efficiently requires the tools we developed above.

- *Calendrical Calculations* — As demonstrated with the birthday example, computing the day of the week a certain number of days from today, or the time a certain number of seconds from now, are both applications of modular arithmetic.

7.4   Congruences

Congruences are an alternate notation for representing modular arithmetic. We say that $a \equiv b(\bmod \, m)$ if $m|(a - b)$. By definition, if $a \bmod m$ is b, then $a \equiv b(\bmod \, m)$.

Congruences are an alternate notation for modular arithmetic, not an inherently different idea. Yet the notation is important. It gets us thinking about the *set* of integers with a given remainder n, and gives us equations for representing them. Suppose that x is a variable. What integers x satisfy the congruence $x \equiv 3(\bmod \, 9)$?

For such a simple congruence, the answer is easy. Clearly $x = 3$ must be a solution. Further, adding or deleting the modulus (9 in this instance) gives another solution. The set of solutions is all integers of the form $9y + 3$, where y is any integer.

What about complicated congruences, such as $2x \equiv 3(\bmod \, 9)$ and $2x \equiv 3(\bmod \, 4)$? Trial and error should convince you that exactly the integers of the form $9y + 6$ satisfy the first example, while the second has no solutions at all.

There are two important problems on congruences, namely, performing arithmetic operations on them, and solving them. These are discussed in the sections below.

7.4.1   Operations on Congruences

Congruences support addition, subtraction, and multiplication, as well as a limited form of division – provided they share the same modulus:

- *Addition and Subtraction* — Suppose $a \equiv b(\bmod \, n)$ and $c \equiv d(\bmod \, n)$. Then $a + c \equiv b + d(\bmod \, n)$. For example, suppose I know that $4x \equiv 7(\bmod \, 9)$ and $3x \equiv 3(\bmod \, 9)$. Then

$$4x - 3x \equiv 7 - 3(\bmod \, 9) \rightarrow x \equiv 4(\bmod \, 9)$$

- *Multiplication* — It is apparent that $a \equiv b(\bmod \, n)$ implies that $a \cdot d \equiv b \cdot d(\bmod \, n)$ by adding the reduced congruence to itself d times. In fact, general multiplication also holds, i.e., $a \equiv b(\bmod \, n)$ and $c \equiv d(\bmod \, n)$ implies $ac \equiv bd(\bmod \, n)$.

- *Division* — However, we cannot cavalierly cancel common factors from congruences. Note that $6 \cdot 2 \equiv 6 \cdot 1(\bmod \, 3)$, but clearly $2 \not\equiv 1(\bmod \, 3)$. To see what the problem is, note that we can redefine division as multiplication by an inverse, so a/b is equivalent to ab^{-1}. Thus we can compute $a/b(\bmod \, n)$ if we can find the inverse b^{-1} such that $bb^{-1} \equiv 1(\bmod \, n)$. This inverse does not always exist – try to find a solution to $2x \equiv 1(\bmod \, 4)$.

  We *can* simplify a congruence $ad \equiv bd(\bmod \, dn)$ to $a \equiv b(\bmod \, n)$, so we can divide all three terms by a mutually common factor if one exists. Thus $170 \equiv 30(\bmod \, 140)$ implies that $17 \equiv 3(\bmod \, 14)$. However, the congruence $a \equiv b(\bmod \, n)$ must be false (i.e., has no solution) if $gcd(a, n)$ does not divide b.

7.4.2 Solving Linear Congruences

A linear congruence is an equation of the form $ax \equiv b(\text{mod } n)$. Solving this equation means identifying which values of x satisfy it.

Not all such equations have solutions. We have seen integers which do not have multiplicative inverses over a given modulus, meaning that $ax \equiv 1(\text{mod } n)$ has no solution. In fact, $ax \equiv 1(\text{mod } n)$ has a solution if and only if the modulus and the multiplier are relatively prime, i.e., $gcd(a, n) = 1$. We may use Euclid's algorithm to find this inverse through the solution to $a \cdot x' + n \cdot y' = gcd(a, n) = 1$. Thus

$$ax \equiv 1(\text{mod } n) \rightarrow ax \equiv a \cdot x' + n \cdot y'(\text{mod } n)$$

Clearly $n \cdot y' \equiv 0(\text{mod } n)$, so in fact this inverse is simply the x' from Euclid's algorithm.

In general, there are three cases, depending on the relationship between a, b, and n:

- $gcd(a, b, n) > 1$ — Then we can divide all three terms by this divisor to get an equivalent congruence. This gives us a single solution mod the new base, or equivalently $gcd(a, b, n)$ solutions (mod n).

- $gcd(a, n)$ *does not divide* b — Then, as described above, the congruence can have no solution.

- $gcd(a, n) = 1$ — Then there is one solution (mod n). Further, $x = a^{-1}b$ works, since $aa^{-1}b \equiv b(\text{mod } n)$. As shown above, this inverse exists and can be found using Euclid's algorithm.

The *Chinese remainder theorem* gives us a tool for working with systems of congruences over different moduli. Suppose there is exists an integer x such that $x \equiv a_1(\text{mod } m_1)$ and $x \equiv a_2(\text{mod } m_2)$. Then x is uniquely determined (mod $m_1 m_2$) if m_1 and m_2 are relatively prime.

To find this x, and thus solve the system of two congruences, we begin by solving the linear congruences $m_2 b_1 \equiv 1(\text{mod } m_1)$ and $m_1 b_1 \equiv 1(\text{mod } m_2)$ to find b_1 and b_2 respectively. Then it can be readily verified that

$$x = a_1 b_1 m_2 + a_2 b_2 m_1$$

is a solution to both of the original congruences. Further, the theorem readily extends to systems of an arbitrary number of congruences whose moduli are all pairwise relatively prime.

7.4.3 Diophantine Equations

Diophantine equations are formulae in which the variables are restricted to integers. For example, Fermat's last theorem concerned answers to the equation $a^n + b^n = c^n$. Solving such an equation for real numbers is no big deal. It is only if all variables are restricted to integers that the problem becomes difficult.

Diophantine equations are difficult to work with because division is not a routine operation with integer formulae. However, there are certain classes of Diophantine equations which are known to be solvable and these tend to arise frequently.

The most important class are linear Diophantine equations of the form $ax - ny = b$, where x and y are the integer variables and a, b, and n are integer constants. These are readily shown to be equivalent to the solving the congruence $ax \equiv b(\bmod n)$ and hence can be solved using the techniques of the previous section.

More advanced Diophantine analysis is beyond the scope of this book, but we refer the reader to standard references in number theory such as Niven and Zuckerman [ZMNN91] and Hardy and Wright [HW79] for more on this fascinating subject.

7.5   Number Theoretic Libraries

The Java `BigInteger` class (`java.math.BigInteger`) includes a variety of useful number-theoretic functions. Most important, of course, is the basic support for arithmetic operations on arbitrary-precision integers as discussed in Chapter 5. But there are also several functions of purely number-theoretic interest:

- *Greatest Common Divisor* — `BigInteger gcd(BigInteger val)` returns the BigInteger whose value is the gcd of abs(this) and abs(val).

- *Modular Exponentiation* — `BigInteger modPow(BigInteger exp, BigInteger m)` returns a BigInteger whose value is $this^{exp} \bmod m$.

- *Modular Inverse* — `BigInteger modInverse(BigInteger m)` returns a BigInteger whose value is $this^{-1}(\bmod m)$, i.e. solves the congruence $y \cdot this \equiv 1(\bmod m)$ by returning an appropriate integer y if it exists.

- *Primality Testing* — `public boolean isProbablePrime(int certainty)` uses a randomized primality test to return true if this BigInteger is probably prime and false if it's definitely composite. If the call returns true, the probability of primality is $\geq 1 - 1/2^{certainty}$.

7.6   Problems

7.6.1   Light, More Light

PC/UVa IDs: 110701/10110, **Popularity:** A, **Success rate:** average **Level:** 1

There is man named Mabu who switches on-off the lights along a corridor at our university. Every bulb has its own toggle switch that changes the state of the light. If the light is off, pressing the switch turns it on. Pressing it again will turn it off. Initially each bulb is off.

He does a peculiar thing. If there are n bulbs in a corridor, he walks along the corridor back and forth n times. On the ith walk, he toggles only the switches whose position is divisible by i. He does not press any switch when coming back to his initial position. The ith walk is defined as going down the corridor (doing his peculiar thing) and coming back again. Determine the final state of the last bulb. Is it on or off?

Input

The input will be an integer indicating the nth bulb in a corridor, which is less than or equal to $2^{32} - 1$. A zero indicates the end of input and should not be processed.

Output

Output "**yes**" or "**no**" to indicate if the light is on, with each case appearing on its own line.

Sample Input

```
3
6241
8191
0
```

Sample Output

```
no
yes
no
```

7.6.2 Carmichael Numbers

PC/UVa IDs: 110702/10006, **Popularity:** A, **Success rate:** average **Level:** 2

Certain cryptographic algorithms make use of big prime numbers. However, checking whether a big number is prime is not so easy.

Randomized primality tests exist that offer a high degree of confidence of accurate determination at low cost, such as the Fermat test. Let a be a random number between 2 and $n-1$, where n is the number whose primality we are testing. Then, n is *probably* prime if the following equation holds:

$$a^n \bmod n = a$$

If a number passes the Fermat test several times, then it is prime with a high probability.

Unfortunately, there is bad news. Certain composite numbers (non-primes) still pass the Fermat test with every number smaller than themselves. These numbers are called Carmichael numbers.

Write a program to test whether a given integer is a Carmichael number.

Input

The input will consist of a series of lines, each containing a small positive number n ($2 < n < 65,000$). A number $n = 0$ will mark the end of the input, and must not be processed.

Output

For each number in the input, print whether it is a Carmichael number or not as shown in the sample output.

Sample Input

```
1729
17
561
1109
431
0
```

Sample Output

```
The number 1729 is a Carmichael number.
17 is normal.
The number 561 is a Carmichael number.
1109 is normal.
431 is normal.
```

7.6.3 Euclid Problem

PC/UVa IDs: 110703/10104, **Popularity:** A, **Success rate:** average **Level:** 1

From Euclid, it is known that for any positive integers A and B there exist such integers X and Y that $AX + BY = D$, where D is the greatest common divisor of A and B. The problem is to find the corresponding X, Y, and D for a given A and B.

Input

The input will consist of a set of lines with the integer numbers A and B, separated with space $(A, B < 1,000,000,001)$.

Output

For each input line the output line should consist of three integers X, Y, and D, separated with space. If there are several such X and Y, you should output that pair for which $X \leq Y$ and $|X| + |Y|$ is minimal.

Sample Input

```
4 6
17 17
```

Sample Output

```
-1 1 2
0 1 17
```

7.6.4   Factovisors

PC/UVa IDs: 110704/10139, **Popularity:** A, **Success rate:** average **Level:** 2

The factorial function, $n!$ is defined as follows for all non-negative integers n:

$$0! = 1$$
$$n! = n \times (n-1)! \quad (n > 0)$$

We say that a divides b if there exists an integer k such that

$$k \times a = b$$

Input

The input to your program consists of several lines, each containing two non-negative integers, n and m, both less than 2^{31}.

Output

For each input line, output a line stating whether or not m divides $n!$, in the format shown below.

Sample Input

```
6 9
6 27
20 10000
20 100000
1000 1009
```

Sample Output

```
9 divides 6!
27 does not divide 6!
10000 divides 20!
100000 does not divide 20!
1009 does not divide 1000!
```

7.6.5   Summation of Four Primes

PC/UVa IDs: 110705/10168, **Popularity:** A, **Success rate:** average **Level:** 2

Waring's prime number conjecture states that every odd integer is either prime or the sum of three primes. Goldbach's conjecture is that every even integer is the sum of two primes. Both problems have been open for over 200 years.

In this problem you have a slightly less demanding task. Find a way to express a given integer as the sum of exactly four primes.

Input

Each input case consists of one integer n ($n \le 10000000$) on its own line. Input is terminated by end of file.

Output

For each input case n, print one line of output containing four prime numbers which sum up to n. If the number cannot be expressed as a summation of four prime numbers print the line "`Impossible.`" in a single line. There can be multiple solutions. Any good solution will be accepted.

Sample Input

```
24
36
46
```

Sample Output

```
3 11 3 7
3 7 13 13
11 11 17 7
```

7.6.6 Smith Numbers

PC/UVa IDs: 110706/10042, **Popularity:** B, **Success rate:** average **Level:** 1

While skimming his phone directory in 1982, mathematician Albert Wilansky noticed that the telephone number of his brother-in-law H. Smith had the following peculiar property: The sum of the digits of that number was equal to the sum of the digits of the prime factors of that number. Got it? Smith's telephone number was 493-7775. This number can be written as the product of its prime factors in the following way:

$$4937775 = 3 \cdot 5 \cdot 5 \cdot 65837$$

The sum of all digits of the telephone number is $4 + 9 + 3 + 7 + 7 + 7 + 5 = 42$, and the sum of the digits of its prime factors is equally $3 + 5 + 5 + 6 + 5 + 8 + 3 + 7 = 42$. Wilansky named this type of number after his brother-in-law: the Smith numbers.

As this property is true for every prime number, Wilansky excluded them from the definition. Other Smith numbers include 6,036 and 9,985.

Wilansky was not able to find a Smith number which was larger than the telephone number of his brother-in-law. Can you help him out?

Input

The input consists of several test cases, the number of which you are given in the first line of the input. Each test case consists of one line containing a single positive integer smaller than 10^9.

Output

For every input value n, compute the smallest Smith number which is larger than n and print it on a single line. You can assume that such a number exists.

Sample Input

```
1
4937774
```

Sample Output

```
4937775
```

7.6.7 Marbles

PC/UVa IDs: 110707/10090, **Popularity:** B, **Success rate:** low **Level:** 1

I collect marbles (colorful small glass balls) and want to buy boxes to store them. The boxes come in two types:

Type 1: each such box costs c_1 dollars and can hold exactly n_1 marbles

Type 2: each such box costs c_2 dollars and can hold exactly n_2 marbles

I want each box to be filled to its capacity, and also to minimize the total cost of buying them. Help me find the best way to distribute my marbles among the boxes.

Input

The input file may contain multiple test cases. Each test case begins with a line containing the integer n ($1 \leq n \leq 2{,}000{,}000{,}000$). The second line contains c_1 and n_1, and the third line contains c_2 and n_2. Here, c_1, c_2, n_1, and n_2 are all positive integers having values smaller than 2,000,000,000.

A test case containing a zero for the number of marbles terminates the input.

Output

For each test case in the input print a line containing the minimum cost solution (two nonnegative integers m_1 and m_2, where m_i = number of type i boxes required if one exists. Otherwise print "`failed`".

If a solution exists, you may assume that it is unique.

Sample Input

```
43
1 3
2 4
40
5 9
5 12
0
```

Sample Output

```
13 1
failed
```

7.6.8 *Repackaging*

PC/UVa IDs: 110708/10089, **Popularity:** C, **Success rate:** low **Level:** 2

Coffee cups of three different sizes (size 1, size 2, and size 3) are manufactured by the Association of Cup Makers (ACM) and are sold in various packages. Each type of package is identified by three positive integers (S_1, S_2, S_3), where S_i $(1 \leq i \leq 3)$ denotes the number of size i cups included in the package. Unfortunately, there is no package such that $S_1 = S_2 = S_3$.

Market research has discovered there is great demand for packages containing equal numbers of cups of all three sizes. To exploit this opportunity, ACM has decided to unpack the cups from some of the packages in its unlimited stock of unsold products and repack them as packages having equal number of cups of all three sizes. For example, suppose ACM has the following packages in its stock: $(1, 2, 3)$, $(1, 11, 5)$, $(9, 4, 3)$, and $(2, 3, 2)$. Then we can unpack three $(1, 2, 3)$ packages, one $(9, 4, 3)$ package, and two $(2, 3, 2)$ packages and repack the cups to produce sixteen $(1, 1, 1)$ packages. One can even produce eight $(2, 2, 2)$ packages or four $(4, 4, 4)$ packages or two $(8, 8, 8)$ packages or one $(16, 16, 16)$ package, etc. Note that all the unpacked cups must be used to produce the new packages; i.e., no unpacked cup is wasted.

ACM has hired you to write a program to decide whether it is possible to produce packages containing an equal number of all three types of cups using all the cups that can be found by unpacking any combination of existing packages in stock.

Input

The input may contain multiple test cases. Each test case begins with a line containing an integer N $(3 \leq N \leq 1,000)$ indicating the number of different types of packages that can be found in the stock. Each of the next N lines contains three positive integers denoting, respectively, the number of size 1, size 2, and size 3 cups in a package. No two packages in a test case will have the same specification.

A test case containing a zero for N in the first line terminates the input.

Output

For each test case print a line containing "**Yes**" if packages can be produced as desired. Print "**No**" if they cannot be produced.

Sample Input

```
4
1 2 3
1 11 5
9 4 3
2 3 2
4
```

```
1 3 3
1 11 5
9 4 3
2 3 2
0
```

Sample Output

```
Yes
No
```

7.7 Hints

7.1 Can we figure out the state of the nth bulb without testing all numbers from 1 to n?

7.2 How can we compute $a^n (\bmod n)$ efficiently?

7.3 Are we sure the construction in the text gives the minimal such pair?

7.4 Can we test the divisibility without explicitly computing $n!$?

7.7 Can you compute the possible exact solutions independent of cost? Which one of these will be the cheapest?

7.8 Can we solve these Diophantine equations using the techniques discussed in this chapter?

7.8 Notes

7.5 The Goldbach and Waring conjectures are almost certainly true, but perhaps because of brute force instead of deep properties of the primes. Do a back-of-the-envelope calculation of the expected number of solutions for each problem, assuming that there are $n/\ln n$ primes less than n. Is it promising to hunt further for a counter-example when none has been found before $n = 1{,}000{,}000$?

7.6 Papers on the properties of Smith numbers include [Wil82, McD87].

8
Backtracking

Modern computers are so fast that brute force can be an effective and honorable way to solve problems. For example, sometimes it is easier to count the number of items in a set by actually constructing them than by using sophisticated combinatorial arguments. Of course, this requires the number of items searched to be small enough for the computation to complete.

A modern personal computer has a clock rate of about 1 gigahertz, meaning one billion operations per second. Figure that doing anything interesting takes a few hundred instructions or even more. Thus you can hope to search a few million items per second on contemporary machines.

It is important to realize how big (or how small) one million is. One million permutations means all arrangements of roughly 10 or 11 objects, but not more. One million subsets means all combinations of roughly 20 items, but not more. Solving significantly larger problems requires carefully pruning the search space to make sure we look at only the elements which really matter.

In this chapter, we look at backtracking algorithms for exhaustive search and designing effective pruning techniques to make them as powerful as possible.

8.1   Backtracking

Backtracking is a systematic method to iterate through all the possible configurations of a search space. It is a general algorithm/technique which must be customized for each individual application.

In the general case, we will model our solution as a vector $a = (a_1, a_2, ..., a_n)$, where each element a_i is selected from a finite ordered set S_i. Such a vector might represent an arrangement where a_i contains the ith element of the permutation. Or the vector might represent a given subset S, where a_i is true if and only if the ith element of the universe is in S. The vector can even represent a sequence of moves in a game or a path in a graph, where a_i contains the ith event in the sequence.

At each step in the backtracking algorithm, we start from a given partial solution, say, $a = (a_1, a_2, ..., a_k)$, and try to extend it by adding another element at the end. After extending it, we must test whether what we have so far is a solution – if so, we should print it, count it, or do what we want with it. If not, we must then check whether the partial solution is still potentially extendible to some complete solution. If so, recur and continue. If not, we delete the last element from a and try another possibility for that position, if one exists.

The honest working code is given below. We include a global finished flag to allow for premature termination, which could be set in any application-specific routine.

```
bool finished = FALSE;                  /* found all solutions yet? */

backtrack(int a[], int k, data input)
{
        int c[MAXCANDIDATES];           /* candidates for next position */
        int ncandidates;                /* next position candidate count */
        int i;                          /* counter */

        if (is_a_solution(a,k,input))
                process_solution(a,k,input);
        else {
                k = k+1;
                construct_candidates(a,k,input,c,&ncandidates);
                for (i=0; i<ncandidates; i++) {
                        a[k] = c[i];
                        backtrack(a,k,input);
                        if (finished) return;   /* terminate early */
                }
        }
}
```

The application-specific parts of this algorithm consists of three subroutines:

- is_a_solution(a,k,input) — This Boolean function tests whether the first k elements of vector a are a complete solution for the given problem. The last argument, input, allows us to pass general information into the routine. We will use it to specify n, the size of a target solution. This makes sense when constructing permutations of size n or subsets of n elements, but may not be relevant when constructing variable-sized objects such as sequences of moves in a game. In such applications, this last argument can be ignored.

- `construct_candidates(a,k,input,c,ncandidates)` — This routine fills an array c with the complete set of possible candidates for the kth position of a, given the contents of the first $k-1$ positions. The number of candidates returned in this array is denoted by `ncandidates`. Again, `input` may be used to pass auxiliary information, particularly the desired solution-size.

- `process_solution(a,k)` — This routine prints, counts, or somehow processes a complete solution once it is constructed. Note that the auxiliary `input` is unnecessary here, since k denotes the number of elements in the solution.

Backtracking ensures correctness by enumerating all possibilities. It ensures efficiency by never visiting a state more than once.

Study how recursion yields an elegant and easy implementation of the backtracking algorithm. Because a new candidates array c is allocated with each recursive procedure call, the subsets of not-yet-considered extension candidates at each position will not interfere with each other. We will see that depth-first traversal in graphs (Chapter 9) uses essentially the same recursive algorithm as `backtrack`. Backtracking can be thought of as depth-first search over an implicit graph instead of an explicit one.

We now provide two examples of backtracking in action, by giving specific implementations of these three functions which iterate through all subsets and permutations of n elements.

8.2   Constructing All Subsets

As mentioned above, we can construct the 2^n subsets of n items by iterating through all possible 2^n length-n vectors of *true* or *false*, letting the ith element denote whether item i is or is not in the subset.

Using the notation of the general backtrack algorithm, $S_k = (true, false)$, and a is a solution whenever $k \geq n$. We can now construct all subsets with simple implementations for `is_a_solution()`, `construct_candidates()`, and `process_solution()`. Printing each subset out after constructing it actually proves to be the most complicated of the three routines!

```
is_a_solution(int a[], int k, int n)
{
        return (k == n);                    /* is k == n? */
}


construct_candidates(int a[], int k, int n, int c[], int *ncandidates)
{
        c[0] = TRUE;
        c[1] = FALSE;
        *ncandidates = 2;
}
```

```
process_solution(int a[], int k)
{
        int i;                                  /* counter */

        printf("{");
        for (i=1; i<=k; i++)
                if (a[i] == TRUE) printf(" %d",i);

        printf(" }\n");
}
```

Finally, we must instantiate the call to **backtrack** with the right arguments. Specifically, this means giving a pointer to the empty solution vector, setting $k = 0$ to denote that it is empty, and specifying the number of elements in the universal set:

```
generate_subsets(int n)
{
        int a[NMAX];                            /* solution vector */

        backtrack(a,0,n);
}
```

In what order will this routine generate the subsets of $\{1, 2, 3\}$? The critical issue is the order of moves generated in **construct_candidates**. Because *true* always appears before *false*, the subset of all trues is generated first, and the all-false empty set is generated last:

```
                { 1 2 3 }
                { 1 2 }
                { 1 3 }
                { 1 }
                { 2 3 }
                { 2 }
                { 3 }
                { }
```

8.3   Constructing All Permutations

The problem of constructing all permutations is similar to that of generating all subsets, except that the candidates for the next move now depend on the values in the partial solution. To avoid repeating permutation elements, we must ensure that the ith element of the permutation is distinct from all the elements before it.

To use the notation of the general backtrack algorithm, $S_k = \{1, \ldots, n\} - a$, and a is a solution whenever $k = n$:

```
construct_candidates(int a[], int k, int n, int c[], int *ncandidates)
{
        int i;                          /* counter */
        bool in_perm[NMAX];             /* who is in the permutation? */

        for (i=1; i<NMAX; i++) in_perm[i] = FALSE;
        for (i=0; i<k; i++) in_perm[ a[i] ] = TRUE;

        *ncandidates = 0;
        for (i=1; i<=n; i++)
                if (in_perm[i] == FALSE) {
                        c[ *ncandidates] = i;
                        *ncandidates = *ncandidates + 1;
                }
}
```

Testing whether i is a candidate for the kth slot in the permutation can be done by iterating through all $k - 1$ elements of a and verifying that none of them matched, but we prefer to set up a bit-vector data structure (see Chapter 2) to maintain which elements are in the partial solution. This gives a constant-time legality check.

Completing the job of generating permutations requires specifying process_solution and is_a_solution, as well as setting the appropriate arguments to backtrack. All are essentially the same as for subsets:

```
process_solution(int a[], int k)
{
        int i;                          /* counter */

        for (i=1; i<=k; i++) printf(" %d",a[i]);

        printf("\n");
}

is_a_solution(int a[], int k, int n)
{
        return (k == n);
}

generate_permutations(int n)
{
        int a[NMAX];                    /* solution vector */

        backtrack(a,0,n);
}
```

Figure 8.1. A solution to the eight-queens problem.

Note that these routines generate the permutations in *lexicographic*, or sorted order, i.e., 123, 132, 213, 231, 312, and 321.

8.4   Program Design Example: The Eight-Queens Problem

The eight queens problem is a classical puzzle of positioning eight queens on an 8×8 chessboard such that no two queens threaten each other. This means that no two queens may lie on the same row, column or diagonal, as shown in Figure 8.1. It has been studied by many famous mathematicians over the years, including Gauss, as well as countless not-so-famous ones who have taken basic programming courses.

There is nothing in this problem which prevents us from considering larger values than eight. The n-queens problem asks how many distinct ways there are to place n mutually non-attacking queens on an $n \times n$ chessboard. For even modest-sized n, there are far too many solutions to make it interesting to print them out. But to what size n can we count them all in a modest amount of time?

―――――――――――――――   Solution starts below   ―――――――――――――――

Getting a grip on such a problem usually requires trying to construct small solutions by hand. You should be able to convince yourself that there is no solution for $n = 2$, since the second queen must threaten the first along a row, column, or diagonal. There is more room to maneuver for $n = 3$, but trial and error should convince you there is still no solution. We encourage you to try to construct a solution for $n = 4$, the smallest interesting case.

Implementing a `backtrack` search requires us to think carefully about the most concise, efficient way to represent our solutions as a vector. What is a reasonable representation for an n-queens solution, and how big must it be?

The most straightforward representation might be to emulate our subset generator, and use a solution vector where a_i is true if and only if there is a queen on the ith square. This requires giving each square a unique name from 1 to n^2. The set of candidate solutions for the ith square will be *true* if none of the previously placed queens threaten this square, and *false* otherwise. We have a solution after all n^2 squares have values where exactly n of them are *true*.

Is this a good representation? It doesn't seem very concise, since almost all the elements end up with *false* in a successful solution. This means it is also very expensive. There are $2^{64} \approx 1.84 \times 10^{19}$ different true/false vectors for an 8×8 board, and while not all of them will be completely constructed it is a frightening number to contemplate.

What about having the ith element of the solution vector explicitly list the square where the ith queen resides? In this representation, a_i will be an integer from 1 to n^2, giving us a solution whenever we have successfully filled in the first n elements of a. The candidates for the ith position are all the squares which are not threatened by any of the first $i - 1$ queens.

Is this better than the previous solution? There are "only" $64^8 \approx 2.81 \times 10^{14}$ possible vectors with this representation for an 8×8 board. This is a huge improvement, but still far above the order-of-one million (10^6) search space that starts to restrict feasibility. Making backtracking work requires eliminating, or *pruning*, the vast majority of these possibilities before they are constructed.

8.5 Pruning Search

The combinatorial explosion implies that the size of most search spaces grows exponentially with the size of the problem. Thus even modest-sized problems quickly hit a wall beyond which they cannot continue to make progress in reasonable amounts of time. To make a backtracking program efficient enough to solve interesting problems, we must prune the search space by terminating every search path the instant it becomes clear it cannot lead to a solution.

The term *prune* for this operation is particularly appropriate. The gardener prunes his trees by cutting back dead and misshapen branches so the tree can focus its energies productively. Similarly, the recursive calls of `backtrack` define a tree. Pruning this tree, by establishing that the set of candidate extensions at a position is in fact empty, keeps it from growing uncontrollably.

So how can we prune search with the positional representation described above? First, we can remove symmetries. As thus far stated, there is no difference between the queen in the first position of the vector (a_1) and the queen in the second position (a_2). Left unchecked, this will generate each solution $8! = 40,320$ times! This can be easily corrected by ensuring that the queen in a_i sits on a higher number square than the queen in a_{i-1}. This simple change will reduce the search space to $\binom{64}{8} = 4.426 \times 10^9$.

Thinking more deeply about the problem leads to an even better representation. Note that there must be exactly one queen per row for an n-queens solution. Why? If there were zero queens in one row, then there must be at least two queens in some other row to get a total of n queens. But two queens in the same row are impossible, because they threaten each other. Limiting the candidates of the ith queen to the eight squares on the ith row reduces our search space to $8^8 \approx 1.677 \times 10^7$, a large but manageable size.

But we can do even better! Since no two queens can occupy the same column, we know that the n columns of a complete solution must form a permutation of n. By avoiding repetitive elements, we reduce our search space to just $8! = 40{,}320$ – clearly short work for any reasonably fast machine.

Now we are ready to code up our solution. The critical routine is the candidate constructor. We repeatedly check whether the kth square on the given row is threatened by any previously positioned queen. If so, we move on, but if not we include it as a possible candidate:

```
construct_candidates(int a[], int k, int n, int c[], int *ncandidates)
{
        int i,j;                        /* counters */
        bool legal_move;                /* might the move be legal? */

        *ncandidates = 0;
        for (i=1; i<=n; i++) {
            legal_move = TRUE;
            for (j=1; j<k; j++) {
                    if (abs((k)-j) == abs(i-a[j]))  /* diagonal threat */
                            legal_move = FALSE;
                    if (i == a[j])                  /* column threat */
                            legal_move = FALSE;
            }
            if (legal_move == TRUE) {
                    c[*ncandidates] = i;
                    *ncandidates = *ncandidates + 1;
            }
        }
}
```

The remaining routines are simple, particularly since we are only interested in counting the solutions, not displaying them:

```
process_solution(int a[], int k)
{
        int i;                          /* counter */

        solution_count ++;
}

is_a_solution(int a[], int k, int n)
{
        return (k == n);
}
```

```
nqueens(int n)
{
        int a[NMAX];                    /* solution vector */

        solution_count = 0;
        backtrack(a,0,n);
        printf("n=%d  solution_count=%d\n",n,solution_count);
}
```

The modest laptop computer we wrote this on solved up to $n = 9$ instantly. Beyond that, it started laboring. The fan on the laptop turned on around $n = 10$ because the computation started generating enough heat to require cooling. By $n = 14$ it was taking several minutes, enough for us to lose interest in larger n. Besides, the fan was giving us a headache. Our counts:

```
n=1   solution_count=1
n=2   solution_count=0
n=3   solution_count=0
n=4   solution_count=2
n=5   solution_count=10
n=6   solution_count=4
n=7   solution_count=40
n=8   solution_count=92
n=9   solution_count=352
n=10  solution_count=724
n=11  solution_count=2680
n=12  solution_count=14200
n=13  solution_count=73712
n=14  solution_count=365596
```

More efficient programs could certainly go a little farther. Our candidate generator can be made faster by terminating the inner for-loop soon as the Boolean variable turns false. More time might be saved by additional pruning. In the current implementation, we backtrack as soon as the kth row has no legal moves. But if some subsequent row (say, the $(k + 2)$nd) has no legal moves, anything we do on the kth row is ultimately futile. The sooner we figure this out, the better.

More profitably, we can try to exploit symmetry. Rotating any solution by 90 degrees yields a different solution, as does reflecting it through the center of the board. By carefully generating only one solution in each equivalence class and counting the symmetries, we can substantially reduce the amount of search needed.

It is fun to try to make a search program as efficient as possible. Why don't you give the queens a try and see how high a value of n you can search within one minute? Don't expect to get *too* much farther than we did, because solving to $n + 1$ should require about ten times as much computation as getting to n in this size range. Even very small increases in solvable problem size thus represents a substantial victory.

8.6   Problems

8.6.1   Little Bishops

PC/UVa IDs: 110801/861, **Popularity:** C, **Success rate:** high **Level:** 2

A bishop is a piece used in the game of chess which can only move diagonally from its current position. Two bishops attack each other if one is on the path of the other. In the figure below, the dark squares represent the reachable locations for bishop B_1 from its current position. Bishops B_1 and B_2 are in attacking position, while B_1 and B_3 are not. Bishops B_2 and B_3 are also in non-attacking position.

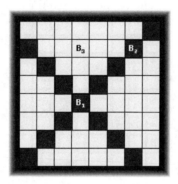

Given two numbers n and k, determine the number of ways one can put k bishops on an $n \times n$ chessboard so that no two of them are in attacking positions.

Input

The input file may contain multiple test cases. Each test case occupies a single line in the input file and contains two integers $n(1 \leq n \leq 8)$ and $k(0 \leq k \leq n^2)$.

A test case containing two zeros terminates the input.

Output

For each test case, print a line containing the total number of ways one can put the given number of bishops on a chessboard of the given size so that no two of them lie in attacking positions. You may safely assume that this number will be less than 10^{15}.

Sample Input

8 6
4 4
0 0

Sample Output

5599888
260

8.6.2   15-Puzzle Problem

PC/UVa IDs: 110802/10181, **Popularity:** B, **Success rate:** average **Level:** 3

The 15-puzzle is a very popular game: you have certainly seen it even if you don't know it by that name. It is constructed with 15 sliding tiles, each with a different number from 1 to 15, with all tiles packed into a 4 by 4 frame with one tile missing. The object of the puzzle is to arrange the tiles so that they are ordered as below:

The only legal operation is to exchange the missing tile with one of the 2, 3, or 4 tiles it shares an edge with. Consider the following sequence of moves:

| A random puzzle position | The missing tile moves right (R) | The missing tile moves upwards (U) | The missing tile moves left (L) |

We denote moves by the neighbor of the missing tile is swapped with it. Legal values are "R," "L," "U," and "D" for right, left, up, and down, based on the movements of the hole.

Given an initial configuration of a 15-puzzle you must determine a sequence of steps that take you to the final state. Each *solvable* 15-puzzle input requires at most 45 steps to be solved with our judge solution; you are limited to using at most 50 steps to solve the puzzle.

Input

The first line of the input contains an integer n indicating the number of puzzle set inputs. The next $4n$ lines contain n puzzles at four lines per puzzle. Zero denotes the missing tile.

Output

For each input set you must produce one line of output. If the given initial configuration is not solvable, print the line "This puzzle is not solvable." If the puzzle is solvable, then print the move sequence as described above to solve the puzzle.

Sample Input

```
2
2 3 4 0
1 5 7 8
9 6 10 12
13 14 11 15
13 1 2 4
5 0 3 7
9 6 10 12
15 8 11 14
```

Sample Output

```
LLLDRDRDR
This puzzle is not solvable.
```

8.6.3   Queue

PC/UVa IDs: 110803/10128, **Popularity:** B, **Success rate:** high **Level:** 2

Consider a queue with N people, each of a different height. A person can see out to the left of the queue if he or she is taller than all the people to the left; otherwise the view is blocked. Similarly, a person can see to the right if he or she is taller than all the people to the right.

A crime has been committed, where a person to the left of the queue has killed a person to the right of the queue using a boomerang. Exactly P members of the queue had unblocked vision to the left and and exactly R members had unblocked vision to the right, thus serving as potential witnesses.

The defense has retained you to determine how many permutations of N people have this property for a given P and R.

Input

The input consists of T test cases, with T $(1 \leq T \leq 10{,}000)$ given on the first line of the input file.

Each test case consists of a line containing three integers. The first integer N indicates the number of people in a queue $(1 \leq N \leq 13)$. The second integer corresponds to the number of people who have unblocked vision to their left (P). The third integer corresponds to the number of people who have unblocked vision to their right (R).

Output

For each test case, print the number of permutations of N people where P people can see out to the left and R people can see out to the right.

Sample Input

```
3
10 4 4
11 3 1
3 1 2
```

Sample Output

```
90720
1026576
1
```

8.6.4 Servicing Stations

PC/UVa IDs: 110804/10160, **Popularity:** B, **Success rate:** low **Level:** 3

A company offers personal computers for sale in N towns ($3 \leq N \leq 35$), denoted by $1, 2, \ldots, N$. There are direct routes connecting M pairs among these towns. The company decides to build servicing stations to ensure that for any town X, there will be a station located either in X or in some immediately neighboring town of X.

Write a program to find the minimum number of stations the company has to build.

Input

The input consists of multiple problem descriptions. Every description starts with number of towns N and number of town-pairs M, separated by a space. Each of the next M lines contains a pair of integers representing connected towns, at one pair per line with each pair separated by a space. The input ends with $N = 0$ and $M = 0$.

Output

For each input case, print a line reporting the minimum number of servicing stations needed.

Sample Input

```
8 12
1 2
1 6
1 8
2 3
2 6
3 4
3 5
4 5
4 7
5 6
6 7
6 8
0 0
```

Sample Output

```
2
```

8.6.5   Tug of War

PC/UVa IDs: 110805/10032, **Popularity:** B, **Success rate:** low **Level:** 2

Tug of war is a contest of brute strength, where two teams of people pull in opposite directions on a rope. The team that succeeds in pulling the rope in their direction is declared the winner.

A tug of war is being arranged for the office picnic. The picnickers must be fairly divided into two teams. Every person must be on one team or the other, the number of people on the two teams must not differ by more than one, and the total weight of the people on each team should be as nearly equal as possible.

Input

The input begins with a single positive integer on a line by itself indicating the number of test cases following, each described below and followed by a blank line.

The first line of each case contains n, the number of people at the picnic. Each of the next n lines gives the weight of a person at the picnic, where each weight is an integer between 1 and 450. There are at most 100 people at the picnic.

Finally, there is a blank line between each two consecutive inputs.

Output

For each test case, your output will consist of a single line containing two numbers: the total weight of the people on one team, and the total weight of the people on the other team. If these numbers differ, give the smaller number first.

The output of each two consecutive cases will be separated by a blank line.

Sample Input

```
1

3
100
90
200
```

Sample Output

```
190 200
```

8.6.6   Garden of Eden

PC/UVa IDs: 110806/10001, **Popularity:** B, **Success rate:** average   **Level:** 2

Cellular automata are mathematical idealizations of physical systems in which both space and time are discrete, and the physical quantities take on a finite set of discrete values. A cellular automaton consists of a lattice (or array) of discrete-valued variables. The state of such automaton is completely specified by the values of the variables at each position in the lattice. Cellular automata evolve in discrete time steps, with the value at each position (cell) being affected by the values of variables at sites in its neighborhood on the previous time step. For each automaton there is a set of rules that define its evolution.

For most cellular automata there are configurations (states) that are unreachable: no state will produce them by the application of the evolution rules. These states are called Gardens of Eden, because they can only appear as initial states. As an example, consider a trivial set of rules that evolve every cell into 0. For this automaton, any state with non-zero cells is a Garden of Eden.

In general, finding the ancestor of a given state (or the non-existence of such an ancestor) is a very hard, computing-intensive, problem. For the sake of simplicity we will restrict the problem to one-dimensional binary finite cellular automata. In other words, the number of cells is a finite number, the cells are arranged in a linear fashion, and their state will be either "0" or "1." To simplify the problem further, each cell state will depend only on its previous state and that of its immediate left and right neighbors.

The actual arrangement of the cells will be along a circle, so that the last cell is a neighbor of the first cell.

Problem definition

Given a circular binary cellular automaton, you must determine whether a given state is a Garden of Eden or a reachable state. The cellular automaton will be described in terms of its evolution rules. For example, the table below shows the evolution rules for the automaton: $Cell = XOR(Left, Right)$.

Left $[i-1]$	Cell $[i]$	Right $[i+1]$	New State		
0	0	0	0	$0 * 2^0$	
0	0	1	1	$1 * 2^1$	
0	1	0	0	$0 * 2^2$	
0	1	1	1	$1 * 2^3$	
1	0	0	1	$1 * 2^4$	
1	0	1	0	$0 * 2^5$	
1	1	0	1	$1 * 2^6$	
1	1	1	0	$0 * 2^7$	
				90	= Automaton Identifier

With the restrictions imposed on this problem, there are only 256 different automata. An identifier for each automaton can be generated by taking the *new state* vector and interpreting it as a binary number, as shown in the table. The example automaton has identifier 90, while the *identity* automaton (where every state evolves to itself) has identifier 204.

Input

The input will consist of several test cases. Each input case describes a cellular automaton and a state on a single line. The first item on the line will be the identifier of the cellular automaton you must work with. The second item in the line will be a positive integer N ($4 \leq N \leq 32$) indicating the number of cells for this test case. Finally, the third item in the line will be a state represented by a string of exactly N zeros and ones. Your program must keep reading lines until the end of file.

Output

If an input case describes a Garden of Eden, output the string GARDEN OF EDEN. If the input does not describe a Garden of Eden (it is a reachable state) you must output the string REACHABLE.

The output for each test case must be on a different line.

Sample Input

```
0 4 1111
204 5 10101
255 6 000000
154 16 1000000000000000
```

Sample Output

```
GARDEN OF EDEN
REACHABLE
GARDEN OF EDEN
GARDEN OF EDEN
```

8.6.7   Color Hash

PC/UVa IDs: 110807/704, **Popularity:** B, **Success rate:** average **Level:** 3

This puzzle consists of two wheels. Both wheels can rotate clockwise and counterclockwise. They contain 21 colored pieces, 10 of which are rounded triangles and 11 of which are separators. The left panel in Figure 8.2 shows the final puzzle position. Note that to perform a one-step rotation you must turn the wheel until you have advanced a triangle and a separator.

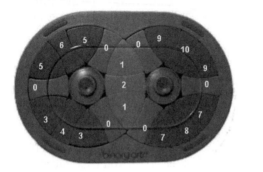 

Figure 8.2. Final puzzle configuration (l), with the puzzle after rotating the left wheel on step clockwise from the final configuration (r).

Your job is to write a program that reads the puzzle configuration and prints the minimum sequence of movements required to reach the final position. We will use the following integer values to encode each type of piece:

0	gray separator
1	yellow triangle
2	yellow separator
3	cyan triangle
4	cyan separator
5	violet triangle
6	violet separator
7	green triangle
8	green separator
9	red triangle
10	red separator

A puzzle configuration will be described using 24 integers; the first 12 describe the left wheel configuration; the last 12, the right wheel. The first integer represents the bottom right separator of the left wheel and the next 11 integers describe the left wheel clockwise. The 13th integer represents the bottom left separator of the right wheel and the next 11 integers describe the right wheel counterclockwise.

The final position is therefore encoded

0 3 4 3 0 5 6 5 0 1 2 1 0 7 8 7 0 9 10 9 0 1 2 1

If we rotate the left wheel clockwise one position from the final configuration (as shown in the right-hand figure) the puzzle configuration would be encoded

2 1 0 3 4 3 0 5 6 5 0 1 0 7 8 7 0 9 10 9 0 5 0 1

Input

Input for your program consists of several puzzles. The first line of the input will contain an integer n specifying the number of puzzles. There will then be n lines, each containing 24 integers separated with one white space, describing the initial puzzle configuration as explained above.

Output

For each configuration, your program should output one line with just one number representing the solution. Each movement is encoded using one digit from 1 to 4 in the following way:

1   Left Wheel Clockwise rotation
2   Right Wheel Clockwise rotation
3   Left Wheel Counterclockwise rotation
4   Right Wheel Counterclockwise rotation

No space should be printed between each digit. Since multiple solutions could be found, you should print the solution that is encoded as the smallest number. The solution will never require more than 16 movements.

If no solution is found you should print, "NO SOLUTION WAS FOUND IN 16 STEPS". If you are given the final position you should print, "PUZZLE ALREADY SOLVED".

Sample Input

```
3
0 3 4 3 0 5 6 5 0 1 2 1 0 7 8 7 0 9 10 9 0 1 2 1
0 3 4 5 0 3 6 5 0 1 2 1 0 7 8 7 0 9 10 9 0 1 2 1
0 9 4 3 0 5 6 5 0 1 2 1 0 7 8 7 0 9 10 3 0 1 2 1
```

Sample Output

```
PUZZLE ALREADY SOLVED
1434332334332323
NO SOLUTION WAS FOUND IN 16 STEPS
```

8.6.8 Bigger Square Please...

PC/UVa IDs: 110808/10270, **Popularity:** C, **Success rate:** high **Level:** 3

Tomy has many paper squares. The side length (size) of them ranges from 1 to $N-1$, and he has an unlimited number of squares of each kind. But he really wants to have a bigger one – a square of size N.

He can make such a square by building it up from the squares he already has. For example, a square of size 7 can be built from nine smaller squares as shown below:

There should be no empty space in the square, no extra paper outside the square, and the small squares should not overlap. Further, Tomy wants to make his square using the minimal number of possible squares. Can you help?

Input

The first line of the input contains a single integer T indicating the number of test cases. Each test case consists of a single integer N, where $2 \leq N \leq 50$.

Output

For each test case, print a line containing a single integer K indicating the minimal number of squares needed to build the target square. On the following K lines, print three integers x, y, l indicating the coordinates of top-left corner ($1 \leq x, y \leq N$) and the side length of the corresponding square.

Sample Input

```
3
4
3
7
```

Sample Output

```
4
1 1 2
1 3 2
3 1 2
3 3 2
6
1 1 2
1 3 1
2 3 1
3 1 1
3 2 1
3 3 1
9
1 1 2
1 3 2
3 1 1
4 1 1
3 2 2
5 1 3
4 4 4
1 5 3
3 4 1
```

8.7 Hints

8.1 In what ways do we have to modify our eight-queens solution to solve the bishop's problem? Does separating the problem of positioning white bishops from that of black bishops help?

8.2 How can we prevent repeating any puzzle state in the course of our search, which is both inefficient and might lead to excessively long move sequences?

8.3 How can we represent the solution for efficient search? Are we better off constructing permutations, or identifying the subsets of the people with unblocked vision?

8.5 The potential size of this problem makes it a challenge, perhaps too large for backtracking even with sophisticated pruning. Can we keep track of all *team weights* realizable by some subset of the first i people, without explicitly enumerating the 2^i subsets? Note that the number of distinct possible team weights is much smaller than 2^i.

8.7 What is the best way to represent the state of a solution?

8.8 Does it pay to try to position the largest squares first?

8.8 Notes

8.1 There is a nice combinatorial solution to the bishops problem which counts the answers without exhaustive search. This enables us to determine the number of placements for much larger chessboards. UVa judge problem 10237 poses the bishops problem for large enough inputs to make such a solution necessary.

8.4 A set of vertices S in a graph G such that every vertex is either in S or a neighbor of a vertex in S is known as a *dominating set* of the graph. This problem of finding a minimum dominating set is NP-complete, so exhausive search is the only available algorithm if you demand an optimal solution.

8.6 Cellular automata have been proposed as models for a wide variety of natural phenomenon. Read Wolfram's controversal book *A New Kind of Science* [Wol02] to see what all the fuss is about.

8.7 Binary Arts Corp., the creater of Color Hash and many other great puzzles of combinatorial interest, also runs the website *www.puzzles.com*. Check them out.

9

Graph Traversal

Graphs are one of the unifying themes of computer science – an abstract representation which describes the organization of transportation systems, electrical circuits, human interactions, and telecommunication networks. That so many different structures can be modeled using a single formalism is a source of great power to the educated programmer.

In this chapter, we focus on problems which require only an elementary knowledge of graph algorithms, specifically the appropriate use of graph data structures and traversal algorithms. In Chapter 10, we will present problems relying on more advanced graph algorithms that find minimum spanning trees, shortest paths, and network flows.

9.1 Flavors of Graphs

A graph $G = (V, E)$ is defined by a set of *vertices* V, and a set of *edges* E consisting of ordered or unordered pairs of vertices from V. In modeling a road network, the vertices may represent the cities or junctions, certain pairs of which are connected by roads/edges. In analyzing the source code of a computer program, the vertices may represent lines of code, with an edge connecting lines x and y if y can be the next statement executed after x. In analyzing human interactions, the vertices typically represent people, with edges connecting pairs of related souls.

There are several fundamental properties of graphs which impact the choice of data structures used to represent them and algorithms available to analyze them. The first step in any graph problem is determining which flavor of graph you are dealing with:

- *Undirected vs. Directed* — A graph $G = (V, E)$ is *undirected* if edge $(x, y) \in E$ implies that (y, x) is also in E. If not, we say that the graph is *directed*. Road

networks *between* cities are typically undirected, since any large road has lanes
going in both directions. Street networks *within* cities are almost always directed,
because there are typically at least a few one-way streets lurking about. Program-
flow graphs are typically directed, because the execution flows from one line into
the next and changes direction only at branches. Most graphs of graph-theoretic
interest are undirected.

- *Weighted vs. Unweighted* — In *weighted* graphs, each edge (or vertex) of G is
  assigned a numerical value, or weight. Typical application-specific edge weights for
  road networks might be the distance, travel time, or maximum capacity between
  x and y. In *unweighted* graphs, there is no cost distinction between various edges
  and vertices.

  The difference between weighted and unweighted graphs becomes particularly
  apparent in finding the shortest path between two vertices. For unweighted graphs,
  the shortest path must have the fewest number of edges, and can be found using
  the breadth-first search algorithm discussed in this chapter. Shortest paths in
  weighted graphs requires more sophisticated algorithms, discussed in Chapter 10.

- *Cyclic vs. Acyclic* — An *acyclic* graph does not contain any cycles. *Trees* are
  connected acyclic *undirected* graphs. Trees are the simplest interesting graphs, and
  inherently recursive structures since cutting any edge leaves two smaller trees.

  Directed acyclic graphs are called *DAGs*. They arise naturally in scheduling
  problems, where a directed edge (x, y) indicates that x must occur before y. An
  operation called *topological sorting* orders the vertices of a DAG so as to respect
  these precedence constraints. Topological sorting is typically the first step of any
  algorithm on a DAG, and will be discussed in Section 9.5.

- *Simple vs. Non-simple* — Certain types of edges complicate the task of working
  with graphs. A *self-loop* is an edge (x, x) involving only one vertex. An edge (x, y)
  is a *multi-edge* if it occurs more than once in the graph.

  Both of these structures require special care in implementing graph algorithms. Hence any graph which avoids them is called *simple*.

- *Embedded vs. Topological* — A graph is *embedded* if the vertices and edges have
  been assigned geometric positions. Thus any drawing of a graph is an embedding,
  which may or may not have algorithmic significance.

  Occasionally, the structure of a graph is completely defined by the geometry
  of its embedding. For example, if we are given a collection of points in the plane,
  and seek the minimum cost tour visiting all of them (i.e., the traveling salesman
  problem), the underlying topology is the *complete graph* connecting each pair of
  vertices. The weights are typically defined by the Euclidean distance between each
  pair of points.

  Another example of topology from geometry arises in grids of points. Many problems on an $n \times m$ grid involve walking between neighboring points, so the edges
  are implicitly defined from the geometry.

- *Implicit vs. Explicit* — Many graphs are not explicitly constructed and then traversed, but built as we use them. A good example is in backtrack search. The vertices of this implicit search graph are the states of the search vector, while edges link pairs of states which can be directly generated from each other. It is often easier to work with an implicit graph than explicitly constructing it before analysis.

- *Labeled vs. Unlabeled* — In *labeled* graphs, each vertex is assigned a unique name or identifier to distinguish it from all other vertices. In *unlabeled* graphs, no such distinctions have been made.

  Most graphs arising in applications are naturally and meaningfully labeled, such as city names in a transportation network. A common problem arising on graphs is that of *isomorphism testing*, determining whether the topological structure of two graphs are in fact identical if we ignore any labels. Such problems are typically solved using backtracking, by trying to assign each vertex in each graph a label such that the structures are identical.

9.2 Data Structures for Graphs

There are several possible ways to represent graphs. We discuss four useful representations below. We assume the graph $G = (V, E)$ contains n vertices and m edges.

- *Adjacency Matrix* — We can represent G using an $n \times n$ matrix M, where element $M[i, j]$ is, say, 1, if (i, j) is an edge of G, and 0 if it isn't. This allows fast answers to the question "is (i, j) in G?", and rapid updates for edge insertion and deletion. It may use excessive space for graphs with many vertices and relatively few edges, however.

  Consider a graph which represents the street map of Manhattan in New York City. Every junction of two streets will be a vertex of the graph, with neighboring junctions connected by edges. How big is this graph? Manhattan is basically a grid of 15 avenues, each crossing roughly 200 streets. This gives us about 3,000 vertices and 6,000 edges, since each vertex neighbors four other vertices and each edge is shared between two vertices. Such a small amount of data should easily and efficiently stored, but the adjacency matrix will have 3,000 × 3,000 = 9,000,000 cells, almost all of them empty!

- *Adjacency Lists in Lists* — We can more efficiently represent sparse graphs by using linked lists to store the neighbors adjacent to each vertex. Adjacency lists require pointers but are not frightening once you have experience with linked structures.

  Adjacency lists make it harder to ask whether a given edge (i, j) is in G, since we have to search through the appropriate list to find the edge. However, it is often surprisingly easy to design graph algorithms which avoid any need for such queries. Typically, we sweep through all the edges of the graph in one pass via a breadth-first or depths-first traversal, and update the implications of the current edge as we visit it.

- *Adjacency Lists in Matrices* — Adjacency lists can also embedded in matrices, thus eliminating the need for pointers. We can represent a list in an array (or equivalently, a row of a matrix) by keeping a count k of how many elements there are, and packing them into the first k elements of the array. Now we can visit successive the elements from the first to last just like a list, but by incrementing an index in a loop instead of cruising through pointers.

  This data structure looks like it combines the worst properties of adjacency matrices (large space) with the worst properties of adjacency lists (the need to search for edges). However, there is a method to its madness. First, it is the simplest data structure to program, particularly for static graphs which do not change after they are built. Second, the space problem can in principle be eliminated by allocating the rows for each vertex dynamically, and making them exactly the right size.

  To prove our point, we will use this representation in all our examples below.

- *Table of Edges* — An even simpler data structure is just to maintain an array or linked list of the edges. This is not as flexible as the other data structures at answering "who is adjacent to vertex x?" but it works just fine for certain simple procedures like Kruskal's minimum spanning tree algorithm.

As stated above, we will use adjacency lists in matrices as our basic data structure to represent graphs. It is not complicated to convert these routines to honest pointer-based adjacency lists. Sample code for adjacency lists and matrices can be found in many books, including [Sed01].

We represent a graph using the following data type. For each graph, we keep count of the number of vertices, and assign each vertex a unique number from 1 to nvertices. We represent the edges in an MAXV × MAXDEGREE array, so each vertex can be adjacent to MAXDEGREE others. By defining MAXDEGREE to be MAXV, we can represent any simple graph, but this is wasteful of space for low-degree graphs:

```
#define MAXV            100           /* maximum number of vertices */
#define MAXDEGREE       50            /* maximum vertex outdegree */

typedef struct {
        int edges[MAXV+1][MAXDEGREE];  /* adjacency info */
        int degree[MAXV+1];            /* outdegree of each vertex */
        int nvertices;                 /* number of vertices in graph */
        int nedges;                    /* number of edges in graph */
} graph;
```

We represent a directed edge (x, y) by the integer y in x's adjacency list, which is located in the subarray graph->edges[x]. The degree field counts the number of meaningful entries for the given vertex. An undirected edge (x, y) appears twice in any adjacency-based graph structure, once as y in x's list, and once as x in y's list.

To demonstrate the use of this data structure, we show how to read in a graph from a file. A typical graph format consists of an initial line featuring the number of vertices and edges in the graph, followed by a listing of the edges at one vertex pair per line.

```
read_graph(graph *g, bool directed)
{
        int i;                          /* counter */
        int m;                          /* number of edges */
        int x, y;                       /* vertices in edge (x,y) */

        initialize_graph(g);

        scanf("%d %d",&(g->nvertices),&m);

        for (i=1; i<=m; i++) {
                scanf("%d %d",&x,&y);
                insert_edge(g,x,y,directed);
        }
} .
```

```
initialize_graph(graph *g)
{
        int i;                          /* counter */

        g -> nvertices = 0;
        g -> nedges = 0;

        for (i=1; i<=MAXV; i++) g->degree[i] = 0;
}
```

The critical routine is insert_edge. We parameterize it with a Boolean flag directed to identify whether we need to insert two copies of each edge or only one. Note the use of recursion to solve the problem:

```
insert_edge(graph *g, int x, int y, bool directed)
{
        if (g->degree[x] > MAXDEGREE)
            printf("Warning: insertion(%d,%d) exceeds max degree\n",x,y);

        g->edges[x][g->degree[x]] = y;
        g->degree[x] ++;

        if (directed == FALSE)
                insert_edge(g,y,x,TRUE);
        else
                g->nedges ++;
```

```
}
```

Printing the associated graph is now simply a matter of nested loops:

```
print_graph(graph *g)
{
        int i,j;                            /* counters */

        for (i=1; i<=g->nvertices; i++) {
                printf("%d: ",i);
                for (j=0; j<g->degree[i]; j++)
                        printf(" %d",g->edges[i][j]);
                printf("\n");
        }
}
```

9.3   Graph Traversal: Breadth-First

The basic operation in most graph algorithms is completely and systematically travers-
ing the graph. We want to visit every vertex and every edge exactly once in some
well-defined order. There are two primary traversal algorithms: *breadth-first search*
(BFS) and *depth-first search* (DFS). For certain problems, it makes absolutely no
different which one you use, but in other cases the distinction is crucial.

Both graph traversal procedures share one fundamental idea, namely, that it is necessary to mark the vertices we have seen before so we don't try to explore them again.
Otherwise we get trapped in a maze and can't find our way out. BFS and DFS differ
only in the order in which they explore vertices.

Breadth-first search is appropriate if (1) we don't care which order we visit the vertices
and edges of the graph, so any order is appropriate or (2) we are interested in shortest
paths on unweighted graphs.

9.3.1   Breadth-First Search

Our breadth-first search implementation **bfs** uses two Boolean arrays to maintain our
knowledge about each vertex in the graph. A vertex is **discovered** the first time we
visit it. A vertex is considered **processed** after we have traversed all outgoing edges
from it. Thus each vertex passes from undiscovered to discovered to processed over the
course of the search. This information could be maintained using one enumerated type
variable; we used two Boolean variables instead.

Once a vertex is discovered, it is placed on a queue, such as we implemented in Section
2.1.2. Since we process these vertices in first-in, first-out order, the oldest vertices are
expanded first, which are exactly those closest to the root:

```
bool processed[MAXV];    /* which vertices have been processed */
bool discovered[MAXV];   /* which vertices have been found */
```

```
int parent[MAXV];        /* discovery relation */

bfs(graph *g, int start)
{
        queue q;                         /* queue of vertices to visit */
        int v;                           /* current vertex */
        int i;                           /* counter */

        init_queue(&q);
        enqueue(&q,start);
        discovered[start] = TRUE;

        while (empty(&q) == FALSE) {
                v = dequeue(&q);
                process_vertex(v);
                processed[v] = TRUE;
                for (i=0; i<g->degree[v]; i++)
                    if (valid_edge(g->edges[v][i]) == TRUE) {
                        if (discovered[g->edges[v][i]] == FALSE) {
                                enqueue(&q,g->edges[v][i]);
                                discovered[g->edges[v][i]] = TRUE;
                                parent[g->edges[v][i]] = v;
                        }
                        if (processed[g->edges[v][i]] == FALSE)
                                process_edge(v,g->edges[v][i]);
                    }
        }
}

initialize_search(graph *g)
{
        int i;                           /* counter */

        for (i=1; i<=g->nvertices; i++) {
                processed[i] = discovered[i] = FALSE;
                parent[i] = -1;
        }
}
```

9.3.2 Exploiting Traversal

The exact behavior of bfs depends upon the functions process_vertex() and
process_edge(). Through these functions, we can easily customize what the traversal does as it makes one official visit to each edge and each vertex. By setting the
functions to

```
process_vertex(int v)
{
        printf("processed vertex %d\n",v);
}
```

```
process_edge(int x, int y)
{
        printf("processed edge (%d,%d)\n",x,y);
}
```

we print each vertex and edge exactly once. By setting the functions to

```
process_vertex(int v)
{
}
```

```
process_edge(int x, int y)
{
        nedges = nedges + 1;
}
```

we get an accurate count of the number of edges. Many problems perform different actions on vertices or edges as they are encountered. These functions give us the freedom to easily customize our response.

One final degree of customization is provided by the Boolean predicate `valid_edge`, which allows us ignore the existence of certain edges in the graph during our traversal. Setting `valid_edge` to return true for all edges results in a full breadth-first search of the graph, and will be the case for our examples except `netflow` in Section 10.4.

9.3.3 Finding Paths

The `parent` array set within `bfs()` is very useful for finding interesting paths through a graph. The vertex which discovered vertex i is defined as `parent[i]`. Every vertex is discovered during the course of traversal, so except for the root every node has a parent. The parent relation defines a tree of discovery with the initial search node as the root of the tree.

Because vertices are discovered in order of increasing distance from the root, this tree has a very important property. The unique tree path from the root to any node $x \in V$ uses the smallest number of edges (or equivalently, intermediate nodes) possible on any root-to-x path in the graph.

We can reconstruct this path by following the chain of ancestors from x to the root. Note that we have to work backward. We cannot find the path from the root to x, since that does not follow the direction of the parent pointers. Instead, we must find the path from x to the root.

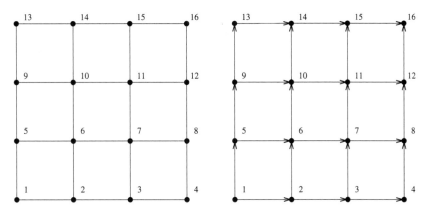

Figure 9.1. An undirected 4 × 4 grid-graph (l), with the DAG defined by edges going to higher-numbered vertices (r).

Since this is the reverse of how we normally want the path, we can either (1) store it and then explicitly reverse it using a stack, or (2) let recursion reverse it for us, as in the following slick routine:

```
find_path(int start, int end, int parents[])
{
        if ((start == end) || (end == -1))
                printf("\n%d",start);
        else {
                find_path(start,parents[end],parents);
                printf(" %d",end);
        }
}
```

On our grid graph example (Figure 9.1) our algorithm generated the following parent relation:

vertex	1	2	3	4	5	6	7	8	9	10	11	12	13	14	15	16
parent	-1	1	2	3	1	2	3	4	5	6	7	8	9	10	11	12

For the shortest path from the lower-left corner of the grid to the upper-right corner, this parent relation yields the path $\{1, 2, 3, 4, 8, 12, 16\}$. Of course, this shortest path is not unique; the number of such paths in this graph is counted in Section 6.3.

There are two points to remember about using breadth-first search to find a shortest path from x to y: First, the shortest path tree is only useful if BFS was performed with x as the root of the search. Second, BFS only gives the shortest path if the graph is unweighted. We will present algorithms for finding shortest paths in weighted graphs in Section 10.3.1.

9.4   Graph Traversal: Depth-First

Depth-first search uses essentially the same idea as backtracking. Both involve exhaustively searching all possibilities by advancing if it is possible, and backing up as soon as there is no unexplored possibility for further advancement. Both are most easily understood as recursive algorithms.

Depth-first search can be thought of as breadth-first search with a stack instead of a queue. The beauty of implementing dfs recursively is that recursion eliminates the need to keep an explicit stack:

```
dfs(graph *g, int v)
{
        int i;                          /* counter */
        int y;                          /* successor vertex */

        if (finished) return;           /* allow for search termination */

        discovered[v] = TRUE;
        process_vertex(v);

        for (i=0; i<g->degree[v]; i++) {
                y = g->edges[v][i];
                if (valid_edge(g->edges[v][i]) == TRUE) {
                        if (discovered[y] == FALSE) {
                                parent[y] = v;
                                dfs(g,y);
                        } else
                                if (processed[y] == FALSE)
                                        process_edge(v,y);
                }
                if (finished) return;
        }

        processed[v] = TRUE;
}
```

Rooted trees are a special type of graph (directed, acyclic, in-degrees of at most 1, with an order defined on the outgoing edges of each node). In-order, pre-order, and post-order traversals are all basically DFS, differing only in how they use the ordering of out-edges and when they process the vertex.

9.4.1   Finding Cycles

Depth-first search of an undirected graph partitions the edges into two classes, *tree edges* and *back edges*. The tree edges those encoded in the **parent** relation, the edges which discover new vertices. Back edges are those whose other endpoint is an ancestor of the vertex being expanded, so they point back into the tree.

That all edges fall into these two classes is an amazing property of depth-first search. Why can't an edge go to a brother or cousin node instead of an ancestor? In DFS, all nodes reachable from a given vertex v are expanded before we finish with the traversal from v, so such topologies are impossible for undirected graphs. The case of DFS on directed graphs is somewhat more complicated but still highly structured.

Back edges are the key to finding a cycle in an undirected graph. If there is no back edge, all edges are tree edges, and no cycle exists in a tree. But any back edge going from x to an ancestor y creates a cycle with the path in the tree from y to x. Such a cycle is easy to find using `dfs`:

```
process_edge(int x, int y)
{
        if (parent[x] != y) {   /* found back edge! */
                printf("Cycle from %d to %d:",y,x);
                find_path(y,x,parent);
                finished = TRUE;
        }
}

process_vertex(int v)
{
}
```

We use the `finished` flag to terminate after finding the first cycle in our 4×4 grid graph, which is 3 4 8 7 with $(7, 3)$ as the back edge.

9.4.2 Connected Components

A *connected component* of an undirected graph is a maximal set of vertices such that there is a path between every pair of vertices. These are the separate "pieces" of the graph such that there is no connection between the pieces.

An amazing number of seemingly complicated problems reduce to finding or counting connected components. For example, testing whether a puzzle such as Rubik's cube or the 15-puzzle can be solved from any position is really asking whether the graph of legal configurations is connected.

Connected components can easily be found using depth-first search or breadth-first search, since the vertex order does not matter. Basically, we search from the first vertex. Anything we discover during this search must be part of the same connected component. We then repeat the search from any undiscovered vertex (if one exists) to define the next component, and so on until all vertices have been found:

```
connected_components(graph *g)
{
        int c;                          /* component number */
```

```
        int i;                              /* counter */

        initialize_search(g);

        c = 0;
        for (i=1; i<=g->nvertices; i++)
                if (discovered[i] == FALSE) {
                        c = c+1;
                        printf("Component %d:",c);
                        dfs(g,i);
                        printf("\n");
                }
}

process_vertex(int v)
{
        printf(" %d",v);
}

process_edge(int x, int y)
{
}
```

Variations on connected components are discussed in Section 10.1.2.

9.5   Topological Sorting

Topological sorting is the fundamental operation on directed acyclic graphs (DAGs). It constructs an ordering of the vertices such that all directed edges go from left to right. Such an ordering clearly cannot exist if the graph contains any directed cycles, because there is no way you can keep going right on a line and still return back to where you started from!

The importance of topological sorting is that it gives us a way to process each vertex before any of its successors. Suppose the edges represented precedence constraints, such that edge (x, y) means job x must be done before job y. Then any topological sort defines a legal schedule. Indeed, there can be many such orderings for a given DAG.

But the applications go deeper. Suppose we seek the shortest (or longest) path from x to y in a DAG. Certainly no vertex appearing after y in the topological order can contribute to any such path, because there will be no way to get back to y. We can appropriately process all the vertices from left to right in topological order, considering the impact of their outgoing edges, and know that we will look at everything we need before we need it.

Topological sorting can be performed efficiently by using a version of depth-first search. However, a more straightforward algorithm is based on an analysis of the in-degrees of each vertex in a DAG. If a vertex has no incoming edges, i.e., has in-degree 0, we may safely place it first in topological order. Deleting its outgoing edges may create new in-degree 0 vertices. This process will continue until all vertices have been placed in the ordering; if not, the graph contained a cycle and was not a DAG in the first place.

Study the following implementation:

```
topsort(graph *g, int sorted[])
{
        int indegree[MAXV];             /* indegree of each vertex */
        queue zeroin;                   /* vertices of indegree 0 */
        int x, y;                       /* current and next vertex */
        int i, j;                       /* counters */

        compute_indegrees(g,indegree);
        init_queue(&zeroin);
        for (i=1; i<=g->nvertices; i++)
                if (indegree[i] == 0) enqueue(&zeroin,i);

        j=0;
        while (empty(&zeroin) == FALSE) {
                j = j+1;
                x = dequeue(&zeroin);
                sorted[j] = x;
                for (i=0; i<g->degree[x]; i++) {
                        y = g->edges[x][i];
                        indegree[y] --;
                        if (indegree[y] == 0) enqueue(&zeroin,y);
                }
        }

        if (j != g->nvertices)
                printf("Not a DAG -- only %d vertices found\n",j);
}


compute_indegrees(graph *g, int in[])
{
        int i,j;                        /* counters */

        for (i=1; i<=g->nvertices; i++) in[i] = 0;

        for (i=1; i<=g->nvertices; i++)
                for (j=0; j<g->degree[i]; j++) in[ g->edges[i][j] ] ++;
}
```

There are several things to observe. Our first step is computing the in-degrees of each vertex of the DAG, since the **degree** field of the graph data type records the out-degree of a vertex. These are the same for undirected graphs, but not directed ones.

Next, note that we use a queue here to maintain the in-degree 0 vertices, but only because we had one sitting around from Section 2.1.2. Any container will do, since the processing order does not matter for correctness. Different processing orders will yield different topological sorts.

The impact of processing orders is apparent in topologically sorting the directed grid in Figure 9.1, where all edges go from lower- to higher-numbered vertices. The sorted permutation $\{1, 2, \ldots, 15, 16\}$ is a topological ordering, but our program repeatedly stripped off diagonals to find

$$1 \ 2 \ 5 \ 3 \ 6 \ 9 \ 4 \ 7 \ 10 \ 13 \ 8 \ 11 \ 14 \ 12 \ 15 \ 16$$

Many other orderings are also possible.

Finally, note that this implementation does not actually delete the edges from the graph! It is sufficient to consider their impact on the in-degree and traverse them rather than delete them.

9.6   Problems

9.6.1   Bicoloring

PC/UVa IDs: 110901/10004, **Popularity:** A, **Success rate:** high **Level:** 1

The *four-color theorem* states that every planar map can be colored using only four colors in such a way that no region is colored using the same color as a neighbor. After being open for over 100 years, the theorem was proven in 1976 with the assistance of a computer.

Here you are asked to solve a simpler problem. Decide whether a given connected graph can be bicolored, i.e., can the vertices be painted red and black such that no two adjacent vertices have the same color.

To simplify the problem, you can assume the graph will be connected, undirected, and not contain self-loops (i.e., edges from a vertex to itself).

Input

The input consists of several test cases. Each test case starts with a line containing the number of vertices n, where $1 < n < 200$. Each vertex is labeled by a number from 0 to $n - 1$. The second line contains the number of edges l. After this, l lines follow, each containing two vertex numbers specifying an edge.

An input with $n = 0$ marks the end of the input and is not to be processed.

Output

Decide whether the input graph can be bicolored, and print the result as shown below.

Sample Input	*Sample Output*
3	NOT BICOLORABLE.
3	BICOLORABLE.
0 1	
1 2	
2 0	
9	
8	
0 1	
0 2	
0 3	
0 4	
0 5	
0 6	
0 7	
0 8	
0	

9.6.2 Playing With Wheels

PC/UVa IDs: 110902/10067, **Popularity:** C, **Success rate:** average **Level:** 2

Consider the following mathematical machine. Digits ranging from 0 to 9 are printed consecutively (clockwise) on the periphery of each wheel. The topmost digits of the wheels form a four-digit integer. For example, in the following figure the wheels form the integer 8,056. Each wheel has two buttons associated with it. Pressing the button marked with a *left arrow* rotates the wheel one digit in the clockwise direction and pressing the one marked with the *right arrow* rotates it by one digit in the opposite direction.

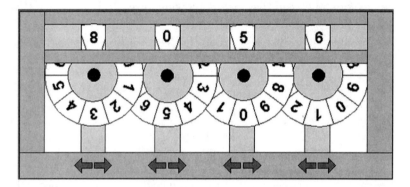

We start with an initial configuration of the wheels, with the topmost digits forming the integer $S_1 S_2 S_3 S_4$. You will be given a set of n forbidden configurations $F_{i_1} F_{i_2} F_{i_3} F_{i_4}$ ($1 \leq i \leq n$) and a target configuration $T_1 T_2 T_3 T_4$. Your job is to write a program to calculate the minimum number of button presses required to transform the initial configuration to the target configuration without passing through a forbidden one.

Input

The first line of the input contains an integer N giving the number of test cases. A blank line then follows.

The first line of each test case contains the initial configuration of the wheels, specified by four digits. Two consecutive digits are separated by a space. The next line contains the target configuration. The third line contains an integer n giving the number of forbidden configurations. Each of the following n lines contains a forbidden configuration. There is a blank line between two consecutive input sets.

Output

For each test case in the input print a line containing the minimum number of button presses required. If the target configuration is not reachable print "-1".

Sample Input

```
2

8 0 5 6
6 5 0 8
5
8 0 5 7
8 0 4 7
5 5 0 8
7 5 0 8
6 4 0 8

0 0 0 0
5 3 1 7
8
0 0 0 1
0 0 0 9
0 0 1 0
0 0 9 0
0 1 0 0
0 9 0 0
1 0 0 0
9 0 0 0
```

Sample Output

```
14
-1
```

9.6.3   The Tourist Guide

PC/UVa IDs: 110903/10099, **Popularity:** B, **Success rate:** average   **Level:** 3

Mr. G. works as a tourist guide in Bangladesh. His current assignment is to show a group of tourists a distant city. As in all countries, certain pairs of cities are connected by two-way roads. Each pair of neighboring cities has a bus service that runs only between those two cities and uses the road that directly connects them. Each bus service has a particular limit on the maximum number of passengers it can carry. Mr. G. has a map showing the cities and the roads connecting them, as well as the service limit for each each bus service.

It is not always possible for him to take all the tourists to the destination city in a single trip. For example, consider the following road map of seven cities, where the edges represent roads and the number written on each edge indicates the passenger limit of the associated bus service.

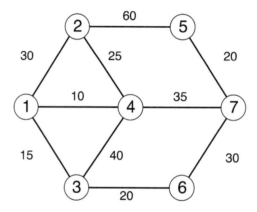

It will take at least five trips for Mr. G. to take 99 tourists from city 1 to city 7, since he has to ride the bus with each group. The best route to take is 1 - 2 - 4 - 7.

Help Mr. G. find the route to take all his tourists to the destination city in the minimum number of trips.

Input

The input will contain one or more test cases. The first line of each test case will contain two integers: N ($N \leq 100$) and R, representing the number of cities and the number of road segments, respectively. Each of the next R lines will contain three integers (C_1, C_2, and P) where C_1 and C_2 are the city numbers and P ($P > 1$) is the maximum number of passengers that can be carried by the bus service between the two cities. City numbers are positive integers ranging from 1 to N. The $(R+1)$th line will contain three integers (S, D, and T) representing, respectively, the starting city, the destination city, and the number of tourists to be guided.

The input will end with two zeros for N and R.

Output

For each test case in the input, first output the scenario number and then the minimum number of trips required for this case on a separate line. Print a blank line after the output for each test case.

Sample Input

```
7 10
1 2 30
1 3 15
1 4 10
2 4 25
2 5 60
3 4 40
3 6 20
4 7 35
5 7 20
6 7 30
1 7 99
0 0
```

Sample Output

```
Scenario #1
Minimum Number of Trips = 5
```

9.6.4   Slash Maze

PC/UVa IDs: 110904/705, **Popularity:** B, **Success rate:** average **Level:** 2

By filling a rectangle with slashes (/) and backslashes (\\), you can generate nice little mazes. Here is an example:

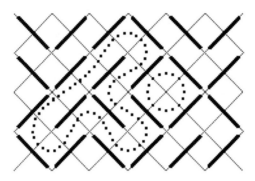

As you can see, paths in the maze cannot branch, so the whole maze contains only (1) cyclic paths and (2) paths entering somewhere and leaving somewhere else. We are only interested in the cycles. There are exactly two of them in our example.

Your task is to write a program that counts the cycles and finds the length of the longest one. The length is defined as the number of small squares the cycle consists of (the ones bordered by gray lines in the picture). In this example, the long cycle has length 16 and the short one length 4.

Input

The input contains several maze descriptions. Each description begins with one line containing two integers w and h ($1 \leq w, h \leq 75$), representing the width and the height of the maze. The next h lines describe the maze itself and contain w characters each; all of these characters will be either "/" or "\\".

The input is terminated by a test case beginning with $w = h = 0$. This case should not be processed.

Output

For each maze, first output the line "Maze #n:", where n is the number of the maze. Then, output the line "k Cycles; the longest has length l.", where k is the number of cycles in the maze and l the length of the longest of the cycles. If the maze is acyclic, output "There are no cycles."

Output a blank line after each test case.

Sample Input

```
6 4
\//\\/
\///\/
//\\/\
\/\///
3 3
///
\//
\\\
0 0
```

Sample Output

```
Maze #1:
2 Cycles; the longest has length 16.

Maze #2:
There are no cycles.
```

9.6.5 Edit Step Ladders

PC/UVa IDs: 110905/10029, **Popularity:** B, **Success rate:** low **Level:** 3

An *edit step* is a transformation from one word x to another word y such that x and y are words in the dictionary, and x can be transformed to y by adding, deleting, or changing one letter. The transformations from *dig* to *dog* and from *dog* to *do* are both edit steps. An *edit step ladder* is a lexicographically ordered sequence of words $w_1, w_2, \ldots, w_n$ such that the transformation from w_i to w_{i+1} is an edit step for all i from 1 to $n-1$.

For a given dictionary, you are to compute the length of the longest edit step ladder.

Input

The input to your program consists of the dictionary: a set of lowercase words in lexicographic order at one word per line. No word exceeds 16 letters and there are at most 25,000 words in the dictionary.

Output

The output consists of a single integer, the number of words in the longest edit step ladder.

Sample Input

```
cat
dig
dog
fig
fin
fine
fog
log
wine
```

Sample Output

```
5
```

9.6.6 Tower of Cubes

PC/UVa IDs: 110906/10051, **Popularity:** C, **Success rate:** high **Level:** 3

You are given N colorful cubes, each having a distinct weight. Cubes are not monochromatic – indeed, every face of a cube is colored with a different color. Your job is to build the tallest possible tower of cubes subject to the restrictions that (1) we never put a heavier cube on a lighter one, and (2) the bottom face of every cube (except the bottom one) must have the same color as the top face of the cube below it.

Input

The input may contain several test cases. The first line of each test case contains an integer N ($1 \leq N \leq 500$) indicating the number of cubes you are given. The ith of the next N lines contains the description of the ith cube. A cube is described by giving the colors of its faces in the following order: front, back, left, right, top, and bottom face. For your convenience colors are identified by integers in the range 1 to 100. You may assume that cubes are given in increasing order of their weights; that is, cube 1 is the lightest and cube N is the heaviest.

The input terminates with a value 0 for N.

Output

For each case, start by printing the test case number on its own line as shown in the sample output. On the next line, print the number of cubes in the tallest possible tower. The next line describes the cubes in your tower from top to bottom with one description per line. Each description gives the serial number of this cube in the input, followed by a single whitespace character and then the identification string (`front`, `back`, `left`, `right`, `top`, or `bottom` of the top face of the cube in the tower. There may be multiple solutions, but any one of them is acceptable.

Print a blank line between two successive test cases.

Sample Input

```
3
1 2 2 2 1 2
3 3 3 3 3 3
3 2 1 1 1 1
10
1 5 10 3 6 5
2 6 7 3 6 9
5 7 3 2 1 9
1 3 3 5 8 10
6 6 2 2 4 4
1 2 3 4 5 6
```

```
10 9 8 7 6 5
6 1 2 3 4 7
1 2 3 3 2 1
3 2 1 1 2 3
0
```

Sample Output

```
Case #1
2
2 front
3 front

Case #2
8
1 bottom
2 back
3 right
4 left
6 top
8 front
9 front
10 top
```

9.6.7 From Dusk Till Dawn

PC/UVa IDs: 110907/10187, **Popularity:** B, **Success rate:** average **Level:** 3

Vladimir has white skin, very long teeth and is 600 years old, but this is no problem because Vladimir is a vampire. Vladimir has never had any problems with being a vampire. In fact, he is a successful doctor who always takes the night shift and so has made many friends among his colleagues. He has an impressive trick which he loves to show at dinner parties: he can tell blood group by taste. Vladimir loves to travel, but being a vampire he must overcome three problems.

1. He can only travel by train, because he must take his coffin with him. Fortunately he can always travel first class because he has made a lot of money through long term investments.

2. He can only travel from dusk till dawn, namely, from 6 P.M. to 6 A.M. During the day he has must stay inside a train station.

3. He has to take something to eat with him. He needs one litre of blood per day, which he drinks at noon (12:00) inside his coffin.

Help Vladimir to find the shortest route between two given cities, so that he can travel with the minimum amount of blood. If he takes too much with him, people ask him funny questions like, "What are you doing with all that blood?"

Input

The first line of the input will contain a single number telling you the number of test cases.

Each test case specification begins with a single number telling you how many route specifications follow. Each route specification consists of the names of two cities, the departure time from city one, and the total traveling time, with all times in hours. Remember, Vladimir cannot use routes departing earlier than 18:00 or arriving later than 6:00.

There will be at most 100 cities and less than 1,000 connections. No route takes less than 1 hour or more than 24 hours, but Vladimir can use only routes within the 12 hours travel time from dusk till dawn.

All city names are at most 32 characters long. The last line contains two city names. The first is Vladimir's start city; the second is Vladimir's destination.

Output

For each test case you should output the number of the test case followed by "Vladimir needs # litre(s) of blood." or "There is no route Vladimir can take."

Sample Input

```
2
3
Ulm Muenchen 17 2
Ulm Muenchen 19 12
Ulm Muenchen 5 2
Ulm Muenchen
10
Lugoj Sibiu 12 6
Lugoj Sibiu 18 6
Lugoj Sibiu 24 5
Lugoj Medias 22 8
Lugoj Medias 18 8
Lugoj Reghin 17 4
Sibiu Reghin 19 9
Sibiu Medias 20 3
Reghin Medias 20 4
Reghin Bacau 24 6
Lugoj Bacau
```

Sample Output

```
Test Case 1.
There is no route Vladimir can take.
Test Case 2.
Vladimir needs 2 litre(s) of blood.
```

9.6.8 Hanoi Tower Troubles Again!

PC/UVa IDs: 110908/10276, **Popularity:** B, **Success rate:** high **Level:** 3

There are many interesting variations on the Tower of Hanoi problem. This version consists of N pegs and one ball containing each number from $1, 2, 3, \ldots, \infty$. Whenever the sum of the numbers on two balls is *not* a perfect square (i.e., c^2 for some integer c), they will repel each other with such force that they can never touch each other.

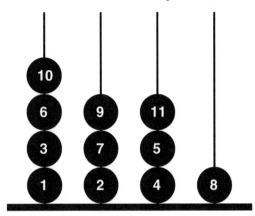

The player must place balls on the pegs one by one, in order of increasing ball number (i.e., first ball 1, then ball 2, then ball 3...). The game ends where there is no non-repelling move.

The goal is to place as many balls on the pegs as possible. The figure above gives a best possible result for 4 pegs.

Input

The first line of the input contains a single integer T indicating the number of test cases $(1 \le T \le 50)$. Each test case contains a single integer N $(1 \le N \le 50)$ indicating the number of pegs available.

Output

For each test case, print a line containing an integer indicating the maximum number of balls that can be placed. Print "-1" if an infinite number of balls can be placed.

Sample Input	Sample Output
2	11
4	337
25	

9.7   Hints

9.1 Can we color the graph during a single traversal?

9.2 What is the graph underlying this problem?

9.3 Can we reduce this problem to connectivity testing?

9.4 Does it pay to represent the graph explicitly, or just work on the matrix of slashes?

9.5 What is the graph underlying this problem?

9.6 Can we define a directed graph on the cubes such that the desired tower is a path in the graph?

9.7 Can this be represented as an *unweighted* graph problem for BFS?

9.8 Can the constraints be usefully modeled using a DAG?

10
Graph Algorithms

The graph representations and traversal algorithms of Chapter 9 provide the basic building blocks for any computation on graph structures. In this chapter, we consider more advanced graph theory and algorithms.

Graph theory is the study of the properties of graph structures. It provides us with a language with which to talk about graphs. The key to solving many problems is identifying the fundamental graph-theoretic notion underlying the situation and then using classical algorithms to solve the resulting problem.

We begin with a overview of basic graph theory and follow with algorithms for finding important structures such as minimum spanning trees, shortest paths, and maximum flows.

10.1   Graph Theory

In this section, we provide a quick review of basic graph theory. Several excellent books on graph theory [PS03, Wes00] are available for more detailed information. We outline relevant algorithms which should be fairly simple to program given the machinery developed in the previous chapter.

10.1.1   Degree Properties

Graphs are made up of vertices and edges. The simplest property of a vertex is its *degree*, the number of edges incident upon it.

There are several important properties of vertex degrees. The sum of the vertex degrees in any undirected graph is twice the number of edges, since every edge contributes one to the degree of both adjacent vertices. A corollary to this is that every graph contains an even number of odd degree vertices. For directed graphs, the relevant degree condition is that the sum of the in-degrees of all vertices equals the sum of all out-degrees. The parity of vertex degrees has an important role in recognizing Eulerian cycles as discussed in Section 10.1.3.

Trees are undirected graphs which contain no cycles. Vertex degrees are important in the analysis of trees. A *leaf* of a tree is a vertex of degree 1. Every n-vertex tree contains $n-1$ edges, so all non-trivial trees contain at least two leaf vertices. Deleting a leaf leaves a smaller tree, trimming the tree instead of disconnecting it.

Rooted trees are directed graphs where every node except the root has in-degree 1. The leaves are the nodes with out-degree 0. *Binary trees* are rooted trees where every vertex has an out-degree of 0 or 2. At least half the vertices of all such binary trees must be leaves.

A *spanning tree* of a graph $G = (V, E)$ is a subset of edges $E' \subset E$ such that E' is a tree on V. Spanning trees exist for any connected graph; the parent relation encoding vertex discovery for either breadth-first or depth-first search suffices to construct one. The *minimum spanning tree* is an important property of weighted graphs, and discussed in Section 10.2.

10.1.2   Connectivity

A graph is *connected* if there is an undirected path between every pair of vertices. The existence of a spanning tree is sufficient to prove connectivity. A depth-first search-based connected components algorithm was presented in Section 9.4.2.

However, there are other notions of connectivity to be aware of. The *vertex (edge) connectivity* is the smallest number of vertices (edges) which must be deleted to disconnect the graph. The most interesting special case when there is a single weak link in the graph. A single vertex whose deletion disconnects the graph is called an *articulation vertex*; any graph without such a vertex is said to be *biconnected*. A single edge whose deletion disconnects the graph is called a *bridge*; any graph without such an edge is said to be *edge-biconnected*.

Testing for articulation vertices or bridges is easy via brute force. For each vertex/edge, delete it from the graph and test whether the resulting graph remains connected. Be sure to add that vertex/edge back before doing the next deletion!

In directed graphs we are often concerned with *strongly connected components*, that is, partitioning the graph into chunks such that there are directed paths between all pairs of vertices within a given chunk. Road networks should be strongly connected, or else there will be places you can drive to but not drive home from without violating one-way signs.

The following idea enables us to identify the strongly connected components in a graph. It is easy to find a directed cycle using depth-first search, since any back edge plus the down path in the DFS tree gives such a cycle. All vertices in this cycle must be in the same strongly connected component. Thus we can shrink (contract) the vertices on this cycle down to a single vertex representing the component, and then repeat. This process terminates when no directed cycle remains, and each vertex represents one strongly connected component.

10.1.3 Cycles in Graphs

All non-tree connected graphs contain cycles. Particularly interesting are cycles which visit all the edges or vertices of the graph.

An *Eulerian cycle* is a tour which visits every edge of the graph exactly once. The children's puzzle of drawing a geometric figure without ever lifting your pencil from the paper is an instance of finding an Eulerian cycle (or path), where the vertices are the junctions in the drawing and the edges represent the lines to trace. A mailman's route is ideally an Eulerian cycle, so he can visit every street (edge) in the neighborhood once before returning home. Strictly speaking, Eulerian cycles are *circuits*, not cycles, because they may visit vertices more than once.

An undirected graph contains an Eulerian cycle if it is connected and every vertex is of even degree. Why? The circuit must enter and exit every vertex it encounters, implying that all degrees must be even. This idea also suggests a way to find an Eulerian cycle, by building it one cycle at a time. We can find a simple cycle in the graph using the DFS-based algorithm discussed in Section 9.4.1. Deleting the edges on this cycle leaves each vertex with even degree. Once we have partitioned the edges into edge-disjoint cycles, we can merge these cycles arbitrarily at common vertices to build an Eulerian cycle.

In the case of directed graphs, the relevant condition is that all vertices have the same in-degree as out-degree. Peeling off any cycle preserves this property, and thus Eulerian cycles of directed graphs can be built in the same manner. *Eulerian paths* are tours that visit every edge exactly once but might not end up where they started from. These allow exactly two vertices to have parity violations, one of which must be the starting node and the other the ending node.

A *Hamiltonian cycle* is a tour which visits every vertex of the graph exactly once. The traveling salesman problem asks for the shortest such tour on a weighted graph. An Eulerian cycle problem in $G = (V, E)$ can be reduced to a Hamiltonian cycle problem by constructing a graph $G' = (V', E')$ such that each vertex in V' represents an edge of E and there are edges in E' connecting all neighboring pair of edges from G.

Unfortunately, no efficient algorithm exists for solving Hamiltonian cycle problems. Thus you have two options on encountering one. If the graph is sufficiently small, it can be solved via backtracking. Each Hamiltonian cycle is described by a permutation of the vertices. We backtrack whenever there does not exist an edge from the latest vertex to an unvisited one. If the graph is too large for such an attack we must try to find an alternate formulation of the problem, perhaps as an Eulerian cycle problem on a different graph.

10.1.4 Planar Graphs

Planar graphs are those which can be drawn in the plane such that no two edges cross each other. Many of the graphs we commonly encounter are planar. Every tree is planar: can you describe how to construct a non-crossing drawing for a given tree? Every road network in the absence of concrete/steel bridges must be planar. The adjacency structure of convex polyhedra also yield planar graphs.

Planar graphs have several important properties. First, there is a tight relation between the number of vertices n, edges m, and faces f of any planar graph. *Euler's formula* states that $n - m + f = 2$. Trees contain $n - 1$ edges, so any planar drawing of a tree has exactly one face, namely, the outside face. Any embedding of a cube (8 vertices and 12 edges) must contain six faces, as those who have played dice can attest to.

Efficient algorithms exist for testing the planarity of a graph and finding non-crossing embeddings, but all are fairly complicated to implement. Euler's formula gives an easy way to prove that certain graphs are *not* planar, however. Every planar graph contains at most $3n - 6$ edges for $n > 2$. This bound means that every planar graph must contain a vertex of degree at most 5, and deleting this vertex leaves a smaller planar graph with this same property. Testing whether a given drawing is a planar embedding is the same as testing whether any of a given set of line segments intersect, which will be discussed when we get to geometric algorithms.

10.2 Minimum Spanning Trees

A *spanning tree* of a graph $G = (V, E)$ is a subset of edges from E forming a tree connecting all vertices of V. For edge-weighted graphs, we are particularly interested in the *minimum spanning tree*, the spanning tree whose sum of edge weights is the smallest possible.

Minimum spanning trees are the answer whenever we need to connect a set of points (representing cities, junctions, or other locations) by the smallest amount of roadway, wire, or pipe. Any tree is the smallest possible connected graph in terms of number of edges, while the minimum spanning tree is the smallest connected graph in terms of edge weight.

The two main algorithms for computing minimum spanning trees are Kruskal's and Prim's, and both are covered in most any algorithms course. We will present Prim's algorithm here because we think it is simpler to program, and because it gives us Dijkstra's shortest path algorithm with very minimal changes.

First, we must generalize the graph data structure from Chapter 9 to support edge-weighted graphs. Each edge-entry previously contained only the other endpoint of the given edge. We must replace this by a record allowing us to annotate the edge with weights:

```
typedef struct {
        int v;                          /* neighboring vertex */
```

```
        int weight;                          /* edge weight */
} edge;

typedef struct {
        edge edges[MAXV+1][MAXDEGREE];   /* adjacency info */
        int degree[MAXV+1];              /* outdegree of each vertex */
        int nvertices;                   /* number of vertices in graph */
        int nedges;                      /* number of edges in graph */
} graph;
```

and update the various initialization and traversal algorithms appropriately. This is not a complicated task.

Prim's algorithm grows the minimum spanning tree in stages starting from a given vertex. At each iteration, we add one new vertex into the spanning tree. A greedy algorithm suffices for correctness: we always add the lowest-weight edge linking a vertex in the tree to a vertex on the outside.

The simplest implementation of this idea would assign each vertex a Boolean variable denoting whether it is already in the tree (the array **intree** in the code below), and then searches all edges at each iteration to find the minimum weight edge with exactly one **intree** vertex.

Our implementation is somewhat smarter. It keeps track of the cheapest edge from any tree vertex to every non-tree vertex in the graph. The cheapest edge over all remaining non-tree vertices gets added in each iteration. We must update the costs of getting to the non-tree vertices after each insertion. However, since the new vertex is the only change in the tree all possible edge-weight updates come from its outgoing edges:

```
prim(graph *g, int start)
{
        int i,j;                          /* counters */
        bool intree[MAXV];                /* is vertex in the tree yet? */
        int distance[MAXV];               /* vertex distance from start */
        int v;                            /* current vertex to process */
        int w;                            /* candidate next vertex */
        int weight;                       /* edge weight */
        int dist;                         /* shortest current distance */

        for (i=1; i<=g->nvertices; i++) {
                intree[i] = FALSE;
                distance[i] = MAXINT;
                parent[i] = -1;
        }

        distance[start] = 0;
        v = start;
```

```
while (intree[v] == FALSE) {
    intree[v] = TRUE;
    for (i=0; i<g->degree[v]; i++) {
        w = g->edges[v][i].v;
        weight = g->edges[v][i].weight;
        if ((distance[w] > weight) && (intree[w]==FALSE)) {
                distance[w] = weight;
                parent[w] = v;
        }
    }

    v = 1;
    dist = MAXINT;
    for (i=2; i<=g->nvertices; i++)
        if ((intree[i]==FALSE) && (dist > distance[i])) {
                dist = distance[i];
                v = i;
        }
}
}
```

The minimum spanning tree itself or its cost can be reconstructed in two different ways. The simplest method would be to augment this procedure with statements that print the edges as they are found or total the weight of all selected edges in a variable for later return. Alternately, since the tree topology is encoded by the **parent** array it plus the original graph tells you everything about the minimum spanning tree.

This minimum spanning tree algorithm has several interesting properties which help solve many closely related problems:

- *Maximum Spanning Trees* — Suppose we hire an evil telephone company to connect a bunch of houses together, and that this company will be paid a price proportional to the amount of wire they install. Naturally, they will want to build as expensive a spanning tree as possible. The *maximum spanning tree* of any graph can be found by simply negating the weights of all edges and running Prim's algorithm. The most negative tree in the negated graph is the maximum spanning tree in the original.

    Most graph algorithms do not adapt so nicely to negative numbers. Indeed, shortest path algorithms have trouble with negative numbers, and certainly do *not* generate the longest possible path using this technique.

- *Minimum Product Spanning Trees* — Suppose we want the spanning tree with the smallest product of edge weights, assuming all edge weights are positive. Since $\lg(a \cdot b) = \lg(a) + \lg(b)$, the minimum spanning tree on a graph where each edge weight is replaced with its logarithm gives the minimum product spanning tree.

- *Minimum Bottleneck Spanning Tree* — Sometimes we seek a spanning tree which minimizes the maximum edge weight over all such trees. In fact, the minimum spanning tree has this property. The proof follows directly from the correctness of Kruskal's algorithm.

  Such bottleneck spanning trees have interesting applications when the edge weights are interpreted as costs, capacities, or strengths. A less efficient but simpler way to solve such problems might be to delete all "heavy" edges from the graph and ask whether the result is still connected. These kind of tests can be done with simple BFS/DFS.

The minimum spanning tree of a graph is unique if all m edge weights in the graph are distinct. If not, the order in which Prim's algorithm breaks ties determines which minimum spanning tree the algorithm returns.

10.3   Shortest Paths

The problem of finding shortest paths in unweighted graphs was discussed in Section 9.3.1; breadth-first search does the job, and that is all she wrote. BFS does *not* suffice for finding shortest paths in weighted graphs, because the shortest weighted path from a to b does not necessarily contain the fewest number of edges. We all have favorite back-door driving/walking routes which use more turns than the simplest path, but which magically get us there faster by avoiding traffic, lights, etc.

In this section, we will implement two distinct algorithms for finding shortest paths in weighted graphs.

10.3.1   Dijkstra's Algorithm

Dijkstra's algorithm is the method of choice for finding the shortest path between two vertices in an edge- and/or vertex-weighted graph. Given a particular start vertex s, it finds the shortest path from s to every other vertex in the graph, including your desired destination t.

The basic idea is very similar to Prim's algorithm. In each iteration, we are going to add exactly one vertex to the tree of vertices for which we *know* the shortest path from s. Just as in Prim's, we will keep track of the best path seen to date for all vertices outside the tree, and insert them in order of increasing cost.

The difference between Dijkstra's and Prim's algorithms is how they rate the desirability of each outside vertex. In the minimum spanning tree problem, all we care about is the weight of the next potential tree edge. In shortest path, we want to include the outside vertex which is closest (in shortest-path distance) to the start. This is a function of both the new edge weight *and* the distance from the start of the tree-vertex it is adjacent to.

In fact, this change is very minor. Below we give an implementation of Dijkstra's algorithm based on changing exactly three lines from our Prim's implementation – one of which is simply the name of the function!

```
dijkstra(graph *g, int start)          /* WAS prim(g,start) */
{
        int i,j;                       /* counters */
        bool intree[MAXV];             /* is vertex in the tree yet? */
        int distance[MAXV];            /* vertex distance from start */
        int v;                         /* current vertex to process */
        int w;                         /* candidate next vertex */
        int weight;                    /* edge weight */
        int dist;                      /* shortest current distance */

        for (i=1; i<=g->nvertices; i++) {
                intree[i] = FALSE;
                distance[i] = MAXINT;
                parent[i] = -1;
        }

        distance[start] = 0;
        v = start;

        while (intree[v] == FALSE) {
            intree[v] = TRUE;
            for (i=0; i<g->degree[v]; i++) {
                w = g->edges[v][i].v;
                weight = g->edges[v][i].weight;
/* CHANGED */   if (distance[w] > (distance[v]+weight)) {
/* CHANGED */           distance[w] = distance[v]+weight;
                        parent[w] = v;
                }
            }

            v = 1;
            dist = MAXINT;
            for (i=2; i<=g->nvertices; i++)
                if ((intree[i]==FALSE) && (dist > distance[i])) {
                        dist = distance[i];
                        v = i;
                }
        }
}
```

How do we use dijkstra to find the length of the shortest path from start to a given vertex t? This is exactly the value of distance[t]. How can we reconstruct the actual path? By following the backward parent pointers from t until we hit start (or -1 if no such path exists), exactly as was done in the find_path() routine of Section 9.3.3.

Unlike Prim's, Dijkstra's algorithm only works on graphs without negative-cost edges. The reason is that midway through the execution we may encounter an edge with weight so negative that it changes the cheapest way to get from s to some other vertex already in the tree. Indeed, the most cost-effective way to get from your house to your next-door neighbor would be through the lobby of any bank offering you enough money to make the detour worthwhile.

Most applications do not feature negative-weight edges, making this discussion academic. Floyd's algorithm, discussed below, works correctly unless there are negative cost cycles, which grossly distort the shortest-path structure. Unless that bank limits its reward to one per customer, you could so benefit by making an infinite number of trips through the lobby that it would *never* pay to actually reach your destination!

10.3.2 All-Pairs Shortest Path

Many applications need to know the length of the shortest path between all pairs of vertices in a given graph. For example, suppose you want to find the "center" vertex, the one which minimizes the longest or average distance to all the other nodes. This might be the best place to start a new business. Or perhaps you need to know the *diameter* of the graph, the longest shortest-path distance between all pairs of vertices. This might correspond to the longest possible time it takes a letter or network packet to be delivered between two arbitrary destinations.

We could solve this problem by calling Dijkstra's algorithm from each of the n possible starting vertices. But Floyd's all-pairs shortest-path algorithm is an amazingly slick way to construct this distance matrix from the original weight matrix of the graph.

Floyd's algorithm is best employed on an adjacency matrix data structure, which is no extravagance since we have to store all n^2 pairwise distances anyway. Our adjacency_matrix type allocates space for the largest possible matrix, and keeps track of how many vertices are in the graph:

```
typedef struct {
        int weight[MAXV+1][MAXV+1];    /* adjacency/weight info */
        int nvertices;                 /* number of vertices in graph */
} adjacency_matrix;
```

A critical issue in any adjacency matrix implementation is how we denote the edges which are not present in the graph. For unweighted graphs, a common convention is that graph edges are denoted by 1 and non-edges by 0. This gives exactly the wrong interpretation if the numbers denote edge weights, for the non-edges get interpreted as a free ride between vertices. Instead, we should initialize each non-edge to MAXINT. This way we can both test whether it is present and automatically ignore it in shortest-path computations, since only real edges will be used unless MAXINT is less than the diameter of your graph.

```
initialize_adjacency_matrix(adjacency_matrix *g)
{
        int i,j;                        /* counters */
```

```
        g -> nvertices = 0;

        for (i=1; i<=MAXV; i++)
                for (j=1; j<=MAXV; j++)
                        g->weight[i][j] = MAXINT;
}

read_adjacency_matrix(adjacency_matrix *g, bool directed)
{
        int i;                          /* counter */
        int m;                          /* number of edges */
        int x,y,w;                      /* placeholder for edge/weight */

        initialize_adjacency_matrix(g);

        scanf("%d %d\n",&(g->nvertices),&m);

        for (i=1; i<=m; i++) {
                scanf("%d %d %d\n",&x,&y,&w);
                g->weight[x][y] = w;
                if (directed==FALSE) g->weight[y][x] = w;
        }
}
```

All this is fairly trivial. How do we find shortest paths in such a matrix? Floyd's algorithm starts by numbering the vertices of the graph from 1 to n, using these numbers not to label the vertices but to order them.

We will perform n iterations, where the kth iteration allows only the first k vertices as possible intermediate steps on the path between each pair of vertices x and y. When $k = 0$, we are allowed no intermediate vertices, so the only allowed paths consist of the original edges in the graph. Thus the initial all-pairs shortest-path matrix consists of the initial adjacency matrix. At each iteration, we allow a richer set of possible shortest paths. Allowing the kth vertex as a new possible intermediary helps only if there is a short path that goes through k, so

$$W[i,j]^k = \min(W[i,j]^{k-1}, W[i,k]^{k-1} + W[k,j]^{k-1})$$

The correctness of this is somewhat subtle, and we encourage you to convince yourself of it. But there is nothing subtle about how short and sweet the implementation is:

```
floyd(adjacency_matrix *g)
{
        int i,j;                        /* dimension counters */
        int k;                          /* intermediate vertex counter */
        int through_k;                  /* distance through vertex k */
```

```
for (k=1; k<=g->nvertices; k++)
      for (i=1; i<=g->nvertices; i++)
            for (j=1; j<=g->nvertices; j++) {
                  through_k = g->weight[i][k]+g->weight[k][j];
                  if (through_k < g->weight[i][j])
                        g->weight[i][j] = through_k;
            }
}
```

The output of Floyd's algorithm, as it is written, does not enable one to reconstruct the actual shortest path between any given pair of vertices. Use Dijkstra's algorithm if you care about the actual path. Note, however, that most all-pairs applications need only the resulting distance matrix. These jobs are what Floyd's algorithm was designed for.

Floyd's algorithm has another important application, that of computing the *transitive closure* of a directed graph. In analyzing a directed graph, we are often interested in which vertices are reachable from a given node.

For example, consider the *blackmail graph* defined on a set of n people, where there is a directed edge (i, j) if i has sensitive-enough private information on j so that i can get him to do whatever he wants. You wish to hire one of these n people to be your personal representative. Who has the most power in terms of blackmail potential?

A simplistic answer would be the vertex of highest degree, but an even better representative would be the person who has blackmail chains to the most other parties. Steve might only be able to blackmail Miguel directly, but if Miguel can blackmail everyone else then Steve is the man you want to hire.

The vertices reachable from any single node can be computed using using breadth-first or depth-first search. But the whole batch can be computed as an all-pairs shortest-path problem. If the shortest path from i to j remains MAXINT after running Floyd's algorithm, you can be sure there is no directed path from i to j. Any vertex pair of weight less than MAXINT must be reachable, both in the graph-theoretic and blackmail senses of the word.

10.4   Network Flows and Bipartite Matching

Any edge-weighted graph can be thought of as a network of pipes, where the weight of edge (i, j) measures the *capacity* of the pipe. Capacities can be thought of as a function of the cross-sectional area of the pipe – a wide pipe might be able to carry 10 units of flow in a given time where a narrower pipe might only be able to carry 5 units. For a given weighted graph G and two vertices s and t, the *network flow problem* asks for the maximum amount of flow which can be sent from s to t while respecting the maximum capacities of each pipe.

While the network flow problem is of independent interest, its primary importance is that of being able to solve other important graph problems. A classic example is bipartite matching. A *matching* in a graph $G = (V, E)$ is a subset of edges $E' \subset E$ such that no two edges in E' share a vertex. Thus a matching pairs off certain vertices such that every vertex is in at most one such pair.

Graph G is *bipartite* or *two-colorable* if the vertices can be divided into two sets, say, L and R, such that all edges in G have one vertex in L and one vertex in R. Many naturally defined graphs are bipartite. For example, suppose certain vertices represent jobs to be done and the remaining vertices people who can potentially do them. The existence of edge (j, p) means that job j can potentially done by person p. Or let certain vertices represent boys and certain vertices girls, with edges representing compatible pairs. Matchings in these graphs have natural interpretations as job assignments or as marriages.

The largest possible bipartite matching can be found using network flow. Create a *source* node s which is connected to every vertex in L by an edge of weight 1. Create a *sink* node t which is connected to every vertex in R by an edge of weight 1. Assign every edge in the bipartite graph G a weight of 1. Now, the maximum possible flow from s to t defines the largest matching in G. Certainly we can find a flow as large as the matching, by taking exactly the matching edges and their source-to-sink connections. Further, there can be no greater possible flow. How can we ever hope to get more than one flow unit through any vertex?

The simplest network flow algorithm to implement is the Ford-Fulkerson augmenting path algorithm. For each edge, we will keep track of both the amount of flow currently going through the edge as well as its remaining *residual* capacity. Thus we must modify our `edge` structure to accommodate the extra fields:

```
typedef struct {
        int v;                          /* neighboring vertex */
        int capacity;                   /* capacity of edge */
        int flow;                       /* flow through edge */
        int residual;                   /* residual capacity of edge */
} edge;
```

We look for any path from source to sink that increases the total flow and use it to augment the total. We terminate on the optimal flow when no such *augmenting* path exists.

```
netflow(flow_graph *g, int source, int sink)
{
        int volume;             /* weight of the augmenting path */

        add_residual_edges(g);

        initialize_search(g);
        bfs(g,source);

        volume = path_volume(g, source, sink, parent);

        while (volume > 0) {
```

```
                augment_path(g,source,sink,parent,volume);
                initialize_search(g);
                bfs(g,source);
                volume = path_volume(g, source, sink, parent);
        }
}
```

Any augmenting path from source to sink increases the flow, so we can use `bfs` to find such a path in the appropriate graph. We are only allowed to walk along network edges which have remaining capacity or, in other words, positive residual flow. We use this predicate to help `bfs` distinguish between saturated and unsaturated edges:

```
bool valid_edge(edge e)
{
        if (e.residual > 0) return (TRUE);
        else return(FALSE);
}
```

Augmenting a path transfers the maximum possible volume from the residual capacity into positive flow. The amount we can move is limited by the path-edge with the smallest amount of residual capacity, just as the rate at which traffic can flow is limited by the most congested point.

```
int path_volume(flow_graph *g, int start, int end, int parents[])
{
        edge *e;                           /* edge in question */
        edge *find_edge();

        if (parents[end] == -1) return(0);

        e = find_edge(g,parents[end],end);

        if (start == parents[end])
                return(e->residual);
        else
                return( min(path_volume(g,start,parents[end],parents),
                        e->residual) );
}

edge *find_edge(flow_graph *g, int x, int y)
{
        int i;                             /* counter */

        for (i=0; i<g->degree[x]; i++)
                if (g->edges[x][i].v == y)
                        return( &g->edges[x][i] );
```

```
        return(NULL);
}
```

Sending an additional unit of flow along directed edge (i, j) reduces the residual capacity of edge (i, j) but *increases* the residual capacity of edge (j, i). Thus the act of augmenting a path requires looking up both forward and reverse edges for each link on the path.

```
augment_path(flow_graph *g, int start, int end, int parents[], int volume)
{
        edge *e;                          /* edge in question */
        edge *find_edge();

        if (start == end) return;

        e = find_edge(g,parents[end],end);
        e->flow += volume;
        e->residual -= volume;

        e = find_edge(g,end,parents[end]);
        e->residual += volume;

        augment_path(g,start,parents[end],parents,volume);
}
```

Initializing the flow graph requires creating directed flow edges (i, j) and (j, i) for each network edge $e = (i, j)$. The initial flows are all set to 0. The initial residual flow of (i, j) is set to the capacity of e, while the initial residual flow of (j, i) is set to 0.

Network flows are an advanced algorithmic technique, and recognizing whether a particular problem can be solved by network flow requires experience. We point the reader to books by Cook and Cunningham [CC97] and Ahuja, Magnanti, and Orlin [AMO93] for more detailed treatments of the subject.

10.5 Problems

10.5.1 Freckles

PC/UVa IDs: 111001/10034, **Popularity:** B, **Success rate:** average **Level:** 2

In an episode of the Dick Van Dyke show, little Richie connects the freckles on his Dad's back to form a picture of the Liberty Bell. Alas, one of the freckles turns out to be a scar, so his Ripley's engagement falls through.

Consider Dick's back to be a plane with freckles at various (x, y) locations. Your job is to tell Richie how to connect the dots so as to minimize the amount of ink used. Richie connects the dots by drawing straight lines between pairs, possibly lifting the pen between lines. When Richie is done there must be a sequence of connected lines from any freckle to any other freckle.

Input

The input begins with a single positive integer on a line by itself indicating the number of test cases, followed by a blank line.

The first line of each test case contains $0 < n \le 100$, giving the number of freckles on Dick's back. For each freckle, a line follows; each following line contains two real numbers indicating the (x, y) coordinates of the freckle.

There is a blank line between each two consecutive test cases.

Output

For each test case, your program must print a single real number to two decimal places: the minimum total length of ink lines that can connect all the freckles. The output of each two consecutive cases must be separated by a blank line.

Sample Input

```
1

3
1.0 1.0
2.0 2.0
2.0 4.0
```

Sample Output

```
3.41
```

10.5.2   The Necklace

PC/UVa IDs: 111002/10054, **Popularity:** B, **Success rate:** low   **Level:** 3

My little sister had a beautiful necklace made of colorful beads. Each two successive beads in the necklace shared a common color at their meeting point, as shown below:

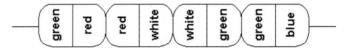

But, alas! One day, the necklace tore and the beads were scattered all over the floor. My sister did her best to pick up all the beads, but she is not sure whether she found them all. Now she has come to me for help. She wants to know whether it is possible to make a necklace using all the beads she has in the same way that her original necklace was made. If so, how can the beads be so arranged?

Write a program to solve the problem.

Input

The first line of the input contains the integer T, giving the number of test cases. The first line of each test case contains an integer N ($5 \leq N \leq 1,000$) giving the number of beads my sister found. Each of the next N lines contains two integers describing the colors of a bead. Colors are represented by integers ranging from 1 to 50.

Output

For each test case, print the test case number as shown in the sample output. If reconstruction is impossible, print the sentence "some beads may be lost" on a line by itself. Otherwise, print N lines, each with a single bead description such that for $1 \leq i \leq N - 1$, the second integer on line i must be the same as the first integer on line $i + 1$. Additionally, the second integer on line N must be equal to the first integer on line 1. There may be many solutions, any one of which is acceptable.

Print a blank line between two successive test cases.

Sample Input

```
2
5
1 2
2 3
3 4
4 5
5 6
5
2 1
```

```
2 2
3 4
3 1
2 4
```

Sample Output

```
Case #1
some beads may be lost

Case #2
2 1
1 3
3 4
4 2
2 2
```

10.5.3   Fire Station

PC/UVa IDs: 111003/10278, **Popularity:** B, **Success rate:** low **Level:** 2

A city is served by a number of fire stations. Residents have complained that the distance between certain houses and the nearest station is too far, so a new station is to be built. You are to choose the location of the new station so as to reduce the distance to the nearest station from the houses of the poorest-served residents.

The city has up to 500 intersections, connected by road segments of various lengths. No more than 20 road segments intersect at a given intersection. The locations of houses and fire stations alike are considered to be at intersections. Furthermore, we assume that there is at least one house associated with every intersection. There may be more than one fire station per intersection.

Input

The input begins with a single line indicating the number of test cases, followed by a blank line. There will also be a blank line between each two consecutive inputs.

The first line of input contains two positive integers: the number of existing fire stations f ($f \leq 100$) and the number of intersections i ($i \leq 500$). Intersections are numbered from 1 to i consecutively. Then f lines follow, each containing the intersection number at which an existing fire station is found. A number of lines follow, each containing three positive integers: the number of an intersection, the number of a different intersection, and the length of the road segment connecting the intersections. All road segments are two-way (at least as far as fire engines are concerned), and there will exist a route between any pair of intersections.

Output

For each test case, output the lowest intersection number at which a new fire station can be built so as to minimize the maximum distance from any intersection to its nearest fire station. Separate the output of each two consecutive cases by a blank line.

Sample Input

```
1

1 6
2
1 2 10
2 3 10
3 4 10
4 5 10
5 6 10
6 1 10
```

Sample Output

```
5
```

10.5.4 Railroads

PC/UVa IDs: 111004/10039, **Popularity:** C, **Success rate:** average **Level:** 3

Tomorrow morning Jill must travel from Hamburg to Darmstadt to compete in the regional programming contest. Since she is afraid of arriving late and being excluded from the contest, she is looking for the train which gets her to Darmstadt as early as possible. However, she dislikes getting to the station too early, so if there are several schedules with the same arrival time then she will choose the one with the latest departure time.

Jill asks you to help her with her problem. You are given a set of railroad schedules from which you must compute the train with the earliest arrival time and the fastest connection from one location to another. Fortunately, Jill is very experienced in changing trains and can do this instantaneously, i.e., in zero time!

Input

The very first line of the input gives the number of scenarios. Each scenario consists of three parts. The first part lists the names of all cities connected by the railroads. It starts with a number $1 < C \leq 100$, followed by C lines containing city names. All names consist only of letters.

The second part describes all the trains running during a day. It starts with a number $T \leq 1,000$ followed by T train descriptions. Each of them consists of one line with a number $t_i \leq 100$ and then t_i more lines, each with a time and a city name, meaning that passengers can get on or off the train at that time at that city.

The final part consists of three lines: the first containing the earliest possible starting time, the second the name of the city where she starts, and the third with the destination city. The start and destination cities are always different.

Output

For each scenario print a line containing "`Scenario` i", where i is the scenario number starting from 1.

If a connection exists, print the two lines containing zero padded timestamps and locations as shown in the example. Use blanks to achieve the indentation. If no connection exists on the same day (i.e., arrival before midnight), print a line containing "`No connection`".

Print a blank line after each scenario.

Sample Input

```
2
3
Hamburg
Frankfurt
```

```
Darmstadt
3
2
0949 Hamburg
1006 Frankfurt
2
1325 Hamburg
1550 Darmstadt
2
1205 Frankfurt
1411 Darmstadt
0800
Hamburg
Darmstadt
2
Paris
Tokyo
1
2
0100 Paris
2300 Tokyo
0800
Paris
Tokyo
```

Sample Output

```
Scenario 1
Departure 0949 Hamburg
Arrival   1411 Darmstadt

Scenario 2
No connection
```

10.5.5   War

PC/UVa IDs: 111005/10158, **Popularity:** B, **Success rate:** average **Level:** 3

A war is being fought between two countries, A and B. As a loyal citizen of C, you decide to help your country by secretly attending the peace talks between A and B. There are n other people at the talks, but you do not know which person belongs to which country. You can see people talking to each other, and by observing their behavior during occasional one-to-one conversations you can guess if they are friends or enemies.

Your country needs to know whether certain pairs of people are from the same country, or whether they are enemies. You can expect to receive such questions from your government during the peace talks, and will have to give replies on the basis of your observations so far.

Now, more formally, consider a black box with the following operations:

setFriends(x,y)	shows that x and y are from the same country
setEnemies(x,y)	shows that x and y are from different countries
areFriends(x,y)	returns true if you are sure that x and y are friends
areEnemies(x,y)	returns true if you are sure that x and y are enemies

The first two operations should signal an error if they contradict your former knowledge. The two relations "friends" (denoted by $\sim$) and "enemies" (denoted by $*$) have the following properties:

$\sim$ is an equivalence relation: i.e.,

1. If $x \sim y$ and $y \sim z$, then $x \sim z$ (The friends of my friends are my friends as well.)
2. If $x \sim y$, then $y \sim x$ (Friendship is mutual.)
3. $x \sim x$ (Everyone is a friend of himself.)

$*$ is symmetric and irreflexive:

1. If $x * y$ then $y * x$ (Hatred is mutual.)
2. Not $x * x$ (Nobody is an enemy of himself.)
3. If $x * y$ and $y * z$ then $x \sim z$ (A common enemy makes two people friends.)
4. If $x \sim y$ and $y * z$ then $x * z$ (An enemy of a friend is an enemy.)

Operations setFriends(x,y) and setEnemies(x,y) must preserve these properties.

Input

The first line contains a single integer, n, the number of people. Each subsequent line contains a triple of integers, $c\ x\ y$, where c is the code of the operation,

$c = 1$,	setFriends
$c = 2$,	setEnemies
$c = 3$,	areFriends
$c = 4$,	areEnemies

and x and y are its parameters, integers in the range $[0, n)$ identifying two different people. The last line contains 0 0 0.

All integers in the input file are separated by at least one space or line break. There are at most 10,000 people, but the number of operations is unconstrained.

Output

For every `areFriends` and `areEnemies` operation write "0" (meaning no) or "1" (meaning yes) to the output. For every `setFriends` or `setEnemies` operation which conflicts with previous knowledge, output a "-1" to the output; such an operation should produce no other effect and execution should continue. A successful `setFriends` or `setEnemies` gives no output.

All integers in the output file must be separated by one line break.

Sample Input

```
10
1 0 1
1 1 2
2 0 5
3 0 2
3 8 9
4 1 5
4 1 2
4 8 9
1 8 9
1 5 2
3 5 2
0 0 0
```

Sample Output

```
1
0
1
0
0
-1
0
```

10.5.6   Tourist Guide

PC/UVa IDs: 111006/10199, **Popularity:** B, **Success rate:** average **Level:** 3

Rio de Janeiro is a very beautiful city, but there are so many places to visit that sometimes you feel overwhelmed, Fortunately, your friend Bruno has promised to be your tour guide.

Unfortunately, Bruno is terrible driver. He has a lot of traffic fines to pay and is eager to avoid paying more. Therefore he wants to know where all the police cameras are located so he can drive more carefully when passing by them. These cameras are strategically distributed over the city, in locations that a driver must pass through in order to travel from one zone of the city to another. A location C will have a camera if and only if there are two city locations A and B such that all paths from A to B pass through a location C.

For instance, suppose that we have six locations (A, B, C, D, E, and F) with seven bidirectional routes $B - C$, $A - B$, $C - A$, $D - C$, $D - E$, $E - F$, and $F - C$. There must be a camera on C because to go from A to E you must pass through C. In this configuration, C is the only camera location.

Given a map of the city, help Bruno avoid further fines during your tour by writing a program to identify where all the cameras are.

Input

The input will consist of an arbitrary number of city maps, where each map begins with an integer N ($2 < N \leq 100$) denoting the total number of locations in the city. Then follow N different place names at one per line, where each place name will consist of least one and at most 30 lowercase letters. A non-negative integer R then follows, denoting the total routes of the city. The next R lines each describe a bidirectional route represented by the two places that the route connects.

Location names in route descriptions will always be valid, and there will be no route from one place to itself. You must read until $N = 0$, which should not be processed.

Output

For each city map you must print the following line:

`City map #d: c camera(s) found`

where d stands for the city map number (starting from 1) and c stands for the total number of cameras. Then should follow c lines with the location names of each camera in alphabetical order. Print a blank line between output sets.

Sample Input

```
6
sugarloaf
```

```
maracana
copacabana
ipanema
corcovado
lapa
7
ipanema copacabana
copacabana sugarloaf
ipanema sugarloaf
maracana lapa
sugarloaf maracana
corcovado sugarloaf
lapa corcovado
5
guanabarabay
downtown
botanicgarden
colombo
sambodromo
4
guanabarabay sambodromo
downtown sambodromo
sambodromo botanicgarden
colombo sambodromo
0
```

Sample Output

```
City map #1: 1 camera(s) found
sugarloaf

City map #2: 1 camera(s) found
sambodromo
```

10.5.7   The Grand Dinner

PC/UVa IDs: 111007/10249, **Popularity:** C, **Success rate:** high **Level:** 4

Each team participating in this year's ACM World Finals is expected to attend the grand banquet arranged for after the award ceremony. To maximize the amount of interaction between members of different teams, no two members of the same team will be allowed to sit at the same table.

Given the number of members on each team (including contestants, coaches, reserves, and guests) and the seating capacity of each table, determine whether it is possible for the teams to sit as described. If such an arrangement is possible, output one such seating assignment. If there are multiple possible arrangements, any one is acceptable.

Input

The input file may contain multiple test cases. The first line of each test case contains two integers, $1 \leq M \leq 70$ and $1 \leq N \leq 50$, denoting the number of teams and tables, respectively. The second line of each test case contains M integers, where the ith integer m_i indicates the number of members of team i. There are at most 100 members of any team. The third line contains N integers, where the jth integer n_j, $2 \leq n_j \leq 100$, indicates the seating capacity of table j.

A test case containing two zeros for M and N terminates the input.

Output

For each test case, print a line containing either 1 or 0, denoting whether there exists a valid seating arrangement of the team members. In case of a successful arrangement, print M additional lines where the ith line contains a table number (from 1 to N) for each of the members of team i.

Sample Input	Sample Output
4 5	1
4 5 3 5	1 2 4 5
3 5 2 6 4	1 2 3 4 5
4 5	2 4 5
4 5 3 5	1 2 3 4 5
3 5 2 6 3	0
0 0	

10.5.8   The Problem With the Problem Setter

PC/UVa IDs: 111008/10092, **Popularity:** C, **Success rate:** average **Level:** 3

So many students are interested in participating in this year's regional programming contest that we have decided to arrange a screening test to identify the most promising candidates. This test may include as many as 100 problems drawn from as many as 20 categories. I have been assigned the job of setting problems for this test.

At first the job seemed to be very easy, since I was told that I would be given a pool of about 1,000 problems divided into appropriate categories. After getting the problems, however, I discovered that the original authors often wrote down multiple category-names in the category fields. Since no problem can used in more than one category and the number of problems needed for each category is fixed, assigning problems for the test is not so easy.

Input

The input file may contain multiple test cases, each of which begins with a line containing two integers, n_k and n_p, where n_k is the number of categories and n_p is the number of problems in the pool. There will be between 2 and 20 categories and at most 1,000 problems in the pool.

The second line contains n_k positive integers, where the ith integer specifies the number of problems to be included in category i $(1 \leq i \leq n_k)$ of the test. You may assume that the sum of these n_k integers will never exceed 100. The jth $(1 \leq j \leq n_p)$ of the next n_p lines contains the category information of the jth problem in the pool. Each such problem category specification starts with a positive integer specifying the number of categories in which this problem can be included, followed by the actual category numbers.

A test case containing two zeros for n_k and n_p terminates the input.

Output

For each test case, print a line reporting whether problems can be successfully selected from the pool under the given restrictions, with 1 for success and 0 for failure.

In case of successful selection, print n_k additional lines where the ith line contains the problem numbers that can be included in category i. Problem numbers are positive integers not greater then n_p and each two problem numbers must be separated by a single space. Any successful selection will be accepted.

Sample Input

```
3 15
3 3 4
2 1 2
1 3
```

```
1 3
1 3
1 3
3 1 2 3
2 2 3
2 1 3
1 2
1 2
2 1 2
2 1 3
2 1 2
1 1
3 1 2 3
3 15
7 3 4
2 1 2
1 1
1 2
1 2
1 3
3 1 2 3 2 2 3
2 2 3
1 2
1 2
2 2 3
2 2 3
2 1 2
1 1
3 1 2 3
0 0
```

Sample Output

```
1
8 11 12
1 6 7
2 3 4 5
0
```

10.6 Hints

10.1 Which problem from the chapter is Richie trying to solve?

10.2 Can this problem be modeled as a Hamiltonian or Eulerian cycle problem?

10.3 How can we use shortest-path information to help us position the station?

10.4 How can we model this as a shortest-path problem? What is the start node of our graph? How can we break ties in favor of trains leaving later in the day?

10.5 Can we propagate some of the implications of an observation through transitive closure?

10.6 What graph-theoretic concept defines the camera locations?

10.7 Does a greedy algorithm do the job, or must we use something like network flow?

10.8 Can this be modeled using network flow, or is there a more elementary approach?

11

Dynamic Programming

As algorithm designers and programmers, we are often charged with building a program to find the *best* solution for all problem instances. It is usually easy to write a program which gives a decent and correct solution, but ensuring that it always returns the absolute best solution requires us to think deeply about the problem.

Dynamic programming is a very powerful, general tool for solving optimization problems on left-right-ordered items such as character strings. Once understood it is relatively easy to apply, but many people have a difficult time understanding it.

Dynamic programming looks like magic until you have seen enough examples. Start by reviewing our binomial coefficient function in Chapter 6, as an example of how we stored partial results to help us compute what we were looking for. Then review Floyd's all-pairs shortest-path algorithm in Section 10.3.2. Only then should you study the two problems in the sections below. The first is a classic example of dynamic programming which appears in every textbook. The second is a more ad hoc example representative of using dynamic programming to design new algorithms.

11.1 Don't Be Greedy

Many problems call for finding the best solution satisfying certain constraints. We have a few tricks available to tackle such jobs. For example, the backtracking problems of Chapter 8 often asked for the largest, smallest, or highest-scoring configuration. Backtracking searches all possible solutions and selects the best one, and hence *must* return the correct answer. But this approach is only feasible for small problem instances.

Correct and efficient algorithms are known for many important graph problems, including shortest paths, minimum spanning trees, and matchings, as discussed in Chapter 10. Always be on the lookout for instances of these problems, so you can just plug in the appropriate solution.

Greedy algorithms focus on making the best local choice at each decision point. For example, a natural way to compute a shortest path from x to y might be to walk out of x, repeatedly following the cheapest edge until we get to y. Natural, but wrong! Indeed, in the absence of a correctness proof such greedy algorithms are very likely to fail.

So what can we do? Dynamic programming gives us a way to design custom algorithms which systematically search all possibilities (thus guaranteeing correctness) while storing results to avoid recomputing (thus providing efficiency).

Dynamic programming algorithms are defined by recursive algorithms/functions that describe the solution to the entire problem in terms of solutions to smaller problems. Backtracking is one such recursive procedure we have seen, as is depth-first search in graphs.

Efficiency in any such recursive algorithm requires storing enough information to avoid repeating computations we have done before. Why is depth-first search in graphs efficient? It is because we mark the vertices we have visited so we don't visit them again. Why is raw backtracking computationally expensive? Because it searches all possible paths/solutions instead of just the ones we haven't seen before.

Dynamic programming is a technique for efficiently implementing a recursive algorithm by storing partial results. The trick is to see that the naive recursive algorithm repeatedly computes the same subproblems over and over and over again. If so, storing the answers to them in a table instead of recomputing can lead to an efficient algorithm. To understand the examples which follow, it will help first to hunt for some kind of recursive algorithm. Only once you have a correct algorithm can you worry about speeding it up by using a results matrix.

11.2   Edit Distance

The problem of searching for patterns in text strings is of unquestionable importance. Indeed, we presented algorithms for string search in Chapter 3. However, there we limited discussion to *exact* string matching, finding where the pattern string s was exactly contained in the text string t. Life is often not that simple. Misspellings in either the text or pattern rob of us exact similarity. Evolutionary changes in genomic sequences or language usage imply that we often search with archaic patterns in mind: "Thou shalt not kill" morphs into "You should not murder."

If we are to deal with inexact string matching, we must first define a cost function telling us how far apart two strings are, i.e., a distance measure between pairs of strings. A reasonable distance measure minimizes the cost of the *changes* which have to be made to convert one string to another. There are three natural types of changes:

- *Substitution* — Change a single character from pattern s to a different character in text t, such as changing "shot" to "spot".

- *Insertion* — Insert a single character into pattern s to help it match text t, such as changing "ago" to "agog".

- *Deletion* — Delete a single character from pattern s to help it match text t, such as changing "hour" to "our".

Properly posing the question of string similarity requires us to set the cost of each of these string transform operations. Setting each operation to cost one step defines the *edit distance* between two strings. Other cost values also yield interesting results, as will be shown in Section 11.4.

But how can we compute the edit distance? We can define a recursive algorithm using the observation that the last character in the string must either be matched, substituted, inserted, or deleted. Chopping off the characters involved in the last edit operation leaves a pair of smaller strings. Let i and j be the last character of the relevant prefix of s and t, respectively. There are three pairs of shorter strings after the last operation, corresponding to the strings after a match/substitution, insertion, or deletion. *If* we knew the cost of editing the three pairs of smaller strings, we could decide which option leads to the best solution and choose that option accordingly. We *can* learn this cost, through the magic of recursion:

```
#define MATCH          0       /* enumerated type symbol for match */
#define INSERT         1       /* enumerated type symbol for insert */
#define DELETE         2       /* enumerated type symbol for delete */

int string_compare(char *s, char *t, int i, int j)
{
        int k;                  /* counter */
        int opt[3];             /* cost of the three options */
        int lowest_cost;        /* lowest cost */

        if (i == 0) return(j * indel(' '));
        if (j == 0) return(i * indel(' '));

        opt[MATCH] = string_compare(s,t,i-1,j-1) + match(s[i],t[j]);
        opt[INSERT] = string_compare(s,t,i,j-1) + indel(t[j]);
        opt[DELETE] = string_compare(s,t,i-1,j) + indel(s[i]);

        lowest_cost = opt[MATCH];
        for (k=INSERT; k<=DELETE; k++)
                if (opt[k] < lowest_cost) lowest_cost = opt[k];

        return( lowest_cost );
}
```

This program is absolutely correct – convince yourself. It is also impossibly slow. Running on our computer, it takes several seconds to compare two 11-character strings, and the computation disappears into never-never land on anything longer.

Why is the algorithm so slow? It takes exponential time because it recomputes values again and again and again. At every position in the string, the recursion branches three ways, meaning it grows at a rate of at least 3^n – indeed, even faster since most of the calls reduce only one of the two indices, not both of them.

So how can we make the algorithm practical? The important observation is that most of these recursive calls are computing things that have already been computed before. How do we know? Well, there can only be $|s| \cdot |t|$ possible unique recursive calls, since there are only that many distinct (i, j) pairs to serve as the parameters of recursive calls. By storing the values for each of these (i, j) pairs in a table, we can avoid recomputing them and just look them up as needed.

A table-based, dynamic programming implementation of this algorithm is given below. The table is a two-dimensional matrix m where each of the $|s| \cdot |t|$ cells contains the cost of the optimal solution of this subproblem, as well as a parent pointer explaining how we got to this location:

```
typedef struct {
        int cost;                  /* cost of reaching this cell */
        int parent;                /* parent cell */
} cell;

cell m[MAXLEN+1][MAXLEN+1];        /* dynamic programming table */
```

The dynamic programming version has three differences from the recursive version. First, it gets its intermediate values using table lookup instead of recursive calls. Second, it updates the **parent** field of each cell, which will enable us to reconstruct the edit-sequence later. Third, it is instrumented using a more general **goal_cell()** function instead of just returning **m[|s|][|t|].cost**. This will enable us to apply this routine to a wider class of problems.

Be aware that we adhere to certain unusual string and index conventions in the following routines. In particular, we assume that each string has been padded with an initial blank character, so the first real character of string **s** sits in **s[1]**. This was done using the following input fragment:

```
s[0] = t[0] = ' ';
scanf("%s",&(s[1]));
scanf("%s",&(t[1]));
```

Why did we do this? It enables us to keep the matrix **m** indices in sync with those of the strings for clarity. Recall that we must dedicate the zeroth row and columns of **m** to store the boundary values matching the empty prefix. Alternatively, we could have left the input strings intact and just adjusted the indices accordingly.

```
int string_compare(char *s, char *t)
{
        int i,j,k;                 /* counters */
        int opt[3];                /* cost of the three options */
```

```c
for (i=0; i<MAXLEN; i++) {
        row_init(i);
        column_init(i);
}

for (i=1; i<strlen(s); i++)
        for (j=1; j<strlen(t); j++) {
                opt[MATCH] = m[i-1][j-1].cost + match(s[i],t[j]);
                opt[INSERT] = m[i][j-1].cost + indel(t[j]);
                opt[DELETE] = m[i-1][j].cost + indel(s[i]);

                m[i][j].cost = opt[MATCH];
                m[i][j].parent = MATCH;
                for (k=INSERT; k<=DELETE; k++)
                        if (opt[k] < m[i][j].cost) {
                                m[i][j].cost = opt[k];
                                m[i][j].parent = k;
                        }
        }

goal_cell(s,t,&i,&j);
return( m[i][j].cost );
}
```

Notice the order that the cells of the matrix are filled in. To determine the value of cell (i, j) we need three values sitting and waiting for us, namely, the cells $(i-1, j-1)$, $(i, j-1)$, and $(i-1, j)$. Any evaluation order with this property will do, including the row-major order used in this program.

Below is an example run, showing the cost and parent values turning "thou shalt not" to "you should not" in five moves:

		y	o	u	-	s	h	o	u	l	d	-	n	o	t
:	0	1	2	3	4	5	6	7	8	9	10	11	12	13	14
t:	1	1	2	3	4	5	6	7	8	9	10	11	12	13	13
h:	2	2	2	3	4	5	5	6	7	8	9	10	11	12	13
o:	3	3	2	3	4	5	6	5	6	7	8	9	10	11	12
u:	4	4	3	2	3	4	5	6	5	6	7	8	9	10	11
-:	5	5	4	3	2	3	4	5	6	6	7	7	8	9	10
s:	6	6	5	4	3	2	3	4	5	6	7	8	8	9	10
h:	7	7	6	5	4	3	2	3	4	5	6	7	8	9	10
a:	8	8	7	6	5	4	3	3	4	5	6	7	8	9	10
l:	9	9	8	7	6	5	4	4	4	4	5	6	7	8	9
t:	10	10	9	8	7	6	5	5	5	5	5	6	7	8	8
-:	11	11	10	9	8	7	6	6	6	6	6	5	6	7	8
n:	12	12	11	10	9	8	7	7	7	7	7	6	5	6	7
o:	13	13	12	11	10	9	8	7	8	8	8	7	6	5	6
t:	14	14	13	12	11	10	9	8	8	9	9	8	7	6	5

		y	o	u	-	s	h	o	u	l	d	-	n	o	t
:	-1	1	1	1	1	1	1	1	1	1	1	1	1	1	1
t:	2	0	0	0	0	0	0	0	0	0	0	0	0	0	0
h:	2	0	0	0	0	0	0	1	1	1	1	1	1	1	1
o:	2	0	0	0	0	0	0	0	1	1	1	1	1	0	1
u:	2	0	2	0	1	1	1	1	0	1	1	1	1	1	1
-:	2	0	2	2	0	1	1	1	1	0	0	0	1	1	1
s:	2	0	2	2	2	0	1	1	1	1	0	0	0	0	0
h:	2	0	2	2	2	2	0	1	1	1	1	1	1	0	0
a:	2	0	2	2	2	2	0	0	0	0	0	0	0	0	0
l:	2	0	2	2	2	2	0	0	0	1	1	1	1	1	1
t:	2	0	2	2	2	2	0	0	0	0	0	0	0	0	0
-:	2	0	2	2	0	2	2	0	0	0	0	0	1	1	1
n:	2	0	2	2	2	2	2	0	0	0	0	2	0	1	1
o:	2	0	0	2	2	2	2	0	0	0	0	2	2	0	1
t:	2	0	2	2	2	2	2	2	0	0	0	2	2	2	0

11.3   Reconstructing the Path

The dynamic programming implementation above returns the cost of the optimal solution, but not the solution itself. Knowing you can convert "thou shalt not" to "you should not" in five moves is fine and dandy, but what is the sequence of editing operations that does it?

The possible solutions to a given dynamic programming problem are described by paths through the dynamic programming matrix, starting from the initial configuration (the pair of empty strings $(0, 0)$) down to the final goal state (the pair of full strings $(|s|, |t|)$). The key to building the solution is to reconstruct the decisions made at every step along the path that lead to the optimal cost. These decisions have been recorded in the `parent` field of each array cell.

Reconstructing these decisions is done by walking backward from the goal state, following the `parent` pointer to an earlier cell. We repeat this process until we arrive back at the initial cell. The `parent` field for `m[i,j]` tells us whether the transform at (i, j) was MATCH, INSERT, or DELETE. The edit sequence from "thou-shalt-not" to "you-should-not" is DSMMMMMISMSMMMM – meaning delete the first "t", replace the "h" with "y", match the next five characters before inserting an "o", replace "a" with "u", and finally replace the "t" with a "d".

Walking backward reconstructs the solution in reverse order. However, clever use of recursion can do the reversing for us:

```
reconstruct_path(char *s, char *t, int i, int j)
{
        if (m[i][j].parent == -1) return;

        if (m[i][j].parent == MATCH) {
                reconstruct_path(s,t,i-1,j-1);
                match_out(s, t, i, j);
                return;
        }
        if (m[i][j].parent == INSERT) {
                reconstruct_path(s,t,i,j-1);
                insert_out(t,j);
                return;
        }
        if (m[i][j].parent == DELETE) {
                reconstruct_path(s,t,i-1,j);
                delete_out(s,i);
                return;
        }
}
```

For many problems, including edit distance, the tour can be reconstructed without explicitly retaining the last-move pointer array. The trick is working backward to see what move took you to the current cell at the given cost.

11.4   Varieties of Edit Distance

The optimization and path reconstruction routines given above reference several functions which we have not yet defined. These fall into four categories:

- *Table Initialization* — The functions `row_init()` and `column_init()` initialize the zeroth row and column of the dynamic programming table, respectively. For the string edit distance problem, cells $(i,0)$ and $(0,i)$ correspond to matching length-i strings against the empty string. This requires exactly i insertions/deletions, so the definition of these functions is clear.

```
row_init(int i)                     column_init(int i)
{                                   {
  m[0][i].cost = i;                   m[i][0].cost = i;
  if (i>0)                            if (i>0)
      m[0][i].parent =  INSERT;           m[i][0].parent = DELETE;
  else                                else
      m[0][i].parent = -1;                m[0][i].parent = -1;
}                                   }
```

- *Penalty Costs* — The functions `match(c,d)` and `indel(c)` present the costs for transforming character c to d and inserting/deleting character c. For standard edit distance, `match` should cost nothing if the characters are identical, and 1 otherwise, while `indel` returns 1 regardless of what the argument is. But more sensitive cost functions are certainly possible, perhaps more forgiving of replacements located near each other on standard keyboard layouts or those which sound or look similar.

```
int match(char c, char d)           int indel(char c)
{                                   {
  if (c == d) return(0);              return(1);
  else return(1);                   }
}
```

- *Goal Cell Identification* — The function `goal_cell` returns the indices of the cell marking the endpoint of the solution. For edit distance, this is defined by the length of the two input strings. However, other applications we shall see do not have fixed goal locations.

```
goal_cell(char *s, char *t, int *i, int *j)
{
  *i = strlen(s) - 1;
  *j = strlen(t) - 1;
}
```

- *Traceback Actions* — The functions `match_out`, `insert_out`, and `delete_out` perform the appropriate actions for each edit-operation during traceback. For edit distance, this might mean printing out the name of the operation or character involved, as determined by the needs of the application.

```
insert_out(char *t, int j)              match_out(char *s, char *t,
{                                                  int i, int j)
        printf("I");                    {
}                                               if (s[i]==t[j]) printf("M");
                                                else printf("S");
delete_out(char *s, int i)              }
{
        printf("D");
}
```

For our edit distance computation all of these functions are quite simple. However, we must confess about the difficulty of getting the boundary conditions and index manipulations correct. Although dynamic programming algorithms are easy to design once you understand the technique, getting the details right requires carefully thinking and thorough testing.

This is a lot of infrastructure to develop for such a simple algorithm. However, there are several important problems which can now be solved as special cases of edit distance using only minor changes to some of these stubs.

- *Substring Matching* — Suppose that we want to find where a short pattern s best occurs within a long text t, say, searching for "Skiena" in all its misspellings (Skienna, Skena, Skina, ...). Plugging this search into our original edit distance function will achieve little sensitivity, since the vast majority of any edit cost will be that of deleting the body of the text.

    We want an edit distance search where the cost of starting the match is independent of the position in the text, so that a match in the middle is not prejudiced against. Likewise, the goal state is not necessarily at the end of both strings, but the cheapest place to match the entire pattern somewhere in the text. Modifying these two functions gives us the correct solution:

```
row_init(int i)
{
        m[0][i].cost = 0;       /* note change */
        m[0][i].parent = -1;    /* note change */
}

goal_cell(char *s, char *t, int *i, int *j)
{
        int k;                  /* counter */

        *i = strlen(s) - 1;
        *j = 0;
        for (k=1; k<strlen(t); k++)
                if (m[*i][k].cost < m[*i][*j].cost) *j = k;
```

}

- *Longest Common Subsequence* — Often we are interested in finding the longest scattered string of characters which is included within both words. The *longest common subsequence* (LCS) between "democrat" and "republican" is *eca*.

  A common subsequence is defined by all the identical-character matches in an edit trace. To maximize the number of such traces, we must prevent substitution of non-identical characters. This is done by changing the match-cost function:

  ```
  int match(char c, char d)
  {
          if (c == d) return(0);
          else return(MAXLEN);
  }
  ```

  Actually, it suffices to make the substitution penalty greater than that of an insertion plus a deletion for substitution to lose any allure as an edit operation.

- *Maximum Monotone Subsequence* — A numerical sequence is *monotonically increasing* if the ith element is at least as big as the $(i-1)$st element. The *maximum monotone subsequence* problem seeks to delete the fewest number of elements from an input string S to leave a monotonically increasing subsequence. Thus a longest increasing subsequence of "243517698" is "23568."

  In fact, this is just a longest common subsequence problem, where the second string is the elements of S sorted in increasing order. Any common sequence of these two must (a) represent characters in proper order in S, and (b) use only characters with increasing position in the collating sequence, so the longest one does the job. Of course, this approach can be modified to give the longest decreasing sequence by simply reversing the sorted order.

As you can see, our simple edit distance routine can be made to do many amazing things easily. The trick is observing that your problem is just a special case of approximate string matching.

11.5   Program Design Example: Elevator Optimization

I work in a very tall building with a very slow elevator. It is especially frustrating for me when people press the buttons for many neighboring floors (say 13, 14, and 15) as I go from ground to the top floor. My trip upward is interrupted three times, once at each of these floors. It would be far more polite for the three of them to agree to press only 14, and have the floor 13 and 15 people take the stairs up or down for one floor. They could use the walk, anyway.

Your task is to write an elevator optimization program. The riders all enter their intended destinations at the beginning of the trip. The elevator then decides which floors it will stop at along the way. We limit the elevator to making at most k stops on any given run, but select the floors so as to minimize the total number of floors people have to walk either up or down. You can assume the elevator is smart enough to know how many people want to get off at each floor.

We assume that the penalty for walking up a flight of stairs is the same as walking down one – remember, these people can use the exercise. In this spirit, management proposes to break ties among equal-cost solutions by giving preference to stopping the elevators at the lowest floor possible, since it uses less electricity. Note that the elevator does not necessarily have to stop at one of the floors the riders specified. If riders specify floors 27 and 29, it can decide to stop at floor 28 instead.

———————————————   Solution starts below   ———————————————

This is an example of a typical programming/algorithm problem which can be neatly solved by dynamic programming. How do we recognize that, and once we do how do we solve it?

Recall that dynamic programming algorithms are based on recursive algorithms. Deciding the best place to put the kth stop depends on the cost of all possible solutions with $k-1$ stops. If you can tell me the cost of the best of the relevant partial solutions, I can make the right decision for the final stop.

Efficient dynamic programming algorithms tend to require *ordered* input. The fact that the passenger's destinations can be ordered from lowest to highest is important. Consider a trip that stops at floor f_2, after an initial stop at f_1. This second stop can be of absolutely no interest to any passenger whose real destination is at or below f_1. This means that the problem can be decomposed into pieces. If I want to add a third stop f_3 above f_2, plotting the best location for it requires no knowledge of f_1.

So we smell dynamic programming here. What is the algorithm? We need to define a cost function for the partial solutions which will let us make bigger decisions. How about —

> Let m[i][j] denote the minimum cost of serving *all* the riders using exactly j stops, the last of which is at floor i.

Can this function help us place the $(j+1)$st stop given smaller values? Yes. The $(j+1)$st stop must, by definition, be higher than the previous (jth) stop at floor i. Further the new stop will only be of interest to the passengers seeking to get above the ith floor. To figure out how much it can help, we must properly divide the passengers between the new stop and i based on which stop they are closer to. This idea defines the following recurrence:

$$m_{i,j+1} = \min_{k=0}^{i}(m_{k,j} - \text{floors\_walked}(k, \infty) + \text{floors\_walked}(k, i) + \text{floors\_walked}(i, \infty))$$

What does the recurrence mean? If the last stop is at i, the previous stop has to be at some $k < i$. What will such a solution cost? We must subtract from $m_{k,j}$ the cost of servicing all passengers above k (i.e., floors_walked(k, ∞)), and replace it by the (presumably) reduced cost of adding a stop at i (i.e., floors_walked(k, i) + floors_walked(i, ∞)).

The key is the function `floors_walked(a,b)`, which counts the total number of floors walked by passengers whose destinations are between the two consecutive stops a and b. Each such passenger goes to the closest such stop:

```
floors_walked(int previous, int current)
{
        int nsteps=0;               /* total distance traveled */
        int i;                      /* counter */

        for (i=1; i<=nriders; i++)
                if ((stops[i] > previous) && (stops[i] <= current))
                        nsteps += min(stops[i]-previous, current-stops[i]);

        return(nsteps);
}
```

Once you buy this logic, the implementation of this algorithm becomes straightforward. We set up global matrices to hold the dynamic programming tables, here separated to store the cost and parent fields:

```
#define NFLOORS         110      /* the building height in floors */
#define MAX_RIDERS      50       /* what is the elevator capacity? */

int stops[MAX_RIDERS];           /* what floor does everyone get off? */
int nriders;                     /* number of riders */
int nstops;                      /* number of allowable stops */

int m[NFLOORS+1][MAX_RIDERS];    /* dynamic programming cost table */
int p[NFLOORS+1][MAX_RIDERS];    /* dynamic programming parent table */
```

The optimization function is a direct implementation of the recurrence, with care taken to order the loops so that all values are ready before they are needed:

```
int optimize_floors()
{
        int i,j,k;              /* counters */
        int cost;               /* costs placeholder */
        int laststop;           /* the elevator's last stop */

        for (i=0; i<=NFLOORS; i++) {
                m[i][0] = floors_walked(0,MAXINT);
                p[i][0] = -1;
        }

        for (j=1; j<=nstops; j++)
                for (i=0; i<=NFLOORS; i++) {
                        m[i][j] = MAXINT;
```

```
        for (k=0; k<=i; k++) {
            cost = m[k][j-1] - floors_walked(k,MAXINT) +
                floors_walked(k,i) + floors_walked(i,MAXINT);
            if (cost < m[i][j]) {
                m[i][j] = cost;
                p[i][j] = k;
            }
        }
    }

    laststop = 0;
    for (i=1; i<=NFLOORS; i++)
        if (m[i][nstops] < m[laststop][nstops])
            laststop = i;

    return(laststop);
}
```

Finally, we need to reconstruct the solution. The logic is exactly the same as the previous examples: follow the parent pointers and work backward:

```
reconstruct_path(int lastfloor, int stops_to_go)
{
    if (stops_to_go > 1)
        reconstruct_path(p[lastfloor][stops_to_go], stops_to_go-1);

    printf("%d\n",lastfloor);
}
```

Running this program on a ten-story European building (which has the ground floor labeled zero) with single passengers seeking to go to every floor from 1 to 10 informs us that the best single stop is at floor 7, for a cost of 18 walked flights (the floor 1, 2, and 3 passengers are told to get out and walk up from the ground floor). The best pair of stops are 3 and 8 for a cost of 11, while the best triple of stops is at 3, 6, and 9 for a total cost of 7 flights.

11.6 Problems

11.6.1 *Is Bigger Smarter?*

PC/UVa IDs: 111101/10131, **Popularity:** B, **Success rate:** high **Level:** 2

Some people think that the bigger an elephant is, the smarter it is. To disprove this, you want to analyze a collection of elephants and place as large a subset of elephants as possible into a sequence whose weights are increasing but IQ's are decreasing.

Input

The input will consist of data for a bunch of elephants, at one elephant per line terminated by the end-of-file. The data for each particular elephant will consist of a pair of integers: the first representing its size in kilograms and the second representing its IQ in hundredths of IQ points. Both integers are between 1 and 10,000. The data contains information on at most 1,000 elephants. Two elephants may have the same weight, the same IQ, or even the same weight and IQ.

Output

The first output line should contain an integer n, the length of elephant sequence found. The remaining n lines should each contain a single positive integer representing an elephant. Denote the numbers on the ith data line as $W[i]$ and $S[i]$. If these sequence of n elephants are $a[1]$, $a[2]$,..., $a[n]$ then it must be the case that

$$W[a[1]] < W[a[2]] < ... < W[a[n]] \text{ and } S[a[1]] > S[a[2]] > ... > S[a[n]]i$$

In order for the answer to be correct, n must be as large as possible. All inequalities are strict: weights must be strictly increasing, and IQs must be strictly decreasing.

Your program can report any correct answer for a given input.

Sample Input	*Sample Output*
6008 1300	4
6000 2100	4
500 2000	5
1000 4000	9
1100 3000	7
6000 2000	
8000 1400	
6000 1200	
2000 1900	

11.6.2 Distinct Subsequences

PC/UVa IDs: 111102/10069, **Popularity:** B, **Success rate:** average **Level:** 3

A subsequence of a given sequence S consists of S with zero or more elements deleted. Formally, a sequence $Z = z_1 z_2 \ldots z_k$ is a subsequence of $X = x_1 x_2 \ldots x_m$ if there exists a strictly increasing sequence $< i_1, i_2, \ldots, i_k >$ of indices of X such that for all $j = 1, 2, \ldots, k$, we have $x_{i_j} = z_j$. For example, $Z = bcdb$ is a subsequence of $X = abcbdab$ with corresponding index sequence $< 2, 3, 5, 7 >$.

Your job is to write a program that counts the number of occurrences of Z in X as a subsequence such that each has a distinct index sequence.

Input

The first line of the input contains an integer N indicating the number of test cases to follow. The first line of each test case contains a string X, composed entirely of lowercase alphabetic characters and having length no greater than 10,000. The second line contains another string Z having length no greater than 100 and also composed of only lowercase alphabetic characters. Be assured that neither Z nor any prefix or suffix of Z will have more than 10^{100} distinct occurrences in X as a subsequence.

Output

For each test case, output the number of distinct occurrences of Z in X as a subsequence.
Output for each input set must be on a separate line.

Sample Input

```
2
babgbag
bag
rabbbit
rabbit
```

Sample Output

```
5
3
```

11.6.3   Weights and Measures

PC/UVa IDs: 111103/10154, **Popularity:** C, **Success rate:** average **Level:** 3

A turtle named Mack, to avoid being cracked, has enlisted your advice as to the order in which turtles should be stacked to form Yertle the Turtle's throne. Each of the 5,607 turtles ordered by Yertle has a different weight and strength. Your task is to build the largest stack of turtles possible.

Input

Standard input consists of several lines, each containing a pair of integers separated by one or more space characters, specifying the weight and strength of a turtle. The weight of the turtle is in grams. The strength, also in grams, is the turtle's overall carrying capacity, including its own weight. That is, a turtle weighing 300 g with a strength of 1,000 g can carry 700 g of turtles on its back. There are at most 5,607 turtles.

Output

Your output is a single integer indicating the maximum number of turtles that can be stacked without exceeding the strength of any one.

Sample Input

```
300 1000
1000 1200
200 600
100 101
```

Sample Output

```
3
```

11.6.4   Unidirectional TSP

PC/UVa IDs: 111104/116, **Popularity:** A, **Success rate:** low **Level:** 3

Given an $m \times n$ matrix of integers, you are to write a program that computes a path of minimal weight from left to right across the matrix. A path starts anywhere in column 1 and consists of a sequence of steps terminating in column n. Each step consists of traveling from column i to column $i + 1$ in an adjacent (horizontal or diagonal) row. The first and last rows (rows 1 and m) of a matrix are considered adjacent; i.e., the matrix "wraps" so that it represents a horizontal cylinder. Legal steps are illustrated below.

The *weight* of a path is the sum of the integers in each of the n cells of the matrix that are visited.

The minimum paths through two slightly different 5×6 matrices are shown below. The matrix values differ only in the bottom row. The path for the matrix on the right takes advantage of the adjacency between the first and last rows.

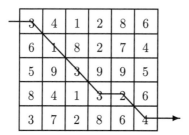 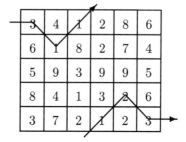

Input

The input consists of a sequence of matrix specifications. Each matrix consists of the row and column dimensions on a line, denoted m and n, respectively. This is followed by $m \cdot n$ integers, appearing in row major order; i.e., the first n integers constitute the first row of the matrix, the second n integers constitute the second row, and so on. The integers on a line will be separated from other integers by one or more spaces. Note: integers are *not* restricted to being positive. There will be one or more matrix specifications in an input file. Input is terminated by end-of-file.

For each specification the number of rows will be between 1 and 10 inclusive; the number of columns will be between 1 and 100 inclusive. No path's weight will exceed integer values representable using 30 bits.

Output

Two lines should be output for each matrix specification. The first line represents a minimal-weight path, and the second line is the cost of this minimal path. The path consists of a sequence of n integers (separated by one or more spaces) representing the rows that constitute the minimal path. If there is more than one path of minimal weight, the lexicographically smallest path should be output.

Sample Input

```
5 6
3 4 1 2 8 6
6 1 8 2 7 4
5 9 3 9 9 5
8 4 1 3 2 6
3 7 2 8 6 4
5 6
3 4 1 2 8 6
6 1 8 2 7 4
5 9 3 9 9 5
8 4 1 3 2 6
3 7 2 1 2 3
2 2
9 10 9 10
```

Sample Output

```
1 2 3 4 4 5
16
1 2 1 5 4 5
11
1 1
19
```

11.6.5   Cutting Sticks

PC/UVa IDs: 111105/10003, **Popularity:** B, **Success rate:** average **Level:** 2

You have to cut a wood stick into several pieces. The most affordable company, Analog Cutting Machinery (ACM), charges money according to the length of the stick being cut. Their cutting saw allows them to make only one cut at a time.

It is easy to see that different cutting orders can lead to different prices. For example, consider a stick of length 10 m that has to be cut at 2, 4, and 7 m from one end. There are several choices. One can cut first at 2, then at 4, then at 7. This leads to a price of $10 + 8 + 6 = 24$ because the first stick was of 10 m, the resulting stick of 8 m, and the last one of 6 m. Another choice could cut at 4, then at 2, then at 7. This would lead to a price of $10 + 4 + 6 = 20$, which is better for us.

Your boss demands that you write a program to find the minimum possible cutting cost for any given stick.

Input

The input will consist of several input cases. The first line of each test case will contain a positive number l that represents the length of the stick to be cut. You can assume $l < 1,000$. The next line will contain the number n ($n < 50$) of cuts to be made.

The next line consists of n positive numbers c_i ($0 < c_i < l$) representing the places where the cuts must be made, given in strictly increasing order.

An input case with $l = 0$ represents the end of input.

Output

Print the cost of the minimum cost solution to cut each stick in the format shown below.

Sample Input

```
100
3
25 50 75
10
4
4 5 7 8
0
```

Sample Output

```
The minimum cutting is 200.
The minimum cutting is 22.
```

11.6.6 Ferry Loading

PC/UVa IDs: 111106/10261, **Popularity:** B, **Success rate:** low **Level:** 3

Ferries are used to transport cars across rivers and other bodies of water. Typically, ferries are wide enough to support two lanes of cars throughout their length. The two lanes of cars drive onto the ferry from one end, the ferry crosses the water, and the cars exit from the other end of the ferry.

The cars waiting to board the ferry form a single queue, and the operator directs each car in turn to drive onto the port (left) or starboard (right) lane of the ferry so as to balance the load. Each car in the queue has a different length, which the operator estimates by inspecting the queue. Based on this inspection, the operator decides which side of the ferry each car should board, and boards as many cars as possible from the queue, subject to the length limit of the ferry. Write a program that will tell the operator which car to load on which side so as to maximize the number of cars loaded.

Input

The input begins with a single positive integer on a line by itself indicating the number of test cases, followed by a blank line.

The first line of each test case contains a single integer between 1 and 100: the length of the ferry (in meters). For each car in the queue there is an additional line of input specifying the length of the car in cm, an integer between 100 and 3,000 inclusive. A final line of input contains the integer 0. The cars must be loaded in order, subject to the constraint that the total length of cars on either side does not exceed the length of the ferry. As many cars should be loaded as possible, starting with the first car in the queue and loading cars in order until the next car cannot be loaded.

There is a blank line between each two consecutive inputs.

Output

For each test case, the first line of output should give the number of cars that can be loaded onto the ferry. For each car that can be loaded onto the ferry, in the order the cars appear in the input, output a line containing "port" if the car is to be directed to the port side and "starboard" if the car is to be directed to the starboard side. If several arrangements of cars meet the criteria above, any one will do.

The output of two consecutive cases will be separated by a blank line.

Sample Input

```
1

50
2500
3000
```

```
1000
1000
1500
700
800
0
```

Sample Output

```
6
port
starboard
starboard
starboard
port
port
```

11.6.7   Chopsticks

PC/UVa IDs: 111107/10271, **Popularity:** B, **Success rate:** average   **Level:** 3

In China, people use pairs of chopsticks to eat food, but Mr. L is a bit different. He uses a set of *three* chopsticks, one pair plus an extra; a long chopstick to get large items by stabbing the food. The length of the two shorter, standard chopsticks should be as close as possible, but the length of the extra one is not important so long as it is the longest. For a set of chopsticks with lengths A, B, C ($A \leq B \leq C$), the function $(A - B)^2$ defines the "*badness*" of the set.

Mr. L has invited K people to his birthday party, and he is eager to introduce his way of using chopsticks. He must prepare $K + 8$ sets of chopsticks (for himself, his wife, his little son, little daughter, his mother, father, mother-in-law, father-in-law, and K other guests). But Mr. L's chopsticks are of many different lengths! Given these lengths, he must find a way of composing the $K + 8$ sets such that the total badness of the sets is minimized.

Input

The first line in the input contains a single integer T indicating the number of test cases ($1 \leq T \leq 20$). Each test case begins with two integers K and N ($0 \leq K \leq 1,000$, $3K + 24 \leq N \leq 5,000$) giving the number of guests and the number of chopsticks. Then follow N positive integers L_i, in non–decreasing order, indicating the lengths of the chopsticks ($1 \leq L_i \leq 32,000$).

Output

For each test case in the input, print a line containing the minimal total badness of all the sets.

Sample Input

```
1
1 40
1 8 10 16 19 22 27 33 36 40 47 52 56 61 63 71 72 75 81 81 84 88 96 98
103 110 113 118 124 128 129 134 134 139 148 157 157 160 162 164
```

Sample Output

```
23
```

Note: A possible collection of the nine chopstick sets for this sample input is $(8, 10, 16)$, $(19, 22, 27)$, $(61, 63, 75)$, $(71, 72, 88)$, $(81, 81, 84)$, $(96, 98, 103)$, $(128, 129, 148)$, $(134, 134, 139)$, and $(157, 157, 160)$.

11.6.8   Adventures in Moving: Part IV

PC/UVa IDs: 111108/10201, **Popularity:** A, **Success rate:** low **Level:** 3

You are considering renting a moving truck to help you move from Waterloo to the big city. Gas prices being so high these days, you want to know how much the gas for this beast will set you back.

The truck consumes a full liter of gas for each kilometer it travels. It has a 200-liter gas tank. When you rent the truck in Waterloo, the tank is half-full. When you return it in the big city, the tank must be at least half-full, or you'll get gouged even more for gas by the rental company. You would like to spend as little as possible on gas, but you don't want to run out along the way.

Input

The input begins with a single positive integer on a line by itself indicating the number of test cases, followed by a blank line.

Each test case is composed only of integers. The first integer is the distance in kilometers from Waterloo to the big city, at most 10,000. Next comes a set of up to 100 gas station specifications, describing all the gas stations along your route, in non-decreasing order by distance. Each specification consists of the distance in kilometers of the gas station from Waterloo, and the price of a liter of gas at the gas station, in tenths of a cent, at most 2,000.

There is a blank line between each two consecutive inputs.

Output

For each test case, output the minimum amount of money that you can spend on gas to get from Waterloo to the big city. If it is not possible to get from Waterloo to the big city subject to the constraints above, print "**Impossible**".

The output of each two consecutive cases will be separated by a blank line.

Sample Input	Sample Output
1	450550

```
500
100 999
150 888
200 777
300 999
400 1009
450 1019
500 1399
```

11.7   Hints

11.1 Can this be reduced to some form of string matching problem?

11.3 Does the original order of the input have any meaning, or are we free to rearrange it? If so, what order is most useful?

11.4 What information do we need about shorter tours to be able to select the optimal last move?

11.5 Can we exploit the fact that each cut leaves two smaller sticks to construct a recursive algorithm?

11.6 Does always putting the next car on the side with the most remaining room solve the problem? Why or why not? Can we exploit the fact that the sum of accumulated car lengths on each lane of the ferry is always an integer?

11.7 How could we solve the problem if we didn't have to worry about the third chopstick?

11.8 What information about the costs of reaching certain places with certain amounts of gas is sufficient to select the optimal last move?

11.8   Notes

11.3 More about Yertle the Turtle can be found in [Seu58].

12
Grids

It is not that polar coordinates are complicated, it is just that Cartesian co-ordinates are simpler than they have a right to be. – Kleppner and Kolenhow, "An Introduction to Mechanics"

Grids underlie a wide variety of natural structures. Chessboards are grids. City blocks are typically arranged on a grid; indeed, the most natural grid distance measure grid is often called the "Manhattan" distance. The system of longitude and latitude defines a grid over the earth, albeit on the surface of a sphere instead of the plane.

Grids are ubiquitous because they are the most natural way to carve space up into regions so that locations can be identified. In the limit, these cells can be individual points, but here we deal with coarser grids whose cells are big enough to have a shape. In *regular* grids, each of these shapes is identical, and they occur in a regular pattern. Rectangular or *rectilinear* subdivisions are the most common grids, due to their simplicity, but triangle-based *hexagonal* grids are also important. Indeed, the honey industry has exploited the efficiency of hexagonal grids for literally millions of years.

12.1   Rectilinear Grids

Rectilinear grids are familiar to anyone who has used a piece of graph paper. In such grids, the cells are typically defined by regularly spaced horizontal and vertical lines. Non-uniform spacing still yields a regular topology, although the size of each cell may differ. Three-dimensional grids are formed by connected regularly spaced layers of planar grids with perpendicular lines across the layers. Three-dimensional grids also have planar faces, defined between any two face-neighboring cubes.

There are three important components of the planar grid: the vertices, the edges, and the cell interiors. Sometimes we are interested in the interiors of the cells, as in geometric applications where each cell describes a region in space. Sometimes we are interested in the vertices of the grid, such as in addressing the pieces on a chessboard. Sometimes we are interested in the edges of the grid, such as when finding routes to travel in a city where buildings occupy the interior of the cells.

Vertices in planar grids each touch four edges and the interiors of four cells, except for vertices on the boundaries. Vertices in 3D grids touch on six edges and eight cells. In d-dimensions, each vertex touches $2d$ edges and 2^d cells. Cells in a planar grid each touch eight faces, four diagonally through vertices and four through edges. Cells in a 3D grid each touch 26 other cells, sharing a face with 6 of them, an edge with 12 of them, and just a vertex with the other 8.

12.1.1 Traversal

It is often necessary to traverse all the cells of an $n \times m$ rectilinear grid. Any such traversal can be thought of as a mapping from each of the nm ordered pairs to a unique integer from 1 to nm. In certain applications the order matters, such as in dynamic programming evaluation strategies. The most important traversal methods are —

- *Row Major* — Here we slice the matrix between rows, so the first m elements visited belong to the first row, the second m elements to the second row, and so forth. Such an ordering is used inside most modern programming language compilers to represent two-dimensional matrices as a single linear array.

```
(1,1)        row_major(int n, int m)
(1,2)        {
(1,3)                int i,j;          /* counters */
(2,1)
(2,2)                for (i=1; i<=n; i++)
(2,3)                        for (j=1; j<=m; j++)
(3,1)                                process(i,j);
(3,2)        }
(3,3)
```

- *Column Major* — Here we slice the matrix between columns, so the first n elements belong to the first column, the second n elements to the second column, and so forth. This can be done by interchanging the order of the nested loops from row-major ordering. Knowing whether your compiler uses row-major or column-major ordering for matrices is important when optimizing for cache performance and when attempting certain pointer-arithmetic operations.

```
(1,1)        column_major(int n, int m)
(2,1)        {
(3,1)                int i,j;          /* counters */
(1,2)
(2,2)                for (j=1; j<=m; j++)
(3,2)                        for (i=1; i<=n; i++)
(1,3)                                process(i,j);
(2,3)        }
(3,3)
```

- *Snake Order* — Instead of starting each row from the first element, we alternate the order of the directions we travel down the rows. The effect is that of a typewriter which can type both left-to-right and right-to-left so as to minimize printing time.

```
(1,1)        snake_order(int n, int m)
(1,2)        {
(1,3)                int i,j;          /* counters */
(2,3)
(2,2)                for (i=1; i<=n; i++)
(2,1)                        for (j=1; j<=m; j++)
(3,1)                                process(i, j + (m+1-2*j) * ((i+1) % 2));
(3,2)        }
(3,3)
```

- *Diagonal Order* — Here we march up and down diagonals. Note that an $n \times m$ grid has $m + n - 1$ diagonals, each with a variable number of elements. This is a trickier task than it appears at first glance.

```
(1,1)        diagonal_order(int n, int m)
(2,1)        {
(1,2)                int d,j;          /* diagonal and point counters */
(3,1)                int pcount;       /* points on diagonal */
(2,2)                int height;       /* row of lowest point */
(1,3)
(4,1)                for (d=1; d<=(m+n-1); d++) {
(3,2)                        height = 1 + max(0,d-m);
(2,3)                        pcount = min(d, (n-height+1));
(4,2)                        for (j=0; j<pcount; j++)
(3,3)                                process(min(m,d)-j, height+j);
(4,3)                }
             }
```

12.1.2 Dual Graphs and Representations

Two-dimensional arrays are the natural choice to represent planar rectilinear grids. We can let m[i][j] denote either the (i, j)th vertex or the (i, j)th face, depending on which we are interested in. The four neighbors of any cell follow by adding ± 1 to either of the coordinates.

A useful concept in thinking about problems on planar subdivisions is that of the *dual graph*, which has one vertex for each region in the subdivision, and edges between the vertices of any two regions which are neighbors of each other.

The four-color theorem states that every planar map can be colored using at most four colors such that all pairs of neighboring regions are colored differently. However, it *really* is a statement about the number of vertex colors needed to color the dual graph of the map. In fact, the dual graph of any planar subdivision must in itself be a planar graph. Can you show why?

Observe that the dual graphs of both rectangular and hexagonal lattices are slightly smaller rectangular and hexagonal lattices. This is why whatever structure we use to represent vertex connectivities can also be used to represent face connectivities.

An adjacency representation is the natural way to represent an edge-weighted rectilinear grid. This might be most easily done by creating a three-dimensional array `m[i][j][d]`, where d ranges over four values (north, east, south, and west) which denote the edge directions from point (i, j).

12.2   Triangular and Hexagonal Grids

The other regular grids of importance are the *triangular* and *hexagonal* lattices. These are very closely related – indeed, hexagonal grids are essentially triangular grids with alternate vertices removed.

12.2.1   Triangular Lattices

Triangular lattices are constructed from three sets of equally spaced lines, consisting of a horizontal "row" axis, a "column" axis 60° from horizontal, and a "diagonal" axis 120° from horizontal. See Figure 12.1 for an example. Vertices of this lattice are formed by the intersection of three axis lines, so each face of the lattice is an equilateral triangle. Each vertex v is connected to six others, those immediately above and below v on each of the three axes.

To manipulate triangular lattices, we need to be able to identify the proper neighbors of each of these vertices as well as their geographical positions. Doing this requires keeping track of two types of coordinate systems:

- *Triangular/Hexagonal Coordinates* — Here, one vertex is designated as the origin of the grid, point $(0, 0)$. We must assign the coordinates such that the logical neighbors of each vertex are easily obtainable. In a standard rectilinear coordinate system, the four neighbors of (x, y) follow by adding ± 1 to either the row or column coordinates.

  Although the intersection of three lines defines each grid vertex, in fact two dimensions suffice to specify location. We will use the row and column dimensions to define our coordinate system. See Figure 12.1 for an example. A vertex (x, y)

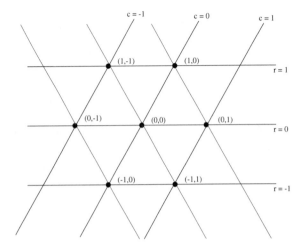

Figure 12.1. A row-column coordinate-system for triangular grids.

lies x rows above the origin, and y ($60°$)-columns to the right of the origin. The neighbors of a vertex v can be found by adding the following pairs to the coordinates of v, in counterclockwise order: $(0, 1)$, $(1, 0)$, $(1, -1)$, $(0, -1)$, $(-1, 0)$, and $(-1, 1)$.

Similar coordinates can be used to represent the faces of the triangular grid, since the dual graph of the faces will also be a triangular grid. Other coordinate choices are also possible; see [LR76] for an alternative.

- *Geometrical Coordinates* — The vertices of a regular triangular grid also correspond to geometric points in the plane. Note that the grid vertices occur in half-staggered rows in Figure 12.1, because the axis lines are $60°$ instead of $90°$ as in rectilinear grids.

  Assume that each lattice point is a distance d from its six nearest neighbors, and that point $(0, 0)$ in triangular coordinates in fact lies at geometric point $(0, 0)$. Then triangular-coordinate point (x_t, y_t) must lie at geometric point

$$(x_g, y_g) = (d(x_t + (y_t \cos(60°))), dy_t \sin(60°))$$

by simple trigonometry. Since $\cos(60°) = 1/2$ and $\sin(60°) = \sqrt{3}/2$, we don't even need to use trigonometric functions for this computation.

We will give code for similar manipulations with hexagonal lattices in the next section.

12.2.2 Hexagonal Lattices

Deleting every other vertex from a triangular lattice leaves us with a *hexagonal* lattice, shown in Figure 12.2. Now the faces of the lattice are regular hexagons, and each

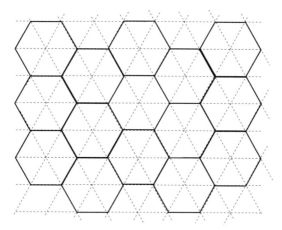

Figure 12.2. Deleting alternate vertices from a triangular lattice yields a hexagonal lattice.

hexagon is adjacent to six other hexagons. The vertices of the lattice now have degree 3, because this lattice is the dual graph of the triangular lattice.

Hexagonal lattices have many interesting and useful properties, primarily because hexagons are "rounder" than squares. Circles enclose the largest amount of area per unit perimeter, so they are the most efficient structures to build. Hexagonal lattices are also more rigid than rectilinear grids, another reason why bees make their honeycombs out of hexagons. Minimizing boundary-per-unit area is also important in minimizing visual artifacts in graphics, so many computer games make images from hexagonal tiles rather than square tiles.

In the previous section, we discussed conversion between triangular/hexagonal co-ordinates and geometrical coordinates. We assume that the origin of both systems is the center of a disk at $(0,0)$. The hexagonal coordinate (xh,yh) refers to the center of the disk on the horizontal row xh and diagonal column yh. The geometric coordinate of such a point is a function of the radius of the disk r, half that of the diameter d described in the previous section:

```
hex_to_geo(int xh, int yh, double r, double *xg, double *yg)
{
        *yg = (2.0 * r) * xh * (sqrt(3)/2.0);
        *xg = (2.0 * r) * xh * (1.0/2.0) + (2.0 * r) * yh;
}
```

```
geo_to_hex(double xg, double yg, double r, double *xh, double *yh)
{
        *xh = (2.0/sqrt(3)) * yg / (2.0 * r);
        *yh = (xg - (2.0 * r) * (*xh) * (1.0/2.0) ) / (2.0 * r);
}
```

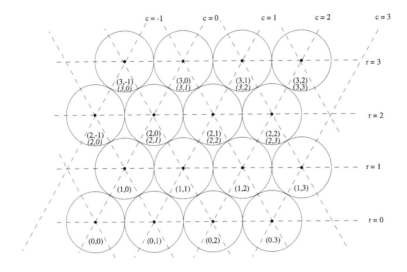

Figure 12.3. A disk packing with hexagonal coordinates, as well as differing array coordinates (below in italics).

The row-column nature of the hexagonal coordinate system implies a very useful property, namely that we can efficiently store a patch of hexagons in a matrix m[row][column]. By using the index offsets described for triangular grids, we can easily find the six neighbors of each hexagon.

There is a problem, however. Under the hexagonal coordinate system, the set of hexagons defined by coordinates (hx, hy), where $0 \le hx \le x_{max}$ and $0 \le hy \le y_{max}$, forms a diamond-shaped patch, not a conventional axis-oriented rectangle. However, for many applications we are interested in rectangles instead of diamonds. To solve this problem, we define array coordinates so that (ax, ay) refers to the position in an axis-oriented rectangle with $(0, 0)$ as the lower-left-hand point in the matrix:

```
array_to_hex(int xa, int ya, int *xh, int *yh)
{
        *xh = xa;
        *yh = ya - xa + ceil(xa/2.0);
}


hex_to_array(int xh, int yh, int *xa, int *ya)
{
        *xa = xh;
        *ya = yh + xh - ceil(xh/2.0);
}
```

Figure 12.3 shows a hexagonal lattice where each vertex is labeled with both its hexagonal coordinates and, below in italics, its array coordinates if they differ.

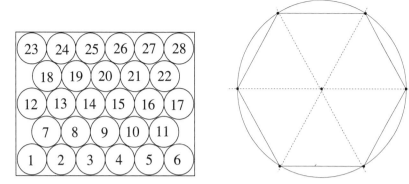

Figure 12.4. Packing plates in a box (l). Viewing a hexagonal grid as a disk packing (r).

12.3   Program Design Example: Plate Weight

A manufacturer of dinner plates seeks to enter the competitive campus dining hall market. Dining halls only buy plates in a single standard size, so they all stack neatly together. Students tend to break a lot of plates during food fights, so selling replacements can be a lucrative business. It is a very cost-sensitive market, however, since the administration gets quite tired of buying extra plates.

Our company seeks an edge in the market through its unique packaging technology. They exploit the fact that hexagonal lattices are denser than rectangular lattices by packaging the plates in $l \times w$ boxes as shown in Figure 12.4(l). Each plate is r units in radius, and the lowest row contains exactly $p = \lfloor w/(2r) \rfloor$ plates. Rows either always contain p plates or alternate between p and $p - 1$ plates, depending on the relationship between w and r. Each plate is assigned a unique identification number as shown in Figure 12.4(l). As many layers as possible are put in the box, subject to its length limit l.

Management needs to know how many plates fit in a box of the given dimensions. They also need to know the maximum number of plates resting on top of any given plate to ensure that the packaging is strong enough to prevent breakage (if the post office will break the plates, who needs the students?). Your job is to identify which plate has the most stress and how many plates lie on top of it, as well as the total number of plates and layers in a box of given dimension.

Solution starts below

The first problem is figuring how many rows of plates fit in the box under the hexagonal grid layout. This is one of the reasons why the Almighty invented trigonometry. The bottom row of plates rests on the floor of the box, so the lowest disk centers sit r units above the floor, where r is the plate radius. The vertical distance between successive rows of disks is $2r \sin(60°) = 2r\sqrt{3}/2$. We could simplify by canceling the 2's, but this obscures the origin of the formula.

```
int dense_layers(double w, double h, double r)
{
        double gap;                          /* distance between layers */

        if ((2*r) > h) return(0);

        gap = 2.0 * r * (sqrt(3)/2.0);
        return( 1 + floor((h-2.0*r)/gap) );
}
```

The number of disks which fit in the box is a function of both the number of rows of plates, and how many plates fit in each row. We always pack the bottom (or zeroth) row starting from the left-hand side of the box, so it contains as many disks as possible constrained by the width of the box. The disks in odd-numbered rows are offset by r, and we might have to remove the last disk from these rows unless there is enough slack ($\geq r$) to accommodate it:

```
int plates_per_row(int row, double w, double r)
{
        int plates_per_full_row;          /* plates in full/even row */

        plates_per_full_row = floor(w/(2*r));

        if ((row % 2) == 0) return(plates_per_full_row);

        if (((w/(2*r))-plates_per_full_row) >= 0.5)   /* odd row full */
                return(plates_per_full_row);
        else
                return(plates_per_full_row - 1);
}
```

Determining how many plates sit on a given plate can be simplified through proper use of our coordinate systems. In an unbounded lattice, two plates in row $r+1$ sit on top of a plate at hexagonal-(r, c), namely, $(r, c-1)$ and (r, c). In general, $i+1$ such plates sit in row $r+i$. However, we must clip these off to reflect the limits of our region. This clipping is easier done in array-coordinates, so we convert to determine the number of plates in our truncated cone:

```
int plates_on_top(int xh, int yh, double w, double l, double r)
{
        int number_on_top = 0;            /* total plates on top */
        int layers;                       /* number of rows in grid */
        int rowlength;                    /* number of plates in row */
        int row;                          /* counter */
        int xla,yla,xra,yra;              /* array coordinates */

        layers = dense_layers(w,l,r);
```

```
    for (row=xh+1; row<layers; row++) {
        rowlength = plates_per_row(row,w,r) - 1;

        hex_to_array(row,yh-row,&xla,&yla);
        if (yla < 0) yla = 0;                    /* left boundary */

        hex_to_array(row,yh,&xra,&yra);
        if (yra > rowlength) yra = rowlength;   /* right boundary */

        number_on_top += yra-yla+1;
    }

    return(number_on_top);
}
```

12.4   Circle Packings

There is an interesting and important connection between hexagonal grids and packing circular disks. The six neighbors of each vertex v in the grid are equidistant from v, so we can draw a circle centered in v through them, as shown in Figure 12.4(r). Each such disk touches the six disks of its neighbors, as shown in Figure 12.3.

The plate packing problem asks us to evaluate two different ways to pack a collection of equal-sized disks, one with the disk centers at the vertices of a rectilinear grid, the other with their centers at the vertices of a hexagonal grid. Which leads to a denser circle packing? It is easy to evaluate both layouts using the routines we have already developed:

```
/* How many radius r plates fit in a hexagonal-lattice packed w*h box? */

int dense_plates(double w, double l, double r)
{
        int layers;                     /* number of layers of balls */

        layers = dense_layers(w,l,r);

        return (ceil(layers/2.0) * plates_per_row(0,w,r) +
                floor(layers/2.0) * plates_per_row(1,w,r) );
}


/* How many radius r plates fit in a grid-lattice packed w*h box?  */

int grid_plates(double w, double h, double r)
```

```
{
        int layers;                        /* number of layers of balls */

        layers = floor(h/(2*r));

        return (layers * plates_per_row(0,w,r));
}
```

For large enough boxes, the hexagonal packing certainly lets us pack more plates than the square grid layout. Indeed, hexagonal packing is the asymptotically densest way to pack disks, and its three-dimensional analog is the densest possible way to pack spheres.

A 4×4 box has room for 16 unit-diameter plates under the square layout versus only 14 with the hexagonal layout, due to boundary effects. But a 10×10 box fits 105 plates in the hexagonal layout, 5 more than the square, and it never looks back from there. A 100×100 box fits 11,443 hex-plates versus 10,000 in a square layout. Thus we can gain a significant advantage with the proposed packaging technology.

12.5   Longitude and Latitude

A particularly important coordinate grid is the system of longitude and latitude which uniquely positions every location on the surface of the Earth.

The lines that run east-west, parallel to the equator, are called lines of *latitude*. The equator has a latitude of $0°$, while the north and south poles have latitudes of $90°$ North and $90°$ South, respectively.

The lines that run north-south are called lines of *longitude* or *meridians*. The *prime meridian* passes through Greenwich, England, and has longitude $0°$, with the entire range of longitudes spanning from $180°$ West to $180°$ East.

Every location on the surface of the Earth is described by the intersection of a latitude line and a longitude line. For example, the center of the universe (Manhattan) lies at $40°47'$ North and $73°58'$ West.

A common problem concerns finding the shortest flying distance between two points on the surface of the Earth. A *great circle* is a circular cross-section of a sphere which passes through the center of the sphere. The shortest distance between points x and y turns out to be the arc length between x and y on the unique great circle which passes through x and y.

We refrain from working through the spherical geometry in favor of stating the result. Denote the position of point p by its longitude-latitude coordinates, (p_{lat}, p_{long}), where all angles are measured in radians. Then the great-circle distance between points p and q is

$$d(p,q) \quad = \quad (\sin(p_{lat})\sin(q_{lat}) + \cos(p_{lat})\cos(q_{lat})\cos(p_{long} - q_{long}))(r)$$

12.6 Problems

12.6.1 Ant on a Chessboard

PC/UVa IDs: 111201/10161, **Popularity:** B, **Success rate:** high **Level:** 1

One day, an ant named Alice came upon an $M \times M$ chessboard. She wanted to explore all the cells of the board. So she began to walk along the board by peeling off a corner of the board.

Alice started at square $(1, 1)$. First, she went up for a step, then a step to the right, and a step downward. After that, she went a step to the right, then two steps upward, and then two grids to the left. In each round, she added one new row and one new column to the corner she had explored.

For example, her first 25 steps went like this, where the numbers in each square denote on which step she visited it.

25	24	23	22	21
10	11	12	13	20
9	8	7	14	19
2	3	6	15	18
1	4	5	16	17

Her 8th step put her on square $(2, 3)$, while her 20th step put her on square $(5, 4)$. Your task is to decide where she was at a given time, assuming the chessboard is large enough to accept all movements.

Input

The input file will contain several lines, each with an integer N denoting the step number where $1 \leq N \leq 2 \times 10^9$. The file will terminate with a line that contains the number 0.

Output

For each input situation, print a line with two numbers (x,y) denoting the column and the row number, respectively. There must be a single space between them.

Sample Input

```
8
20
25
0
```

Sample Output

```
2 3
5 4
1 5
```

12.6.2   The Monocycle

PC/UVa IDs: 111202/10047, **Popularity:** C, **Success rate:** average **Level:** 3

A monocycle is a cycle that runs on one wheel. We will be considering a special one which has a solid wheel colored with five different colors as shown in the figure:

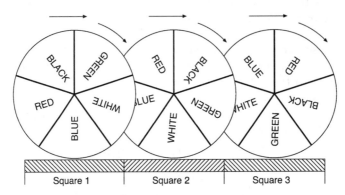

The colored segments make equal angles ($72°$) at the center. A monocyclist rides this cycle on an $M \times N$ grid of square tiles. The tiles are of a size such that moving forward from the center of one tile to that of the next one makes the wheel rotate exactly $72°$ around its center. The effect is shown in the above figure. When the wheel is at the center of square 1, the midpoint of its blue segment is in touch with the ground. But when the wheel moves forward to the center of the next square (square 2) the midpoint of its white segment touches the ground.

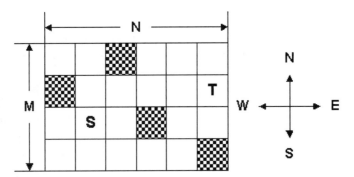

Some of the squares of the grid are blocked and hence the cyclist cannot move to them. The cyclist starts from some square and tries to move to a target square in minimum amount of time. From any square he either moves forward to the next square or he remains in the same square but turns $90°$ left or right. Each of these actions requires exactly 1 second to execute. He always starts his ride facing north and with the midpoint of the green segment of his wheel touching the ground. In the target square, too, the green segment must touch the ground but he does not care which direction he will be facing.

Please help the monocyclist check whether the destination is reachable and if so the minimum amount of time he will require to reach it.

Input

The input may contain multiple test cases.

The first line of each test case contains two integers M and N $(1 \leq M, N \leq 25)$ giving the dimensions of the grid. Then follows the description of the grid in M lines of N characters each. The character "#" will indicate a blocked square, but all other squares are free. The starting location of the cyclist is marked by "S" and the target is marked by "T".

The input terminates with two zeros for M and N.

Output

For each test case first print the test case number on a separate line, as shown in the sample output. If the target location can be reached by the cyclist, print the minimum amount of time (in seconds) required to reach it in the format shown below. Otherwise print "destination not reachable".

Print a blank line between two successive test cases.

Sample Input	Sample Output
1 3	Case #1
S#T	destination not reachable
10 10	
#S......#	Case #2
#..#.##.##	minimum time = 49 sec
#.##.##.##	
.#....##.#	
##.##..#.#	
#..#.##...	
#......##.	
..##.##...	
#.###...#.	
#.....###T	
0 0	

12.6.3 Star

PC/UVa IDs: 111203/10159, **Popularity:** C, **Success rate:** average **Level:** 2

A board contains 48 triangular cells. In each cell is written a digit in a range from 0 through 9. Every cell belongs to two or three lines. These lines are marked by letters from *A* through *L*. See the figure below, where the cell containing digit 9 belongs to lines *D*, *G*, and *I* and the cell containing digit 7 belongs to lines *B* and *I*.

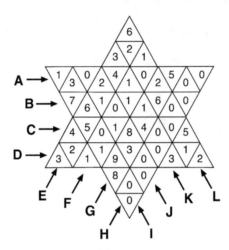

For each line, we can measure the largest digit on the line. Here the largest digit for line *A* is 5, *B* is 7, *E* is 6, *H* is 0, and *J* is 8.

Write a program that reads the largest digit for all 12 of the depicted lines and computes the smallest and the largest possible sums of all digits on the board.

Input

Every line in the input contains 12 digits, each separated by a space. The first of these digits describes the largest digit in line *A*, the second in line *B*, and so on, until the last digit denotes the largest one in line *L*.

Output

For each input line, print the value of the smallest and largest sums of digits possible for the given board. These two values should appear on the same line and be separated by exactly one space. If there does not exists a solution, your program must output "NO SOLUTION".

Sample Input

5 7 8 9 6 1 9 0 9 8 4 6

Sample Output

40 172

12.6.4   Bee Maja

PC/UVa IDs: 111204/10182, **Popularity:** B, **Success rate:** high **Level:** 2

Maja is a bee. She lives in a hive of hexagonal honeycombs with thousands of other bees. But Maja has a problem. Her friend Willi told her where she can meet him, but Willi (a male drone) and Maja (a female worker) have different coordinate systems:

- *Maja's Coordinate System* — Maja (on left) flies directly to a special honeycomb using an advanced two-dimensional grid over the whole hive.

- *Willi's Coordinate System* — Willi (on right) is less intelligent, and just walks around cells in clockwise order starting from 1 in the middle of the hive.

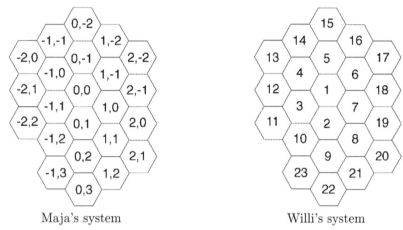

Maja's system   Willi's system

Help Maja to convert Willi's system to hers. Write a program which for a given honeycomb number returns the coordinates in Maja's system.

Input

The input file contains one or more integers each standing on its own line. All honeycomb numbers are less than 100,000.

Output

Output the corresponding Maja coordinates for Willi's numbers, with each coordinate pair on a separate line.

Sample Input	Sample Output
1	0 0
2	0 1
3	-1 1
4	-1 0
5	0 -1

12.6.5 Robbery

PC/UVa IDs: 111205/707, **Popularity:** B, **Success rate:** average **Level:** 3

Inspector Robostop is very angry. Last night, a bank was robbed and the robber escaped. As quickly as possible, all roads leading out of the city were blocked, making it impossible for the robber to escape. The inspector then asked everybody in the city to watch out for the robber, but the only messages he got were "We don't see him."

Robostop is determined to discover exactly how the robber escaped. He asks you to write a program which analyzes all the inspector's information to find out where the robber was at any given time.

The city in which the bank was robbed has a rectangular shape. All roads leaving the city were blocked for a certain period of time t, during which several observations of the form "The robber isn't in the rectangle R_i at time t_i" were reported. Assuming that the robber can move at most one unit per time step, try to find the exact position of the robber at each time step.

Input

The input file describes several robberies. The first line of each description consists of three numbers W, H, and t $(1 \leq W, H, t \leq 100)$, where W is the width, H the height of the city, and t is the length of time during which the city is locked.

The next line contains a single integer n $(0 \leq n \leq 100)$, where n is the number of messages the inspector received. The next n lines each consist of five integers t_i, L_i, T_i, R_i, B_i, where t_i is the time at which the observation has been made $(1 \leq t_i \leq t)$, and L_i, T_i, R_i, B_i are the left, top, right, and bottom, respectively, of the rectangular area which has been observed. The point $(1, 1)$ is the upper-left-hand corner, and (W, H) is the lower-right-hand corner of the city. The messages mean that the robber was not in the given rectangle at time t_i.

The input is terminated by a test case starting with $W = H = t = 0$. This case should not be processed.

Output

For each robbery, output the line "Robbery #k:", where k is the number of the robbery. Then, there are three possibilities:

If it is impossible that the robber is still in the city, output "The robber has escaped."

In all other cases, assume that the robber is still in the city. Output one line of the form "Time step τ: The robber has been at x,y." for each time step in which the exact location can be deduced, and x and y are the column and row, respectively, of the robber in time step τ. Output these lines ordered by time τ.

If nothing can be deduced, output the line "Nothing known." and hope that the inspector does not get even angrier.

Print a blank line after each processed case.

Sample Input

```
4 4 5
4
1 1 1 4 3
1 1 1 3 4
4 1 1 3 4
4 4 2 4 4
10 10 3
1
2 1 1 10 10
0 0 0
```

Sample Output

```
Robbery #1:
Time step 1: The robber has been at 4,4.
Time step 2: The robber has been at 4,3.
Time step 3: The robber has been at 4,2.
Time step 4: The robber has been at 4,1.

Robbery #2:
The robber has escaped.
```

12.6.6   (2/3/4)-D Sqr/Rects/Cubes/Boxes?

PC/UVa IDs: 111206/10177, **Popularity:** B, **Success rate:** high **Level:** 2

How many squares and rectangles are hidden in the 4×4 grid below? Maybe you can count it by hand for such a small grid, but what about for a 100×100 grid or even larger?

What about higher dimensions? Can you count how many cubes or boxes of different size there are in a $10 \times 10 \times 10$ cube, or how many hypercubes and hyperboxes there are in a four-dimensional $5 \times 5 \times 5 \times 5$ hypercube?

Your program needs to be efficient, so be clever. You should assume that squares are not rectangles, cubes are not boxes, and hypercubes are not hyperboxes.

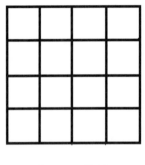

A 4×4 Grid

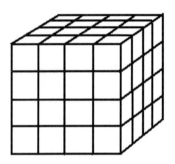

A $4 \times 4 \times 4$ Cube

Input

The input contains one integer N ($0 \le N \le 100$) in each line, which is the length of one side of the grid, cube, or hypercube. In the example above $N = 4$. There may be as many as 100 lines of input.

Output

For each line of input, output six integers $S_2, R_2, S_3, R_3, S_4, R_4$ on a single line, where S_2 denotes the number of squares and R_2 the number of rectangles occurring in a two-dimensional ($N \times N$) grid. The integers S_3, R_3, S_4, R_4 denote similar quantities in higher dimensions.

Sample Input	*Sample Output*
1	1 0 1 0 1 0
2	5 4 9 18 17 64
3	14 22 36 180 98 1198

12.6.7 Dermuba Triangle

PC/UVa IDs: 111207/10233, **Popularity:** C, **Success rate:** high **Level:** 2

Dermuba Triangle is the universally-famous flat and triangular region in the L-PAX planet in the Geometria galaxy. The people of Dermuba live in equilateral-triangular fields with sides exactly equal to 1 km. Houses are always built at the circumcenters of the triangular fields. Their houses are numbered as shown in the figure below.

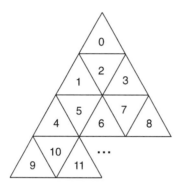

When Dermubian people visit each other, they follow the shortest path from their house to the destination house. This shortest path is obviously the straight-line distance that connects these two houses. Now comes your task. You have to write a program which computes the length of the shortest path between two houses given their house numbers.

Input

The input consists of several lines with two non-negative integer values n and m which specify the start and destination house numbers, where $0 \le n, m \le 2{,}147{,}483{,}647$.

Output

For each line in the input, print the shortest distance between the given houses in kilometers rounded off to three decimal places.

Sample Input	Sample Output
0 7	1.528
2 8	1.528
9 10	0.577
10 11	0.577

12.6.8   Airlines

PC/UVa IDs: 111208/10075, **Popularity:** C, **Success rate:** high **Level:** 3

A leading airline has hired you to write a program that answers the following query: given lists of city locations and direct flights, what is the minimum distance a passenger needs to fly to get from one given city to another? The city locations are specified by latitude and longitude.

To get from a city to another a passenger may take a direct flight if one exists; otherwise he must take a sequence of connecting flights.

Assume that if a passenger takes a direct flight from X to Y he never flies more than the geographical distance between X and Y. The geographical distance between two locations X and Y is the length of the geodetic line segment connecting X and Y. The geodetic line segment between two points on a sphere is the shortest connecting curve lying entirely on the surface of the sphere. Assume that the Earth is a perfect sphere of radius exactly 6,378 km, and that the value of π is approximately 3.141592653589793. Round the geographical distance between every pair of cities to the nearest integer.

Input

The input may contain multiple test cases. The first line of each test case contains three integers $N \leq 100$, $M \leq 300$, and $Q \leq 10,000$, where N indicates the number of cities, M represents the number of direct flights, and Q is the number of queries.

The next N lines contain the list of cities. The ith of these lines contains a string c_i followed by two real numbers lt_i and ln_i, representing the city name, latitude, and longitude, respectively. The city name will be at most 20 characters and will not contain white-space characters. The latitude will be between $-90°$ (South Pole) and $+90°$ (North Pole). The longitude will be between $-180°$ and $+180°$, where negative (positive) numbers denote locations west (east) of the meridian passing through Greenwich, England.

The next M lines contain the direct flight list. The ith of these lines contains two city names a_i and b_i, indicating that there exists a direct flight from city a_i to city b_i. Both city names will occur in the city list.

The next Q lines contain the query list. The ith of these lines will contain city names a_i and b_i asking for the minimum distance a passenger needs to fly to get from a_i to b_i. Be assured that a_i and b_i are not equal and both city names will occur in the city list.

The input will terminate with three zeros for N, M, and Q.

Output

For each test case, first output the test case number (starting from 1) as shown in the sample output. Then for each input query, print a line giving the shortest distance (in km) a passenger needs to fly to get from the first city (a_i) to the second one (b_i). If there exists no route form a_i to b_i, just print the line "no route exists".

Print a blank line between two consecutive test cases.

Sample Input

```
3 4 2
Dhaka 23.8500 90.4000
Chittagong 22.2500 91.8333
Calcutta 22.5333 88.3667
Dhaka Calcutta
Calcutta Dhaka
Dhaka Chittagong
Chittagong Dhaka
Chittagong Calcutta
Dhaka Chittagong
5 6 3
Baghdad 33.2333 44.3667
Dhaka 23.8500 90.4000
Frankfurt 50.0330 8.5670
Hong_Kong 21.7500 115.0000
Tokyo 35.6833 139.7333
Baghdad Dhaka
Dhaka Frankfurt
Tokyo Hong_Kong
Hong_Kong Dhaka
Baghdad Tokyo
Frankfurt Tokyo
Dhaka Hong_Kong
Frankfurt Baghdad
Baghdad Frankfurt
0 0 0
```

Sample Output

```
Case #1
485 km
231 km

Case #2
19654 km
no route exists
12023 km
```

12.7   Hints

12.1 Do we need to walk off the entire path explicitly, or can we compute the final square via some formula?

12.2 What is the right underlying graph to capture the color structure?

12.3 Can we compute the upper and lower bounds for each digit in isolation?

12.4 If we cannot find a formula to compute locations under Willi's system, how can we best simulate his traversal using an explicit data structure?

12.5 What is the right underlying graph to capture both time and space?

12.6 How do the 2-D and 3-D face incidence formulas generalize to 4-D? Is every hypercube still specified by two corner points?

12.7 How do we convert between our previous triangular coordinate systems and this new one?

12.8 Do the distances derived from your longitude/lattitude computations make sense, or is there a bug? What is the underlying graph problem?

13

Geometry

Above the gateway to Plato's academy appeared the inscription, "Let no one who is ignorant of geometry enter here." The organizers of programming competitions feel much the same way, for you can count on seeing at least one geometric problem at every contest.

Geometry is an inherently visual discipline, one that mandates drawing pictures and studying them carefully. Part of the difficulty of geometric programming is that certain "obvious" operations you do with a pencil, such as finding the intersection of two lines, requires non-trivial programming to do correctly with a computer.

Geometry is a subject which everybody studies in high school but which often turns rusty with time. In this chapter, we will refresh your knowledge with programming problems associated with "real" geometry – lines, points, circles, and so forth. After solving a few of these problems you should feel confident enough to walk through Plato's academy once again.

There is more geometry to come. We defer problems associated with line segments and polygons to Chapter 14.

13.1 Lines

Straight *lines* are the shortest distance between any two points. Lines are of infinite length in both directions, as opposed to *line segments*, which are finite. We limit our discussion here to lines in the plane.

- *Representation* — Lines can be represented in two different ways, as either pairs of points or as equations. Every line l is completely represented by any pair of points (x_1, y_1) and (x_2, y_2) which lie on it. Lines are also completely described by equations such as $y = mx + b$, where m is the *slope* of the line and b is the *y-intercept*, i.e., the unique point $(0, b)$ where it crosses the x-axis. The line l has slope $m = \Delta y / \Delta x = (y_1 - y_2)/(x_1 - x_2)$ and intercept $b = y_1 - mx_1$.

Vertical lines cannot be described by such equations, however, because dividing by Δx means dividing by zero. The equation $x = c$ denotes a vertical line that crosses the x-axis at the point $(c, 0)$. This special case, or *degeneracy*, requires extra attention when doing geometric programming. We use the more general formula $ax + by + c = 0$ as the foundation of our line type because it covers all possible lines in the plane:

```
typedef struct {
        double a;                    /* x-coefficient */
        double b;                    /* y-coefficient */
        double c;                    /* constant term */
} line;
```

Multiplying these coefficients by any non-zero constant yields an alternate representation for any line. We establish a canonical representation by insisting that the y-coefficient equal 1 if it is non-zero. Otherwise, we set the x-coefficient to 1:

```
points_to_line(point p1, point p2, line *l)
{
        if (p1[X] == p2[X]) {
                l->a = 1;
                l->b = 0;
                l->c = -p1[X];
        } else {
                l->b = 1;
                l->a = -(p1[Y]-p2[Y])/(p1[X]-p2[X]);
                l->c = -(l->a * p1[X]) - (l->b * p1[Y]);
        }
}


point_and_slope_to_line(point p, double m, line *l)
{
        l->a = -m;
        l->b = 1;
        l->c = -((l->a*p[X]) + (l->b*p[Y]));
}
```

- *Intersection* — Two distinct lines have one *intersection point* unless they are *parallel*; in which case they have none. Parallel lines share the same slope but have different intercepts and by definition never cross.

```
bool parallelQ(line l1, line l2)
{
    return ( (fabs(l1.a-l2.a) <= EPSILON) &&
             (fabs(l1.b-l2.b) <= EPSILON) );
}


bool same_lineQ(line l1, line l2)
{
    return ( parallelQ(l1,l2) && (fabs(l1.c-l2.c) <= EPSILON) );
}
```

A point (x', y') lies on a line $l : y = mx + b$ if plugging x' into the formula for x yields y'. The intersection point of lines $l_1 : y = m_1 x + b_1$ and $l_2 : y_2 = m_2 x + b_2$ is the point where they are equal, namely,

$$x = \frac{b_2 - b_1}{m_1 - m_2}, \qquad y = m_1 \frac{b_2 - b_1}{m_1 - m_2} + b_1$$

```
intersection_point(line l1, line l2, point p)
{
    if (same_lineQ(l1,l2)) {
        printf("Warning: Identical lines, all points intersect.\n");
        p[X] = p[Y] = 0.0;
        return;
    }

    if (parallelQ(l1,l2) == TRUE) {
        printf("Error: Distinct parallel lines do not intersect.\n");
        return;
    }

    p[X] = (l2.b*l1.c - l1.b*l2.c) / (l2.a*l1.b - l1.a*l2.b);

    if (fabs(l1.b) > EPSILON)        /* test for vertical line */
            p[Y] = - (l1.a * (p[X]) + l1.c) / l1.b;
    else
            p[Y] = - (l2.a * (p[X]) + l2.c) / l2.b;
}
```

- *Angles* — Any two non-parallel lines intersect each other at a given angle. Lines $l_1 : a_1 x + b_1 y + c_1 = 0$ and $l_2 : a_2 x + b_2 y + c_2 = 0$, written in the general form, intersect at the angle θ given by:

$$\tan \theta = \frac{a_1 b_2 - a_2 b_1}{a_1 a_2 + b_1 b_2}$$

For lines in slope-intercept form this reduces to $\tan \theta = (m_2 - m_1)/(m_1 m_2 + 1)$.

Two lines are *perpendicular* if they cross at right angles to each other. For example, the x-axis and y-axis of a rectilinear coordinate system are perpendicular, as are the lines $y = x$ and $y = -1/x$. The line perpendicular to $l : y = mx + b$ is $y = (-1/m)x + b'$, for all values of b'.

- *Closest Point* — A very useful subproblem is identifying the point on line l which is closest to a given point p. This closest point lies on the line through p which is perpendicular to l, and hence can be found using the routines we have already developed:

```
closest_point(point p_in, line l, point p_c)
{
        line perp;                      /* perpendicular to l through (x,y) */

        if (fabs(l.b) <= EPSILON) {     /* vertical line */
                p_c[X] = -(l.c);
                p_c[Y] = p_in[Y];
                return;
        }

        if (fabs(l.a) <= EPSILON) {     /* horizontal line */
                p_c[X] = p_in[X];
                p_c[Y] = -(l.c);
                return;
        }

        point_and_slope_to_line(p_in,1/l.a,&perp); /* normal case */
        intersection_point(l,perp,p_c);
}
```

- *Rays* — These are half-lines originating from some vertex v, called the *origin*. Any ray is completely described by a line equation, origin, and direction or the origin and another point on the ray.

13.2   Triangles and Trigonometry

An *angle* is the union of two rays sharing a common endpoint. *Trigonometry* is the branch of mathematics dealing with angles and their measurement.

There are two common units used to measure angles, *radians* and *degrees*. The entire range of angles spans from 0 to 2π radians or, equivalently, 0 to 360 degrees. Using radians is better computationally, because the trigonometric libraries we will see in Section 13.5 assume angles are measured in radians. However, we confess that we think more naturally in degrees. Historically, fractional parts of angles measured in degrees are given in *minutes*, or 1/60th of a degree. But working in degrees and minutes is hopeless, which is why radians (or at least decimal degrees) are the preferred measure.

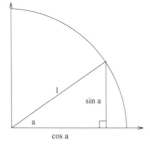 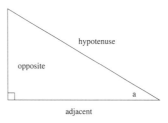

Figure 13.1. Defining sine and cosine (l). Labeling the edges of a right triangle (r).

The geometry of triangles ("three angles") is intimately related to trigonometry, so we will discuss them together in the sections below.

13.2.1 Right Triangles and the Pythagorean Theorem

A *right* angle measures 90° or $\pi/2$ radians. Right angles are formed at the intersection of two perpendicular lines, such as rectilinear coordinate axes. Such lines divide the 360° = 2π radian space into four right angles.

Each pair of rays with a common endpoint actually defines two angles, an *internal angle* of a radians and an *external angle* of $2\pi - a$ radians. The internal angles are the ones we usually claim to be interested in. The three internal (smaller) angles of any triangle add up to 180° = π radians, meaning that the average internal angle is 60° = $\pi/3$ radians. Triangles with three equal angles are called *equilateral*, as was discussed in Section 12.2.

A triangle is called a *right* triangle if it contains a right internal angle. Right triangles are particularly easy to work with because of the *Pythagorean theorem*, which enables us to calculate the length of the third side of any triangle given the length of the other two. Specifically, $|a|^2 + |b|^2 = |c|^2$, where a and b are the two shorter sides, and c is the longest side or *hypotenuse*.

One can go a long way in analyzing triangles with just the Pythagorean theorem. But we can go even farther using trigonometry.

13.2.2 Trigonometric Functions

The trigonometric functions *sine* and *cosine* are defined as the x- and y-coordinates of points on the unit circle centered at $(0, 0)$, as shown in Figure 13.1(l). Thus the values of sine and cosine range from -1 to 1. Further, the two functions are really the same thing, since $\cos(\theta) = \sin(\theta + \pi/2)$.

A third important trigonometric function is the *tangent*, defined as the ratio of sine over cosine. Thus $\tan(\theta) = \sin(\theta)/\cos(\theta)$, which is well-defined except when $\cos(\theta) = 0$ at $\theta = \pi/2$ and $\theta = 3\pi/2$.

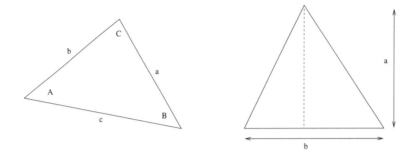

Figure 13.2. Notation for solving triangles (l) and computing their area (r).

These functions are important, because they enable us to relate the lengths of any two sides of a right triangle T with the non-right angles of T. Recall that the hypotenuse of a right triangle is the longest edge in T, that edge opposite the right angle. The other two edges in T can be labeled as *opposite* or *adjacent* edges in relation to a given angle a, as shown in Figure 13.1(r). Then

$$\cos(a) = \frac{|\text{adjacent}|}{|\text{hypotenuse}|}, \quad \sin(a) = \frac{|\text{opposite}|}{|\text{hypotenuse}|}, \quad \tan(a) = \frac{|\text{opposite}|}{|\text{adjacent}|}$$

These relations are worth remembering. As a mnemonic, we use the name of the famous Indian Chief Soh-Cah-Toa, where each syllable of his name encodes a different relation. "Cah" means *C*osine equals *A*djacent over *H*ypotenuse, for example.

Chief Soh-Cah-Toa would not be of much use without inverse functions mapping $\cos(\theta)$, $\sin(\theta)$, and $\tan(\theta)$ back to the original angles. These inverse functions are called arccos, arcsin, and arctan, respectively. With them, we can easily compute the remaining angles of any right triangle given two side lengths.

These trigonometric functions are properly computed using Taylor series expansions, but don't worry: the math library of your favorite programming language already includes them. Trigonometric functions tend to be numerically unstable, so be careful. Do not expect that θ exactly equals $\arcsin(\sin(\theta))$, particularly for large or small angles.

13.2.3 Solving Triangles

Two powerful trigonometric formulae enable us to compute important properties of triangles. The *Law of Sines* provides the relationship between sides and angles in any triangle. For angles A, B, C, and opposing edges a, b, c (shown in Figure 13.2(l)),

$$\frac{a}{\sin A} = \frac{b}{\sin B} = \frac{c}{\sin C}$$

The *Law of Cosines* is a generalization of the Pythagorean theorem beyond right angles. For any triangle with angles A, B, C, and opposing edges a, b, c,

$$a^2 = b^2 + c^2 - 2bc \cos A$$

Solving triangles is the art of deriving the unknown angles and edge lengths of a triangle given a subset of such measurements. Such problems fall into two categories:

- *Given two angles and side, find the rest* — Finding the third angle is easy, since the three angles must sum to $180° = \pi$ radians. The Law of Sines then gives us a way to find the missing edge lengths.

- *Given two sides and an angle, find the rest* — If the angle lies between the two edges, the Law of Cosines gives us the way to find the remaining edge length. The Law of Sines then enables us to mop up the unknown angles. Otherwise, we can use the Law of Sines and the angle sum property to determine all angles, and then the Law of Sines to get the remaining edge length.

The area $A(T)$ of a triangle T is given by $A(T) = (1/2)ab$, where a is the altitude and b is the base of the triangle. The base is any one of the sides while the altitude is the distance from the third vertex to this base, as shown in Figure 13.2(r). This altitude can be easily calculated via trigonometry or the Pythagorean theorem, depending on what is known about the triangle.

Another approach to computing the area of a triangle is directly from its coordinate representation. Using linear algebra and determinants, it can be shown that the *signed* area $A(T)$ of triangle $T = (a, b, c)$ is

$$2 \cdot A(T) = \begin{vmatrix} a_x & a_y & 1 \\ b_x & b_y & 1 \\ c_x & c_y & 1 \end{vmatrix} = a_x b_y - a_y b_x + a_y c_x - a_x c_y + b_x c_y - c_x b_y$$

This formula generalizes nicely to compute $d!$ times the volume of a simplex in d dimensions.

Note that the signed areas can be negative, so we must take the absolute value to compute the actual area. This is a feature, not a bug. We will see how to use the sign of this area to build important primitives for computational geometry in Section 14.1.

```
double signed_triangle_area(point a, point b, point c)
{
        return( (a[X]*b[Y] - a[Y]*b[X] + a[Y]*c[X]
                - a[X]*c[Y] + b[X]*c[Y] - c[X]*b[Y]) / 2.0 );
}

double triangle_area(point a, point b, point c)
{
        return( fabs(signed_triangle_area(a,b,c)) );
}
```

13.3   Circles

A *circle* is defined as the set of points at a given distance (or *radius*) from its *center*, (x_c, y_c). A *disk* is circle plus its interior, i.e., the set of points a distance at most r from its center.

- *Representation* — A circle can be represented in two basic ways, either as triples of boundary points or by its center/radius. For most applications, the center/radius representation is most convenient:

```
typedef struct {
        point c;                    /* center of circle */
        double r;                   /* radius of circle */
} circle;
```

  The equation of a circle follows directly from its center/radius representation. Since the distance between two points is defined by $\sqrt{(x_1 - x_2)^2 + (y_1 - y_2)^2}$, the equation of a circle of radius r is $r = \sqrt{(x - x_c)^2 + (y - y_c)^2}$ or, equivalently, $r^2 = (x - x_c)^2 + (y - y_c)^2$ to get rid of the root.

- *Circumference and Area* — Many important quantities associated with circles are easy to compute. Both the area A and boundary length (circumference) C of a circle depend on the magical constant $\pi = 3.1415926$. Specifically, $A = \pi r^2$ and $C = 2\pi r$. Memorizing π to many more digits is a good way to prove you are a geek. The *diameter*, or longest straight-line distance within the circle, is simply $2r$.

- *Tangents* — A line l most likely intersects the boundary of circle c at either zero or two points; the first case meaning it misses c entirely and the second case meaning it crosses the interior of c. The only remaining case is when the line l intersects the boundary of c but not its interior. Such lines are called *tangent lines*.

  The construction of a line l tangent to c through a given point O is illustrated in Figure 13.3. The point of contact between c and l lies on the line perpendicular to l through the center of c. Since the triangle with side lengths r, d, and x is a right triangle, we can compute the unknown tangent length x using the Pythagorean theorem. From x, we can compute either the tangent point or the angle a. The distance d from O to the center is computed using the distance formula.

- *Interacting Circles* — Two circles c_1 and c_2 of distinct radii r_1 and r_2 can interact in several ways. The circles will intersect if and only if the distance between their centers is at most $r_1 + r_2$. The smaller circle (say, c_1) will be completely contained within c_2 if and only if the distance between their centers plus r_1 is at most r_2. The remaining case is if c_1 and c_2 intersect each other's boundaries at two points. As shown in Figure 13.4, the points of intersection form triangles with the two centers whose edge lengths are totally determined (r_1, r_2, and the distance between the centers), so the angles and coordinates can be computed as needed.

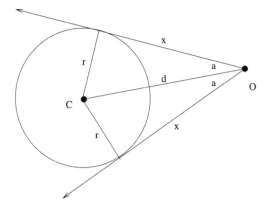

Figure 13.3. Constructing the line tangent to a circle through O.

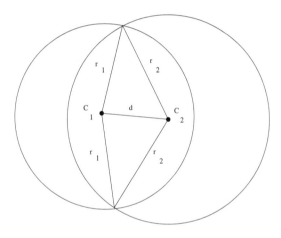

Figure 13.4. The intersection points of two circles.

13.4 Program Design Example: Faster Than a Speeding Bullet

Superman has at least two powers that normal mortals do not possess, namely, x-ray vision and the ability to fly faster than a speeding bullet. Some of his other skills are not so impressive: you or I could probably change clothes in a telephone booth if we put our minds to it.

Superman seeks to demonstrate his powers between his current position $s = (x_s, y_s)$ and a target position $t = (x_t, y_t)$. The environment is filled with circular (or cylindrical) obstacles. Superman's x-ray vision does not have unlimited range, being bounded by

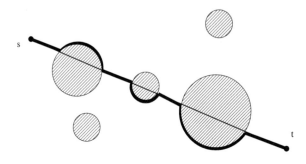

Figure 13.5. Superman's flight plan, with associated x-ray thickness.

the amount of material he has to see through. He is eager to compute the total obstacle intersection length between the two points to know whether to attempt this trick.

Failing this, the Man of Steel would like to fly between his current position and the target. He can see through objects, but not fly through them. His desired path (Figure 13.5) flies straight to the goal, until it bumps into an object. At this point, he flies along the boundary of the circle until he returns to the straight line linking position to his start and end positions. This is not the shortest obstacle-free path, but Superman is not completely stupid – he always takes the shorter of the two arcs around the circle.

You may assume that none of the circular obstacles intersect each other, and that both the start and target positions lie outside of obstacles. Circles are specified by giving the center coordinates and radius.

———————————————   Solution starts below   ———————————————

Solving this problem requires three basic geometric operations. We need to be able to (1) test whether a given circle intersects a given line l between the start and target points, (2) compute the length of the chord intersecting l and circle, and (3) compute the arc length around the smaller piece of a circle cut by l.

The first task is relatively easy. Find the length of the shortest distance from the center of the circle to l. If this is less than the radius, they intersect; if not, they don't. To test whether this intersection occurs between s and t, it suffices to check if the point on l closest to the center of the circle lies within the box defined by s and t.

Measuring the consequences of the intersection appears more difficult. One approach would be to start by computing the coordinates of the intersection points between the line and circle. Although this could be done by setting the circle and line equations equal and solving the resulting quadratic equation, it will be a mess. *There is usually a simpler way to solve a geometric problem than explicitly finding the coordinates of points.*

Such a simpler way is revealed in Figure 13.6. The length of chord intersection is equal to $2x$ on the diagram. We know that d, the shortest length from l to the center, d, lies on a line perpendicular to l. Thus all four angles at the intersection are right

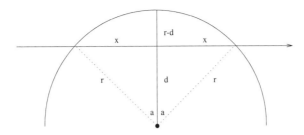

Figure 13.6. Computing chord and arc lengths for line-circle intersection.

angles, including the two angles incident on the triangles with sides r, d, and x. We can now obtain x via an application of the Pythagorean theorem.

The arc length of the shorter walk around the circle can be obtained from angle a of this triangle. The arc we are interested in is defined by the angle $2a$ (in radians), and so is $(2a)/(2\pi)$ times the total circumference of the circle, which is just $2\pi r$. The angle is easily computed from the sides of the triangle using inverse trigonometric functions.

Viewed in this way, and using the subroutines developed earlier, the solution becomes very simple:

```
point s;                      /* Superman's initial position */
point t;                      /* target position */
int ncircles;                 /* number of circles */
circle c[MAXN];               /* circles data structure */

superman()
{
        line l;               /* line from start to target position */
        point close;          /* closest point */
        double d;             /* distance from circle-center */
        double xray = 0.0;    /* length of intersection with circles */
        double around = 0.0;  /* length around circular arcs */
        double angle;         /* angle subtended by arc */
        double travel;        /* total travel distance */
        int i;                /* counter */
        double asin(), sqrt();
        double distance();

        points_to_line(s,t,&l);

        for (i=1; i<=ncircles; i++) {
                closest_point(c[i].c,l,close);
                d = distance(c[i].c,close);
                if ((d>=0) && (d < c[i].r) && point_in_box(close,s,t)) {
```

```
                              xray += 2*sqrt(c[i].r*c[i].r - d*d);
                              angle = acos(d/c[i].r);
                              around += ((2*angle)/(2*PI)) * (2*PI*c[i].r);
                        }
                  }

                  travel = distance(s,t) - xray + around;
                  printf("Superman sees thru %7.3lf units, and flies %7.3lf units\n",
                        xray, travel);
            }
```

13.5   Trigonometric Function Libraries

The trigonometric libraries of different programming languages tend to be very similar. Make sure you know whether your library works in degrees or radians and what angle ranges are returned in the inverse trigonometric functions. Also find out which half-periods the inverse sin and cos functions assume. They cannot determine the angle over the full $360° = 2\pi$ radian range but only a $180° = \pi$ radian period.

Trigonometric Libraries in C/C++

The standard C/C++ math library math.h has all the standard trigonometric functions. Be sure to compile it with the math library included for successful operation:

```
#include <math.h>

double cos(double x);      /* compute the cosine of x radians */
double acos(double x);     /* compute the arc cosine of [-1,1] */

double sin(double x);      /* compute the sine of x radians */
double asin(double x);     /* compute the arc sine of [-1,1] */

double tan(double x)       /* compute the tangent of x radians */
double atan(double x);     /* compute the principal arctan of x */
double atan2(double y, double x); /* compute the arc tan of y/x */
```

The primary reason for two different arctan functions is correctly identifying which of the four quadrants the angle is in. This depends on the signs of both x and y.

Trigonometric Libraries in Java

The Java trigonometric functions reside in java.lang.Math, and assume angles are given in radians. Library functions are provided to convert between degrees and radians. All functions are static, with functionality very similar to the C library:

```
double cos(double a)      Return the trigonometric cosine of angle a.
double acos(double a)     Return the arc cosine of angle a, [0,pi].

double sin(double a)      Return the trigonometric sine of angle a.
double asin(double a)     Return the arc sine of angle a, [-pi/2,pi/2].

double tan(double a)      Return the trigonometric tangent of angle a.
double atan(double a)      Return the arc tangent of angle a, [-pi/2,pi/2]
double atan2(double a, double b)   Convert (b, a) to polar (r, theta)

double toDegrees(double angrad)   Convert a radian angle to degrees.
double toRadians(double angdeg)   Convert a degree angle to radians.
```

13.6   Problems

13.6.1   Dog and Gopher

PC/UVa IDs: 111301/10310, **Popularity:** A, **Success rate:** average **Level:** 1

A large field has a dog and a gopher. The dog wants to eat the gopher, while the gopher wants to run to safety through one of several gopher holes dug in the surface of the field.

Neither the dog nor the gopher is a math major; however, neither is entirely stupid. The gopher decides on a particular gopher hole and heads for that hole in a straight line at a fixed speed. The dog, which is very good at reading body language, anticipates which hole the gopher has chosen. The dog heads at double the speed of the gopher to the hole. If the dog reaches the hole first, the gopher gets gobbled up; otherwise, the gopher escapes.

You have been retained by the gopher to select a hole through which it can escape, if such a hole exists.

Input

The input file contains several sets of input. The first line of each set contains one integer and four floating point numbers. The integer n denotes how many holes are in the set. The four floating point numbers denote the (x, y) coordinates of the gopher followed by the (x, y) coordinates of the dog. The subsequent n lines of input each contain two floating point numbers: the (x, y) coordinates of a gopher hole. All distances are in meters to the nearest millimeter. The input is terminated by end of file and there is a blank line between two consecutive sets.

Output

Print a single line for each set of input. If the gopher can escape, the output line should read, "The gopher can escape through the hole at (x, y)." while identifying the appropriate hole to the nearest millimeter. Otherwise, the output line should read, "The gopher cannot escape." If the gopher can escape through more than one hole, report the one that appears first in the input. There are at most 1,000 gopher holes in a set of input and all coordinates range between −10,000 and +10,000.

Sample Input

```
1 1.000 1.000 2.000 2.000
1.500 1.500

2 2.000 2.000 1.000 1.000
1.500 1.500
2.500 2.500
```

Sample Output

```
The gopher cannot escape.
The gopher can escape through the hole at (2.500,2.500).
```

13.6.2   Rope Crisis in Ropeland!

PC/UVa IDs: 111302/10180, **Popularity:** B, **Success rate:** average **Level:** 2

Rope-pulling (also known as tug of war) is a very popular game in Ropeland, just like cricket is in Bangladesh. Two groups of players hold different ends of a rope and pull. The group that snatches the rope from the other group is declared winner.

Due to a rope shortage, the king of the country has declared that groups will not be allowed to buy longer ropes than they require.

Rope-pulling takes place in a large room, which contains a large round pillar of a certain radius. If two groups are on the opposite side of the pillar, their pulled rope cannot be a straight line. Given the position of the two groups, find out the minimum length of rope required to start rope-pulling. You can assume that a point represents the position of each group.

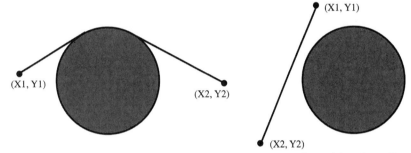

Two groups with the round pillar between them.   Two groups unaffected by the pillar.

Input

The first line of the input file contains an integer N giving the number of input cases. Then follow N lines, each containing five numbers X_1, Y_1, X_2, Y_2, and R, where (X_1, Y_1) and (X_2, Y_2) are the coordinates of the two groups and $R > 0$ is the radius of the pillar.

The center of the pillar is always at the origin, and you may assume that neither team starts in the circle. All input values except for N are floating point numbers, and all have absolute value $\leq 10{,}000$.

Output

For each input set, output a floating point number on a new line rounded to the third digit after the decimal point denoting the minimum length of rope required.

Sample Input

```
2
1 1 -1 -1 1
1 1 -1 1 1
```

Sample Output

```
3.571
2.000
```

13.6.3 The Knights of the Round Table

PC/UVa IDs: 111303/10195, **Popularity:** A, **Success rate:** average **Level:** 2

King Arthur is planning to build the round table in a room which has a triangular window in the ceiling. He wants the sun to shine on his round table. In particular, he wants the table to be totally in the sunlight when the sun is directly overhead at noon.

Thus the table must be built in a particular triangular region of the room. Of course, the king wants to build the largest possible table under the circumstances.

As Merlin is out to lunch, write a program which finds the radius of the largest circular table that fits in the sunlit area.

Input

There will be an arbitrary number of test cases, each represented by three real numbers (a, b, and c), which stand for the side lengths of the triangular region. No side length will be greater than 1,000,000, and you may assume that $\max(a, b, c) \le (a + b + c)/2$.

You must read until you reach the end of the file.

Output

For each room configuration read, you must print the following line:

The radius of the round table is: r

where r is the radius of the largest round table that fits in the sunlit area, rounded to three decimal digits.

Sample Input

```
12.0 12.0 8.0
```

Sample Output

```
The radius of the round table is: 2.828
```

13.6.4   Chocolate Chip Cookies

PC/UVa IDs: 111304/10136, **Popularity:** C, **Success rate:** average **Level:** 3

Making chocolate chip cookies involves mixing flour, salt, oil, baking soda, and chocolate chips to form dough, which is then rolled into a plane about 50 cm square. Circles are cut from this plane, placed on a cookie sheet, and baked in an oven for about 20 minutes. When the cookies are done, they are removed from the oven and allowed to cool before being eaten.

We are concerned here with the process of cutting the first cookie after the dough has been rolled. Each chip is visible in the planar dough, so we simply need to place the cutter so as to maximize the number of chocolate chips contained in its perimeter.

Input

The input begins with a single positive integer on a line by itself indicating the number of test cases. This line is followed by a blank line, and there is also a blank line between two consecutive test cases.

Each input case consists of a number of lines, each containing two floating point numbers indicating the (x, y) coordinates of a chip in the square surface of cookie dough. Each coordinate is between 0.0 and 50.0 (cm). Each chip may be considered a point; i.e., these are not President's Choice cookies. All of the at most 200 chocolate chips are at different positions.

Output

For each test case, the output consists of a single integer: the maximum number of chocolate chips that can be contained in a single cookie whose diameter is 5 cm. The cookie need not be fully contained in the 50-cm square dough (i.e., it may have a flat side).

The output of two consecutive cases must be separated by a blank line.

Sample Input	Sample Output
1	4
4.0 4.0	
4.0 5.0	
5.0 6.0	
1.0 20.0	
1.0 21.0	
1.0 22.0	
1.0 25.0	
1.0 26.0	

13.6.5 Birthday Cake

PC/UVa IDs: 111305/10167, **Popularity:** C, **Success rate:** average **Level:** 2

Lucy and Lily are twins. Today is their birthday, so Mother buys them a birthday cake. There are $2N$ cherries on the cake, where $1 \le N \le 50$. Mother wants to cut the cake into two halves with a single straight-line cut through the center so each twin gets both the same amount of cake *and* the same number of cherries. Can you help her?

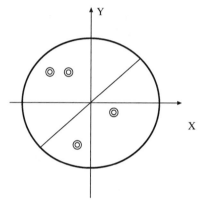

The cake has a radius of 100 and its center is located at $(0,0)$. The coordinates of each cherry are given by two integers (x, y). You must give the line in the form $Ax + By = 0$, where both A and B are integers in $[-500, 500]$. Cherries are not allowed to lie on the cutline. There is at least one solution for each data set.

Input

The input file contains several test cases. The first line of each case contains the integer N. This is followed by $2N$ lines, where each line contains the (x, y) location of a cherry with one space between them. The input is ends with $N = 0$.

Output

For each test case, print a line containing A and B with a space between them. If there are many solutions, any one will suffice.

Sample Input	Sample Output
2	0 1
-20 20	
-30 20	
-10 -50	
10 -5	
0	

13.6.6   The Largest/Smallest Box ...

PC/UVa IDs: 111306/10215, **Popularity:** A, **Success rate:** average **Level:** 2

The following figure shows a rectangular card of width W, length L, and thickness 0. Four $x \times x$ squares are cut from the four corners of the card shown by the dotted lines. The card is then folded along the dashed lines to make a box without a cover.

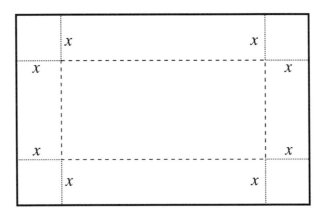

Given the width and height of the box, find the values of x for which the box has maximum and minimum volume.

Input

The input file contains several lines of input. Each line contains two positive floating point numbers L ($0 < L < 10,000$) and W ($0 < W < 10,000$), which indicate the length and width of the card, respectively.

Output

For each line of input, give one line of output containing two or more floating point numbers separated by a single space. Each floating point number should contain three digits after the decimal point. The first number indicates the value which maximizes the volume of the box, while the subsequent values (sorted in ascending order) indicate the cut values which minimize the volume of the box.

Sample Input

```
1 1
2 2
3 3
```

Sample Output

```
0.167 0.000 0.500
0.333 0.000 1.000
0.500 0.000 1.500
```

13.6.7   Is This Integration?

PC/UVa IDs: 111307/10209, **Popularity:** A, **Success rate:** high **Level:** 3

The image below shows a square $ABCD$, where $AB = BC = CD = DA = a$. Four arcs are drawn taking the four vertexes A, B, C, D as centers and a as the radius. The arc that is drawn taking A as center starts at neighboring vertex B and ends at neighboring vertex D. All other arcs are drawn in a similar fashion. Regions of three different shapes are created in this fashion. You must determine the total area of these different shaped regions.

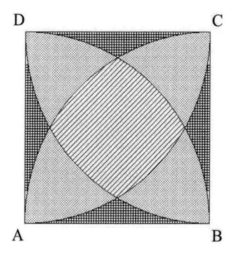

Input

Each line of the input file contains a floating-point number a indicating the side length of the square, where $0 \le a \le 10,000.0$. Input is terminated by end of file.

Output

For each test case, output on a single line the area of the different region types in the image above. Each floating point number should be printed with three digits after the decimal point. The first number of each case will denote the area of the striped region, the second number will denote the total area of the dotted regions, and the third number will denote the rest of the area.

Sample Input	Sample Output
0.1	0.003 0.005 0.002
0.2	0.013 0.020 0.007
0.3	0.028 0.046 0.016

13.6.8   How Big Is It?

PC/UVa IDs: 111308/10012, **Popularity:** B, **Success rate:** low **Level:** 3

Ian is going to California and has to pack his things, including his collection of circles. Given a set of circles, your program must find the smallest rectangular box they fit in.

All circles must touch the bottom of the box. The figure below shows an acceptable packing for a set of circles, although it may not be the optimal packing for these particular circles. In an ideal packing, each circle should touch at least one other circle, but you probably figured that out.

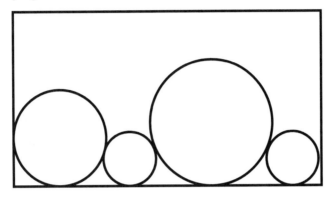

Input

The first line of input contains a single positive decimal integer n, $n \le 50$. This indicates the number of test cases to follow. The subsequent n lines each contain a series of numbers separated by spaces. The first number on each of these lines is a positive integer m, $m \le 8$, which indicates how many other numbers appear on that line. The next m numbers on the line are the radii of the circles which must be packed in a single box. These numbers need not be integers.

Output

For each test case, your program must output the size of the smallest rectangle which can pack the circles. Each case should be output on a separate line by itself, with three places after the decimal point. Do not output leading zeroes unless the number is less than 1, e.g., 0.543.

Sample Input

```
3
3 2.0 1.0 2.0
4 2.0 2.0 2.0 2.0
3 2.0 1.0 4.0
```

Sample Output

```
9.657
16.000
12.657
```

13.7 Hints

13.1 Is the closest hole *really* the safest spot for the gopher?

13.2 Does it help to compute tangent lines to the pillar?

13.3 How many sides of the triangle must the table touch?

13.4 Can we always move the cutter circle to put some chips on its boundary? If so how many? Does this plus the radius define all "interesting" cutter placements?

13.5 There is always a solution to this problem if we remove the constraint that the cutline have integer coordinates – can you prove it? Is there a more efficient solution than trying all possible A, B pairs?

13.6 What are the values of x for which the box has zero volume? Is calculus helpful in maximizing the volume?

13.7 Can we use inclusion-exclusion to give us the area of complicated regions from easy-to-compute parts?

13.8 Is it better to order the circles from largest to smallest, or to interleave them? Does the order ever *not* matter? Will backtracking work for this problem?

14

Computational Geometry

Geometric computing has been become increasingly important in applications such as computer graphics, robotics, and computer-aided design, because shape is an inherent property of real objects. But most real-world objects are not made of lines which go to infinity. Instead, most computer programs represent geometry as arrangements of line segments. Arbitrary closed curves or shapes can be represented by ordered collections of line segments or *polygons*.

Computational geometry can be defined (for our purposes) as the geometry of discrete line segments and polygons. It is a fun and interesting subject, but one not typically taught in required college courses. This gives the ambitious student who learns a little computational geometry a leg up on the competition, and a window into a fascinating area of algorithms still under active research today. Excellent books on computational geometry are available [O'R00, dBvKOS00], but this chapter should be enough to get you started.

14.1   Line Segments and Intersection

A *line segment s* is the portion of a line *l* which lies between two given points inclusive. Thus line segments are most naturally represented by pairs of endpoints:

```
typedef struct {
        point p1,p2;              /* endpoints of line segment */
} segment;
```

The most important geometric primitive on segments, testing whether a given pair of them intersect, proves surprisingly complicated because of tricky special cases that arise. Two segments may lie on parallel lines, meaning they do not intersect at all. One segment may intersect at another's endpoint, or the two segments may lie on top of each other so they intersect in a segment instead of a single point.

This problem of geometric special cases, or *degeneracy*, seriously complicates the problem of building robust implementations of computational geometry algorithms. Degeneracy can be a real pain in the neck to deal with. Read any problem specification carefully to see if it promises no parallel lines or overlapping segments. Without such guarantees, however, you had better program defensively and deal with them.

The right way to deal with degeneracy is to base all computation on a small number of carefully crafted geometric primitives. In Chapter 13, we implemented a general line data type that successfully dealt with vertical lines; those of infinite slope. We can reap the benefits by generalizing our line intersection routines to line segments:

```
bool segments_intersect(segment s1, segment s2)
{
        line l1,l2;               /* lines containing the input segments */
        point p;                  /* intersection point */

        points_to_line(s1.p1,s1.p2,&l1);
        points_to_line(s2.p1,s2.p2,&l2);

        if (same_lineQ(l1,l2))  /* overlapping or disjoint segments */
                return( point_in_box(s1.p1,s2.p1,s2.p2) ||
                        point_in_box(s1.p2,s2.p1,s2.p2) ||
                        point_in_box(s2.p1,s1.p1,s1.p2) ||
                        point_in_box(s2.p1,s1.p1,s1.p2) );

        if (parallelQ(l1,l2)) return(FALSE);

        intersection_point(l1,l2,p);

        return(point_in_box(p,s1.p1,s1.p2) && point_in_box(p,s2.p1,s2.p2));
}
```

We will use our line intersection routines to find an intersection point if one exists. If so, the remaining question is whether this point lies within the region defined by our line segments. This is most easily tested by establishing whether the intersection point lies in the bounding box around each line segment, which is defined by the endpoints of each segment:

```
bool point_in_box(point p, point b1, point b2)
{
        return( (p[X] >= min(b1[X],b2[X])) && (p[X] <= max(b1[X],b2[X]))
              && (p[Y] >= min(b1[Y],b2[Y])) && (p[Y] <= max(b1[Y],b2[Y])) );
}
```

Segment intersection can also be cleanly tested using a primitive to check whether three ordered points turn in a counterclockwise direction. Such a primitive is described in the next section. However, we find the `point_in_box` method more intuitive.

14.2 Polygons and Angle Computations

Polygons are closed chains of non-intersecting line segments. That they are closed means the first vertex of the chain is the same as the last. That they are non-intersecting means that pairs of segments meet only at endpoints.

Polygons are the basic structure to describe shapes in the plane. Instead of explicitly listing the segments (or edges) of polygon, we can implicitly represent them by listing the n vertices in order around the boundary of the polygon. Thus a segment exists between the ith and $(i + 1)$st points in the chain for $0 \leq i \leq n - 1$. These indices are taken mod n to ensure there is an edge between the first and last point:

```
typedef struct {
        int n;                /* number of points in polygon */
        point p[MAXPOLY];     /* array of points in polygon */
} polygon;
```

A polygon P is *convex* if any line segment defined by two points within P lies entirely within P; i.e., there are no notches or bumps such that the segment can exit and re-enter P. This implies that all internal angles in a convex polygon must be *acute*; i.e., at most $180°$ or π radians.

Actually computing the angle defined between three ordered points is a tricky problem. We can avoid the need to know actual angles in most geometric algorithms by using the *counterclockwise predicate* `ccw(a,b,c)`. This routine tests whether point c lies to the right of the directed line which goes from point a to point b. If so, the angle formed by sweeping from a to c in a counterclockwise manner around b is acute, hence the name of the predicate. If not, the point either lies to the left of $\overrightarrow{ab}$ or the three points are collinear.

These predicates can be computed using the `signed_triangle_area()` formula introduced in Section 13.2.3. Negative area results if point c is to the left of $\overrightarrow{ab}$. Zero area results if all three points are collinear. For robustness in the face of floating point errors, we compare it to a tiny constant ϵ instead of zero. This is an imperfect solution; building *provably* robust geometric code with floating point arithmetic is somewhere between difficult and impossible. However, it is better than nothing.

```
bool ccw(point a, point b, point c)
{
        double signed_triangle_area();

        return (signed_triangle_area(a,b,c) > EPSILON);
}
```

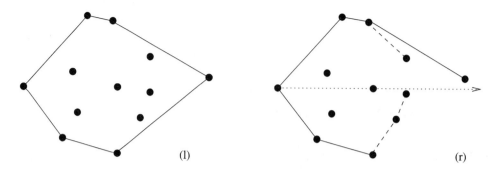

Figure 14.1. The convex hull of a set of points (l), with the change in hull due to inserting the rightmost point (r).

```
bool cw(point a, point b, point c)
{
        double signed_triangle_area();

        return (signed_triangle_area(a,b,c) < EPSILON);
}

bool collinear(point a, point b, point c)
{
        double signed_triangle_area();

        return (fabs(signed_triangle_area(a,b,c)) <= EPSILON);
}
```

14.3 Convex Hulls

Convex hull is to computational geometry what sorting is to other algorithmic problems, a first step to apply to unstructured data so we can do more interesting things with it. The *convex hull* $C(S)$ of a set of points S is the smallest convex polygon containing S, as shown in Figure 14.1(l).

There are almost as many different algorithms for convex hull as there are for sorting. The Graham's scan algorithm for convex hull which we will implement first sorts the points in either angular or left-right order, and then incrementally inserts the points into the hull in this sorted order. Previous hull points rendered obsolete by the last insertion are then deleted.

Our implementation is based on the Gries and Stojmenović [GS87] version of Graham scan, which sorts the vertices by *angle* around the leftmost-lowest point. Observe that both the leftmost and lowest points *must* lie on the hull, because they cannot lie within some other triangle of points. We use the second criteria to break ties for the first, since there might be many different but equally leftmost points. Such considerations are necessary to achieve robustness with degenerate input.

The main loop of the algorithm inserts the points in increasing angular order around this initial point. Because of this ordering, the newly inserted point must sit on the hull of the thus-far-inserted points. This new insertion may form a triangle containing former hull points which now must be deleted. These points-to-be-deleted will sit at the end of the chain as the most recent surviving insertions. The deletion criteria is whether the new insertion makes an obtuse angle with the last two points on the chain – recall that only acute angles appear in convex polygons. If the angle is too large, the last point on the chain has to go. We repeat until a small enough angle is created or we run out of points. We can use our ccw() predicate to test whether the angle is too big:

```
point first_point;              /* first hull point */

convex_hull(point in[], int n, polygon *hull)
{
        int i;                  /* input counter */
        int top;                /* current hull size */
        bool smaller_angle();

        if (n <= 3) {           /* all points on hull! */
                for (i=0; i<n; i++)
                        copy_point(in[i],hull->p[i]);
                hull->n = n;
                return;
        }

        sort_and_remove_duplicates(in,&n);
        copy_point(in[0],&first_point);

        qsort(&in[1], n-1, sizeof(point), smaller_angle);

        copy_point(first_point,hull->p[0]);
        copy_point(in[1],hull->p[1]);

        copy_point(first_point,in[n]);  /* sentinel for wrap-around */
        top = 1;
        i = 2;

        while (i <= n) {
                if (!ccw(hull->p[top-1], hull->p[top], in[i]))
                        top = top-1;    /* top not on hull */
                else {
```

```
                              top = top+1;
                              copy_point(in[i],hull->p[top]);
                              i = i+1;
                       }
               }

               hull->n = top;
}
```

The beauty of this implementation is how naturally it avoids *most* of the problems of degeneracy. A particularly insidious problem is when three or more input points are collinear, particularly when one of these points is the leftmost-lowest hull point which we started with. If we are not careful, we can include three collinear vertices on a hull edge, where in fact only the endpoints belong on the hull.

We resolve this by breaking ties in sorting by angle according to the distance from the initial hull point. By making sure the farthest of these collinear points is inserted last, we ensure that it remains on the final hull instead of its angular brethren:

```
bool smaller_angle(point *p1, point *p2)
{
       if (collinear(first_point,*p1,*p2)) {
               if (distance(first_point,*p1) <= distance(first_point,*p2))
                       return(-1);
               else
                       return(1);
       }

       if (ccw(first_point,*p1,*p2))
               return(-1);
       else
               return(1);
}
```

The remaining degenerate case concerns repeated points. What angle is defined between three occurrences of the same point? To eliminate this problem, we remove duplicate copies of points when we sort to identify the leftmost-lowest hull point:

```
sort_and_remove_duplicates(point in[], int *n)
{
       int i;                   /* counter */
       int oldn;                /* number of points before deletion */
       int hole;                /* index marked for potential deletion */
       bool leftlower();

       qsort(in, *n, sizeof(point), leftlower);

       oldn = *n;
```

```
        hole = 1;
        for (i=1; i<(oldn-1); i++) {
                if ((in[hole-1][X]==in[i][X]) && (in[hole-1][Y]==in[i][Y]))
                        (*n)--;
                else {
                        copy_point(in[i],in[hole]);
                        hole = hole + 1;
                }
        }
        copy_point(in[oldn-1],in[hole]);
}

bool leftlower(point *p1, point *p2)
{
        if ((*p1)[X] < (*p2)[X]) return (-1);
        if ((*p1)[X] > (*p2)[X]) return (1);

        if ((*p1)[Y] < (*p2)[Y]) return (-1);
        if ((*p1)[Y] > (*p2)[Y]) return (1);

        return(0);
}
```

There are a few final things to note about convex_hull. Observe the beautiful use of sentinels to simplify the code. We copy the origin point at the end of the insertion chain to avoid explicitly having to test for the wrap-around condition. We then implicitly delete this duplicated point by setting the return count appropriately.

Finally, note that we sort the points by angle without ever actually computing angles. The ccw predicate is enough to do the job.

14.4   Triangulation: Algorithms and Related Problems

Finding the perimeter of a polygon is easy; just compute the length of each edge using the Euclidean distance formula and add them together. Computing the area of irregular blobs is somewhat harder. The most straightforward approach is to divide the polygon into non-overlapping triangles and then sum the area of each triangle. The operation of partitioning a polygon into triangles is called *triangulation*.

Triangulating a convex polygon is easy, for we can just connect a given vertex v to all $n-1$ other vertices like a fan. This doesn't work for general polygons, however, because the edges might go outside the polygon. We must carve up a polygon P into triangles using non-intersecting chords which lie completely within P.

We can represent the triangulation either by listing the chords or, as we do here, with an explicit list of the vertex indices in each triangle.

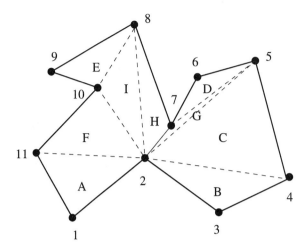

Figure 14.2. Triangulating a polygon via the van Gogh (ear-cutting) algorithm, with triangles labeled in order of insertion $(A - I)$.

```
typedef struct {
        int n;                 /* number of triangles in triangulation */
        int t[MAXPOLY][3];     /* indices of vertices in triangulation */
} triangulation;
```

14.4.1 Van Gogh's Algorithm

Several polygon triangulation algorithms are known, the most efficient of which run in time linear in the number of vertices. But perhaps the simplest algorithm to program is based on ear-cutting. An *ear* of a polygon P is a triangle defined by a vertex v and its left and right neighbors (l and r), such that the triangle (v, l, r) lies completely within P.

Since $\vec{lv}$ and $\vec{vr}$ are boundary segments of P, the chord defining the ear is $\vec{rl}$. Under what conditions can this chord be in the triangulation? First, $\vec{rl}$ must lie completely within the interior of P. To have a chance, lvr must define an acute angle. Second, no other segment of the polygon can be cut by this chord, for if so a bite will be taken out of the triangle.

The important fact is that *every* polygon always contains an ear; in fact at least two of them for $n \geq 3$. This suggests the following algorithm. Test each one of the vertices until we find an ear. Adding the associated chord cuts the ear off, thus reducing the number of vertices by one. The remaining polygon must also have an ear, so we can keep cutting and recurring until only three vertices remain, leaving a triangle.

Testing whether a vertex defines an ear has two parts. For the angle test, we can trot out our ccw/cw predicates again. We must take care that our expectations are consistent with the vertex order of the polygon. We assume the vertices of the polygon to be labeled in counterclockwise order around the virtual center, as in Figure 14.2. Reversing the order of the polygon would require flipping the sign on our angle test.

```
bool ear_Q(int i, int j, int k, polygon *p)
{
        triangle t;                     /* coordinates for points i,j,k */
        int m;                          /* counter */
        bool cw();

        copy_point(p->p[i],t[0]);
        copy_point(p->p[j],t[1]);
        copy_point(p->p[k],t[2]);

        if (cw(t[0],t[1],t[2])) return(FALSE);

        for (m=0; m<p->n; m++) {
                if ((m!=i) && (m!=j) && (m!=k))
                        if (point_in_triangle(p->p[m],t)) return(FALSE);
        }

        return(TRUE);
}
```

For the segment-cutting test, it suffices to test whether there exists any vertex which lies within the induced triangle. If the triangle is empty of points, the polygon must be empty of segments because P does not self-intersect. Testing whether a given point lies within a triangle will be discussed in Section 14.4.3.

Our main triangulation routine is thus limited to testing the earness of vertices, and clipping them off once we find them. A nice property of our array-of-points polygon representation is that the two immediate neighbors of vertex i are easily found, namely, in the $(i-1)$st and $(i+1)$st positions in the array. This data structure does not cleanly support vertex deletion, however. To solve this problem, we define auxiliary arrays l and r that point to the current left and right neighbors of every point remaining in the polygon:

```
triangulate(polygon *p, triangulation *t)
{
        int l[MAXPOLY], r[MAXPOLY];     /* left/right neighbor indices */
        int i;                          /* counter */

        for (i=0; i<p->n; i++) {        /* initialization */
                l[i] = ((i-1) + p->n) % p->n;
                r[i] = ((i+1) + p->n) % p->n;
        }

        t->n = 0;
```

```
        i = p->n-1;
        while (t->n < (p->n-2)) {
                i = r[i];
                if (ear_Q(l[i],i,r[i],p)) {
                        add_triangle(t,l[i],i,r[i],p);
                        l[ r[i] ] = l[i];
                        r[ l[i] ] = r[i];
                }
        }
}
```

14.4.2 Area Computations

We can compute the area of any triangulated polygon by summing the area of all triangles. This is easy to implement using the routines we have already developed.

However, there is an even slicker algorithm based on the notion of signed areas for triangles, which we used as the basis for our ccw routine. By properly summing the signed areas of the triangles defined by an arbitrary point p with each segment of polygon P we get the area of P, because the negatively signed triangles cancel the area outside the polygon. This computation simplifies to the equation

$$A(P) = \frac{1}{2} \sum_{i=0}^{n-1} (x_i \cdot y_{i+1} - x_{i+1} \cdot y_i)$$

where all indices are taken modulo the number of vertices. Thus we don't even need to use our signed_area routine! See [O'R00] for an exposition of why this works, but it certainly leads to a simple solution:

```
double area(polygon *p)
{
        double total = 0.0;        /* total area so far */
        int i, j;                  /* counters */

        for (i=0; i<p->n; i++) {
                j = (i+1) % p->n;
                total += (p->p[i][X]*p->p[j][Y]) - (p->p[j][X]*p->p[i][Y]);
        }

        return(total / 2.0);
}
```

14.4.3 Point Location

Our triangulation algorithm defined a vertex as an ear only when the associated triangle contained no other points. Thus ear testing requires us to test whether a given point p lies within the interior of a triangle t.

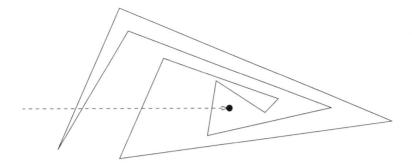

Figure 14.3. The odd/even parity of the number of boundary crossings determines whether a given point is inside or outside a given polygon.

Triangles are always convex polygons, because three vertices does not give the freedom to create bumps and notches. A point lies within a convex polygon if it is to the left of each of the directed lines $\overrightarrow{p_i p_{i+1}}$, where the vertices of the polygon are represented in counterclockwise order. The `ccw` predicate enables us to easily make such left-of decisions:

```
bool point_in_triangle(point p, triangle t)
{
        int i;                            /* counter */
        bool cw();

        for (i=0; i<3; i++)
                if (cw(t[i],t[(i+1)%3],p)) return(FALSE);

        return(TRUE);
}
```

This algorithm works to decide *point location* (in P or out?) for convex polygons. But it breaks down for general polygons. Imagine the task of deciding whether a point is inside or outside the center of a complex spiral-shaped polygon. There is a straightforward solution for general polygons using the code we have already developed. Ear-clipping required us to test whether a given point lies within a given triangle. Thus we can use `triangulate` to divide the polygon into triangular cells and then test each of the cells to see whether they contain the point. If one of them does, the point is in the polygon.

Triangulation is a heavyweight solution for this problem, however, just as it was for area. There is a much simpler algorithm based on the *Jordan curve theorem*, which states that every polygon or other closed figure has an inside and an outside. You can't get from one to the other without crossing the boundary.

This gives the following algorithm, illustrated in Figure 14.3. Suppose we draw a line l that starts from outside the polygon P and goes through point q. If this line crosses the polygon boundary an even number of times before reaching q, it must lie outside

P. Why? If we start outside the polygon, then every pair of boundary crossings leaves us outside. Thus an odd number of boundary crossings puts us inside P.

Important subtleties occur at degenerate cases. Cutting through a vertex of p crosses a boundary only if we enter the interior of p, instead of just clipping off the vertex. We cross a boundary if and only if the vertices neighboring p lie on different sides of line l. Crawling along an edge of the polygon does not change the boundary count, although it raises the application-specific question of whether such a point on the boundary is considered inside or outside p.

14.5   Algorithms on Grids

That polygons drawn on rectilinear and hexagonal grid points can be naturally decomposed into individual cells makes it useful to be able to solve certain computational problems on these cells:

- *Area* — The formula *length* $\times$ *width* computes the area of a rectangle. For triangles, it is $1/2 \times$ *altitude* $\times$ *base*. An equilateral triangle where each side has length r has area $\sqrt{3}r^2/4$; so a regular hexagon with radius r has area $3\sqrt{3}r^2/2$.

- *Perimeter* — The formula $2 \times$ (*length* + *width*) computes the perimeter of a rectangle. For triangles, we sum the side lengths, $a + b + c$, which reduces to $3r$ for equilateral triangles. Regular hexagons of radius r have perimeter $6r$; observe how they approach the circumference of a circle $2\pi r \approx 6.28r$.

- *Convex Hulls* — Squares, equilateral triangles, and regular hexagons are all inherently convex, so they are all their own convex hulls.

- *Triangulation* — Inserting either one of the two diagonals in a square or all three diagonals radiating from any point in a regular hexagon triangulates it. This works only because these figures are convex; notches and bumps make the process harder.

- *Point location* — As we have seen, a point lies in an axis-oriented rectangle if and only if $x_{max} > x > x_{min}$ and $y_{max} > y > y_{min}$. Such tests are slightly more difficult for triangles and hexagons, but surrounding these shapes by a bounding box usually reduces the need for the complicated case.

We conclude this section with two interesting algorithms for geometric computing on grids. They are primarily of interest for rectilinear grids but can be adapted to other lattices if the need arises.

14.5.1   Range Queries

Orthogonal range queries are a common operation in working with $n \times m$ rectilinear grids. We seek a data structure which quickly and easily answers questions of the form: "What is the sum of the values in a given subrectangle of the matrix?"

Any axis-oriented rectangle can be specified by two points, the upper-left-hand corner (x_l, y_l) and the lower-right-hand corner (x_r, y_r). The simplest algorithm is to run nested loops adding up all values `m[i][j]` for $x_l \leq i \leq x_r$ and $y_r \leq j \leq y_l$. But this is inefficient, particularly if you must do it repeatedly in seeking the rectangle of largest or smallest such sum.

Instead, we can construct an alternate rectangular matrix such that element `m1[x][y]` represents the sum of all elements `m[i][j]` where $i \leq x$ and $j \leq y$. This *dominance matrix* `m1` makes it easy to find the sum of the elements in any rectangle, because the sum $S(x_l, y_l, x_r, y_r)$ of elements in such a box is

$$S(x_l, y_l, x_r, y_r) = m_1[x_r, y_l] - m_1[x_l - 1, y_l] - m_1[x_r, y_r - 1] + m_1[x_l - 1, y_r - 1]$$

This is certainly fast, reducing the computation to just four array element lookups. Why it is correct? The term $m1[x_r, y_l]$ contains the sum of all the elements in the desired rectangle, plus all other dominated items. The next two terms subtract this away, but remove the lower-left-hand corner twice so it must be added back again. The argument is that of standard inclusion-exclusion formulas in combinatorics. The array m_1 can be built in $O(mn)$ time by filling in the cells using row-major ordering and similar ideas.

14.5.2 Lattice Polygons and Pick's Theorem

Rectangular grids of unit-spaced points (also called *lattice points*) are at the heart of any grid-based coordinate system. In general, there will be about one grid point per unit-area in the grid, because each grid point can be assigned to be the upper-right-hand corner of a different 1×1 empty rectangle. Thus the number of grid points within a given figure should give a pretty good approximation to the area of the figure.

Pick's theorem gives an exact relation between the area of a lattice polygon P (a non-intersecting figure whose vertices all lie on lattice points) and the number of lattice points on/in the polygon. Suppose there are $I(P)$ lattice points *inside* of P and $B(P)$ lattice points on the boundary of P. Then the area $A(P)$ of P is given by

$$A(P) = I(P) + B(P)/2 - 1$$

as illustrated in Figure 14.4.

For example, consider a triangle defined by coordinates $(x, 1)$, $(y, 2)$, and $(y+k, 2)$. No matter what x, y, and k are there can be no interior points, because the three points lie on consecutive rows of the lattice. Lattice point $(x, 1)$ serves as the apex of the triangle, and there are $k+1$ lattice points on the boundary of the base. Thus $I(P) = 0$, $B(P) = k + 2$, and so the area is $k/2$, precisely what you get from the triangle area formula.

As another example, consider a rectangle defined by corners (x_1, y_1) and (x_2, y_2). The number of boundary points is

$$B(P) = 2|y_2 - y_1 + 1| + 2|x_2 - x_1 + 1| - 4 = 2(\Delta_y - \Delta_x)$$

with the 4-term to avoid double-counting the corners. The interior is the total number of points in or on the rectangle minus the boundary, giving

$$I(P) = (\Delta_x + 1)(\Delta_y + 1) - 2(\Delta_y - \Delta_x)$$

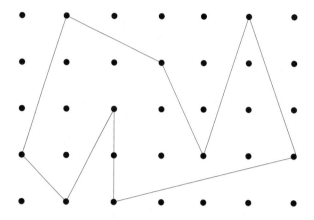

Figure 14.4. A lattice polygon with ten boundary points and nine internal points, and hence area 13 by Pick's theorem.

Pick's theorem correctly computes the area of the rectangle as $\Delta_x \Delta_y$.

Applying Pick's theorem requires counting lattice points accurately. This can in principle be done by exhaustive testing for *small* area polygons using functions that (1) test whether a point lies on a line segment and (2) test whether a point is inside or outside a polygon. More clever sweep-line algorithms would eliminate the need to check all but the boundary points for efficiency. See [GS93] for an interesting discussion of Pick's theorem and related subjects.

14.6   Geometry Libraries

The Java `java.awt.geom` package provides the classes for defining and performing operations on objects related to two-dimensional geometry. The `Polygon` class provides much of the functionality we have developed here, including a `contains` method for point location. The more general *Area* class permits us to union and intersect polygons with other shapes and curves. The `Line2D` class provides much of the functionality we have developed for line segments, including intersection testing and the `ccw` predicate.

14.7 Problems

14.7.1 Herding Frosh

PC/UVa IDs: 111401/10135, **Popularity:** C, **Success rate:** average **Level:** 2

One day, a lawn in the center of campus became infested with frosh. In an effort to beautify the campus, one of our illustrious senior classmen decided to round them up using a length of pink silk. Your job is to compute how much silk was required to complete the task.

The senior classman tied the silk to a telephone post, and walked around the perimeter of the area containing the frosh, drawing the silk taught so as to encircle all of them. He then returned to the telephone post. The senior classman used the minimum amount of silk necessary to encircle all the frosh plus one extra meter at each end to tie it.

You may assume that the telephone post is at coordinates (0,0), where the first dimension is north/south and the second dimension is east/west. The coordinates of the frosh are given in meters relative to the post. There are no more than 1,000 frosh.

Input

The input begins with a single positive integer on a line by itself indicating the number of test cases, followed by a blank line.

Each test case consists of a line specifying the number of frosh, followed by one line per frosh with two real numbers given his or her position.

There is a blank line between two consecutive inputs.

Output

For each test case, the output consists of a single number: the length of silk in meters to two decimal places. The output of two consecutive cases will be separated by a blank line.

Sample Input

```
1

4
1.0 1.0
-1.0 1.0
-1.0 -1.0
1.0 -1.0
```

Sample Output

```
10.83
```

14.7.2   The Closest Pair Problem

PC/UVa IDs: 111402/10245, **Popularity:** A, **Success rate:** low **Level:** 2

A particularly inefficient telephone company seeks to claim they provide high-speed broadband access to customers. It will suffice for marketing purposes if they can create just one such link directly connecting two locations. As the cost for installing such a connection is proportional to the distance between the sites, they need to know which pair of locations are the shortest distance apart so as to provide the cheapest possible implementation of this marketing strategy.

More precisely, given a set of points in the plane, find the distance between the closest pair of points provided this distance is less than some limit. If the closest pair is too far apart, marketing will have to opt for some less expensive strategy.

Input

The input file contains several sets of input. Each set of input starts with an integer N ($0 \leq N \leq 10,000$), which denotes the number of points in this set. The next N lines contain the coordinates of N two-dimensional points. The two numbers denote the x- and y-coordinates, respectively. The input is terminated by a set whose $N = 0$, which should not be processed. All coordinates will have values less than 40,000 and be non-negative.

Output

For each input set, produce a single line of output containing a floating point number (with four digits after the decimal point) which denotes the distance between the closest two points. If there do not exist two points whose distance is less than 10,000, print the line "INFINITY".

Sample Input

```
3
0 0
10000 10000
20000 20000
5
0 2
6 67
43 71
39 107
189 140
0
```

Sample Output

```
INFINITY
36.2215
```

14.7.3 Chainsaw Massacre

PC/UVa IDs: 111403/10043, **Popularity:** B, **Success rate:** low **Level:** 3

The Canadian Lumberjack Society has just held its annual woodcutting competition and the national forests between Montreal and Vancouver are devastated. Now for the social part! In order to lay out an adequate dance floor for the evening party the organizing committee is looking for a large rectangular area without trees. All lumberjacks are already drunk and nobody wants to take the risk of having any of them operate a chainsaw.

The organizing committee has asked you to find the largest free rectangular region which can serve as the dance floor. The area in which you should search is also rectangular and the dance floor must be entirely located in that area. Its sides should be parallel to the borders of the area. The dance floor may be located at the borders of the area, and trees may grow on the borders of the dance floor.

Input

The first line of the input specifies the number of scenarios. For each scenario, the first line provides the length l and width w of the area in meters ($0 < l, w \leq 10,000$, both integers). Each of the following lines describes either a single tree, or a line of trees according to one of the following formats:

- $1 \; x \; y$, where the "1" characterizes a single tree, and x and y provide its coordinates in meters with respect to the upper-left corner.

- $k \; x \; y \; dx \; dy$, where $k > 1$ provides the number of trees in a line with coordinates $(x, y), (x + dx, y + dy), \ldots, (x + (k-1)dx, y + (k-1)dy)$.

- 0 denotes the end of the scenario.

The coordinates x, y, dx, and dy are given as integers. All the trees will be situated in this area, i.e., have coordinates in $[0, l] \times [0, w]$. There will be at most 1,000 trees.

Output

For each scenario print a line containing the maximum size of the dance floor measured in square meters.

Sample Input	Sample Output
2	6
2 3	80
0	
10 10	
2 1 1 8 0	
2 1 9 8 0	
0	

14.7.4 Hotter Colder

PC/UVa IDs: 111404/10084, **Popularity:** C, **Success rate:** low **Level:** 3

The children's game *Hotter Colder* is played as follows. Player A leaves the room while player B hides an object somewhere within. Player A re-enters at position $(0,0)$ and then visits various other locations about the room. When player A visits a new position, player B announces "Hotter" if this position is closer to the object than the previous position, "Colder" if it is farther, and "Same" if it is the same distance.

Input

Input consists of up to 50 lines, each containing an (x, y)-coordinate pair followed by "Hotter", "Colder", or "Same". Each pair represents a position within the room, which may be assumed to be a square with opposite corners at $(0,0)$ and $(10,10)$.

Output

For each line of input, print a line giving the total area of the region in which the object may have been placed, to two decimal places. If there is no such region, output "0.00".

Sample Input

```
10.0 10.0 Colder
10.0 0.0 Hotter
0.0 0.0 Colder
10.0 10.0 Hotter
```

Sample Output

```
50.00
37.50
12.50
0.00
```

14.7.5   Useless Tile Packers

PC/UVa IDs: 111405/10065, **Popularity:** C, **Success rate:** average   **Level:** 3

Useless Tile Packer, Inc., prides itself on efficiency. As their name suggests, they aim to use less space than other companies. Their marketing department has tried to convince management to change the name, believing that "useless" has other connotations, but has thus far been unsuccessful.

Tiles to be packed are of uniform thickness and have a simple polygonal shape. For each tile, a container is custom-built. The floor of the container is a convex polygon that has the minimum possible space inside to hold the tile it is built for.

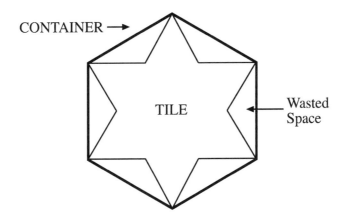

This strategy leads to wasted space inside the container. Your job is to compute the percentage of wasted space for a given tile.

Input

The input file consists of several data blocks. Each data block describes one tile. The first line of a data block contains an integer N ($3 \le N \le 100$) indicating the number of corner points of the tile. Each of the next N lines contains two integers giving the (x, y) coordinates of a corner point (determined using a suitable origin and orientation of the axes) where $0 \le x, y \le 1,000$. The corner points occur in the same order on the boundary of the tile as they appear in the input. No three consecutive points are collinear.

The input file terminates with a value of 0 for N.

Output

For each tile in the input, print the percentage of wasted space rounded to two digits after the decimal point. Each output must be on a separate line.

Print a blank line after each output block.

Sample Input

```
5
0 0
2 0
2 2
1 1
0 2
5
0 0
0 2
1 3
2 2
2 0
0
```

Sample Output

```
Tile #1
Wasted Space = 25.00 %

Tile #2
Wasted Space = 0.00 %
```

14.7.6 Radar Tracking

PC/UVa IDs: 111406/849, **Popularity:** C, **Success rate:** low **Level:** 2

A ground-to-air radar system uses an antenna that rotates clockwise in a horizontal plane with a period of two seconds. Whenever the antenna faces an object, its distance from that antenna is measured and displayed on a circular screen as a white dot. The distance from the dot to the center of the screen is proportional to the horizontal distance from the antenna to the object, and the angle of the line passing through the center and the dot represents the direction of the object from the antenna. A dot directly above the center represents an object that is north of the antenna; an object to the right of the center represents an object to the east; and so on.

There are a number of objects in the sky. Each is moving at a constant velocity, and so the dot on the screen appears in a different position every time the antenna observes it. Your task is to determine where the dot will appear on the screen the next time the antenna observes it, given the previous two observations. If there are several possibilities, you are to find them all.

Input

The input consists of a number of lines, each with four real numbers: a_1, d_1, a_2, d_2. The first pair a_1, d_1 are the angle (in degrees) and distance (in arbitrary distance units) for the first observation while the second pair a_2, d_2 are the angle and distance for the second observation.

Note that the antenna rotates clockwise; that is, if it points north at time $t = 0.0$, it points east at $t = 0.5$, south at $t = 1.0$, west at $t = 1.5$, north at $t = 2$, and so on. If the object is directly on top of the radar antenna, it cannot be observed. Angles are specified as on a compass, where north is $0°$ or $360°$, east is $90°$, south is $180°$, and west is $270°$.

Output

The output consists of one line per input case containing all possible solutions. Each solution consists of two real numbers (with two digits after the decimal place) indicating the angle a_3 and distance d_3 for the next observation.

Sample Input	Sample Output
90.0 100.0 90.0 110.0	90.00 120.00
90.0 100.0 270.0 10.0	270.00 230.00
90.0 100.0 180.0 50.0	199.93 64.96 223.39 130.49

14.7.7 Trees on My Island

PC/UVa IDs: 111407/10088, **Popularity:** C, **Success rate:** average **Level:** 3

I have bought an island where I want to plant trees in rows and columns. The trees will be planted to form a rectangular grid, so each can be thought of as having integer coordinates by taking a suitable grid point as the origin.

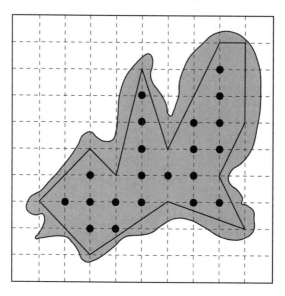

A sample of my island

However, my island is not rectangular. I have identified a simple polygonal area inside the island with vertices on the grid points and have decided to plant trees on grid points lying strictly inside the polygon.

I seek your help in calculating the number of trees that can be planted.

Input

The input file may contain multiple test cases. Each test case begins with a line containing an integer N ($3 \leq N \leq 1,000$) identifying the number of vertices of the polygon. The next N lines contain the vertices of the polygon in either the clockwise or counterclockwise direction. Each of these N lines contains two integers identifying the x- and y-coordinates of a vertex. You may assume that the absolute value of all coordinates will be no larger than 1,000,000.

A test case containing a zero for N in the first line terminates the input.

Output

For each test case, print a line containing the number of trees that can be planted inside the polygon.

Sample Input

```
12
3 1
6 3
9 2
8 4
9 6
9 9
8 9
6 5
5 8
4 4
3 5
1 3
12
1000 1000
2000 1000
4000 2000
6000 1000
8000 3000
8000 8000
7000 8000
5000 4000
4000 5000
3000 4000
3000 5000
1000 3000
0
```

Sample Output

```
21
25990001
```

14.7.8   Nice Milk

PC/UVa IDs: 111408/10117, **Popularity:** C, **Success rate:** low   **Level:** 4

Little Tomy likes to cover his bread with milk. He does this by dipping it so that its bottom side touches the bottom of the cup, as in the picture below:

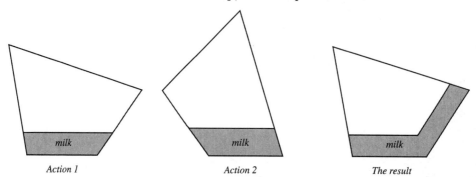

Action 1   Action 2   The result

Since the amount of milk in the cup is limited, only the area between the surface of the milk and the bottom side of the bread is covered. Note that the depth of the milk is always h and remains unchanged with repeated dippings.

Tomy wants to cover this bread with largest possible area of milk in this way, but doesn't want to dip more than k times. Can you help him out? You may assume that the cup is wider than any side of the bread, so it is possible to cover any side completely.

Input

Each test case begins with a line containing three integers n, k, and h ($3 \le n \le 20$, $0 \le k \le 8$, $0 \le h \le 10$). A piece of bread is guaranteed to be a convex polygon of n vertices. Each of the following n lines contains two integers x_i and y_i ($0 \le x_i, y_i \le 1{,}000$) representing the Cartesian coordinates of the ith vertex. The vertices are numbered in counterclockwise order. The test case $n = 0$, $k = 0$, $h = 0$ terminates the input.

Output

Output (to two decimal places) the area of the largest possible bread region which can be covered with milk using k dips. The result for test case should appear on its own line.

Sample Input

```
4 2 1
1 0
3 0
5 2
0 4
0 0 0
```

Sample Output

```
7.46
```

14.8   Hints

14.1 How do we best deal with the telephone pole constraint?

14.2 Comparing each point against each other point might be too slow. Can we use the fact that we are only interested in a *nearby* closest pair to reduce the number of comparisons?

14.3 Is the data better explicitly represented as an $l \times w$ matrix or left compressed as in the input format?

14.4 How can we best represent the region of possible locations? Is it always a convex polygon?

14.5 Is it easier compute the difference between the two areas or compute the area of each external pocket?

14.6 How do multiple solutions possibly arise?

14.7 Is this a candidate for Pick's theorem or is there a better way?

14.8 Does some form of greedy algorithm provably maximize the milk-covered area, or must we use exhaustive search?

A
Appendix

Achieving top performance in a programming contest or any other sporting event is not purely a function of talent. It is important to know the competition, to train correctly, and to develop the proper strategies and tactics in order to compete successfully.

In this chapter, we will introduce the three most important programming contests, namely, the *ACM International Collegiate Programming Competition* for college students, the *International Olympiad in Informatics* for high school students, and finally the *TopCoder Challenge* for all practicing programmers. We discuss the history, format, and entry requirements for each contest. Further, we have interviewed top contestants and coaches so we can pass their training and strategy secrets on to you.

A.1 The ACM International Collegiate Programming Contest

The ACM International Collegiate Programming Contest (ACM ICPC) is the forum where computer science students show the world they have the right stuff. The ICPC has grown steadily in numbers, excitement, and prestige since its founding in 1976. The 2002 competition attracted 3,082 three-person teams representing over 1,300 schools in 67 countries, plus countless other students who participated in associated local and on-line programming contests.

The format of the contest is as follows. Each team is composed of three students, and given a collection of five to ten programming problems. Only one computer is allocated to each team, so coordination and teamwork are essential.

The winner is the team which correctly solves[1] the most problems within the specified time limit, typically about five hours. No partial credit is awarded, so only completely correct programs count. Ties between teams are broken by comparing the elapsed time needed to get the solutions accepted. Thus the fastest programmers (as opposed to the fastest programs) win. No points are given for programming style or efficiency, provided the program completes within the several seconds the judges typically allot for testing. Time penalties of 20 minutes are administered for every unsatisfactory program submitted to the judges, thus providing incentive for students to check their work carefully.

We asked the members and coaches of top teams from the 2002 ACM ICPC for their training and competition secrets. Here is what we learned....

A.1.1 Preparation

Team Selection and Coaching

It is the coach's job to select the members of his/her school's team. Graduate students serve as coaches at some schools, including Cornell and Tsinghua University. Distinguished and caring faculty do the job at others, including Duke and Waterloo. The constant is that good teams require careful selection and effective leadership. Both types of coaches can be highly successful, as the excellent performance of all these schools demonstrates.

Many top teams run local contests to select teams for regional competition. Waterloo Coach Gordon Cormack prefers individual contests to team contests to lower entry barriers for loners, and then selects the best individuals for his team. By using the contest hosting services of the Universidad de Valladolid robot judge, such contests can be relatively easy to organize and administer.

The best teams go through extensive training. For example, Waterloo practices as a team two or three times a week in an environment similar to the one used during the finals.

Resources

ACM ICPC rules permit teams to bring any printed material they wish for use at the contest but allow no access to online material. Books are carefully checked for CD-ROMs, and network connectivity is typically cut or sniffer programs employed make sure no one gets to the web.

What are the best books to study from, beyond the one you are holding in your hands? As a general algorithms reference, we recommend Skiena's *The Algorithm Design Manual* [Ski97], and many contestants and coaches without our degree of self-interest agree. Especially popular are books which contain implementations of algorithms in a real programming language, such as Sedgewick [Sed01] for graph algorithms and O'Rourke [O'R00] for computational geometry. However, expect a painful debugging

---

[1] At least correctly enough to satisfy the judges. Legal battles have been fought over this distinction.

session after typing someone else's routine from a book – unless you really understand it. Warns Cormack, "code is a lot less useful than you think, unless you have actually composed it and/or typed it in." Reference manuals for your favorite programming language and associated libraries are also a must.

Well-prepared teams bring printouts of their solutions to old problems just in case they are given something similar to one they have seen before. Christian Ohler of the University of Oldenburg (Germany) stresses the importance of canned geometry routines. "You're doomed if you don't have them prepared and pre-tested."

Such templates are particularly important if you will be using Java. Subroutines providing exception-less I/O and parsing the most common data types are complicated, yet essential to get anything working. It may be useful to have such routines typed in by a team member at the start of the competition while the rest of the team reads the problems.

Training

The best training resource is the Universidad de Valladolid robot judge. At least 80% of last year's finalists trained on the judge. Regular online contests are held at *http://acm.uva.es/contest/*, with increasing frequency around the time of the regional and international competitions. Check the webpage for schedules and other information.

Ural State University (*http://acm.timus.ru/*) and the Internet Problem Solving Contest (IPSC) (*http://ipsc.ksp.sk/*) also maintain online judges, running contests with similar functionality. The USA Olympiad team website *http://www.usaco.org* contains lots of interesting problems and material.

Many students like to think through solutions to past contests, even if they don't go so far as to implement them. Such problems are available from the official ACM ICPC website *http://www.acmicpc.org*. Rujia Liu of Tsinghua University notices that different types of problems appear in different countries. He finds Asian problems "very strange and difficult" and thus good for think-through analysis. North American problems tend to be better for programming practice under contest conditions but require less deep algorithmics.

A.1.2 Strategies and Tactics

Teamwork

Teams in the ICPC consist of three people. With only one computer per team, there is a premium on teamwork. Teams which fight for the terminal go nowhere. Zhou Jian from Shanghai Jiaotong University (the 2002 world champions) puts it this way: "The goal of everything you do is to make the team's result better, not to do your personal best in the contest."

Most successful teams assign the individual members different roles depending upon their individual skills. A typical organization identifies one student as the *coder*, the jockey who rides the keyboard most of the contest due to his or her superior language and typing skills. Another student is the *algorist*, the one best at cracking the problem and sketching out solutions. The third student is the *debugger*, one who works off-line from printouts of the program and output traces to fix things while freeing the coder and the keyboard for other problems.

Of course, these roles change during the flow of the contest and vary considerably from team to team. Some teams use a designated leader to decide which member gets which problems and who has control of the machine at any given time.

Certain teams adopt special strategies for reading the problems. Most efficient seems to be dividing them up among the team members to read in parallel, since the easiest problems may be in the back of the package. When someone finds an easy problem, they start to go at it, or hand it off to the most appropriate team member. On some international teams, the best English reader is assigned the task of skimming the problems and parceling them out among the team.

Contest Tactics

- *Know Your Limitations* — Since you only get credit for correct solutions, identify the easiest problems and work on them first. Often easy-sounding problems have some dirty trick or ambiguous specification which leads to repeated and frustrating wrong answers. Shahriar Manzoor of the Bangladesh University of Engineering and Technology has the following advice: If your solution to the easiest problem in the contest is rejected for unclear reasons, have another team member redo the problem to avoid the mind traps you fell into.

- *Keep an Eye on the Competition* — If possible, try to view the current standings and find out which problems are being solved most frequently. If your team has not tried this problem, go for it! Odds are it is relatively easy.

- *Avoid Wrong Answers* — Rujia Liu of Tsinghua thinks correctness is much more important than speed. "We missed finishing among the top three teams this year because of time penalties from wrong answers." Reducing such penalties requires adequate testing before submission and discussion among team members to make sure the problem is properly understood.

- *Halting Problems* — The message *time limit exceeded* does not always imply an algorithmic problem. You could be in an infinite loop because of problems reading the input [Man01]. Perhaps your program is waiting for input from standard IO when the judge is expecting you to take input from a file. Or maybe you have the wrong input data format, such as assuming termination with a 0 symbol when the judge terminates input with end of file.

- *Know Your Compiler* — Certain programming environments have options which can make life easier for you. Flags which limit memory allocation can help test solutions when the contest enforces certain memory limits. "Eliminate surprises by anticipating the environment," says Gordon Cormack.

- *Keep the Machine Busy* — Cormack urges his team to "always use the keyboard, even if you are just typing in the shell of a program for reading input."

- *Clean Debugging* — How do you debug in the absence of so little information? All the judge will tell you is that your program is wrong. You cannot see the example you are failing on. Judging problems occasionally occur, but usually you have a bug if your program is not accepted. A clean printout of your program and a cool head are your best tools.

Carefully check the test data you are using to validate your program. One of our teams once lost two hours debugging a correct program because they typed the test data in wrong. But don't abandon incorrect solutions too quickly. Jens Zumbrugel from the University of Oldenburg warns never to "begin a new problem when you have just 90 minutes left and other problems still to debug."

- *Dirty Debugging* — Here is a dirty trick which might help if you really get stuck. Add a time-out loop or divide by zero at a point where you think your program is failing. You can get one bit of information in exchange for a 20-minute penalty. Don't try this too often or you are certain to incur the wrath of your teammates the moment your program is accepted.

- *Make Exceptions* — Daniel Wright of Stanford University recommends the following trick. If your language supports exception handling, use it to return a guess at the answer instead of crashing. For example, catch any exception and output that there is no solution or the input is invalid.

- *Stay Calm Amidst the Confusion* — Try not to get stressed and don't fight with your teammates. "Have fun and don't lose focus," Gordon Cormack urges his students. "You can do well by identifying and solving only the straightforward questions."

A.2   International Olympiad in Informatics

The International Olympiad in Informatics (IOI) is an annual competition in computer science for secondary/high school students. Since its founding in 1989, it has grown to be the second largest of the five international science Olympiads, behind only mathematics. In 2002, 78 countries sent 276 competitors to the finals in Korea, but these finalists were selected from literally hundreds of thousands of students striving to make their national teams.

The goals of the IOI are somewhat different from that of the ACM ICPC. Participants typically have not yet selected a career path; the IOI seeks to stimulate their interest in informatics (computing science). The IOI brings together exceptionally talented pupils from various countries so they can share scientific and cultural experiences.

A.2.1   Participation

The IOI is hosted in a different country each year: Wisconsin, USA, in 2003; Greece in 2004; and Poland in 2005. Each participating nation sends a delegation of four students and two accompanying coaches. The students compete individually and try to maximize their score by solving a set of programming problems during two competition days. Typically, students have five hours to do three questions in each day's session.

Every country has its own procedure to select its national team. Certain countries, such as China and Iran, give screening exams to literally hundreds of thousands of students to identify the most promising prospects. Most nations run more modest screening exams to reduce the field to 20 or so candidates. These students are given intensive training under the eyes of the national coach, who then picks the four best students to represent them.

The USA Computing Olympiad maintains an excellent training program at *http://train.usaco.org* and runs a series of Internet programming competitions which anyone may participate in. To be considered for the United States team, you must compete in the U.S. Open National Championship tournament. This requires proctoring by a teacher at your local high school. Top finishers are invited to the USA training camp for additional training and final team selection. Canada weeds through about 1,000 candidates through screening exams to select 22 for a week-long training camp.

A.2.2 Format

Unlike the ACM ICPC, the Olympiad provides for partial credit. Each problem typically has ten test inputs and you get 10 points for each input you successfully solve. Typically three problems are given on each of the two days, for a maximum possible contest score of 600.

All problems (called *tasks* in IOI lingo) involve computations of an algorithmic nature. Whenever algorithmic efficiency is important, they aim to provide at least one grading input where inefficient program can also score some points. But IOI Scientific Committee member Ian Munro says, "It is hard to design questions that give some credit to most competitors yet are still able to distinguish at the top."

A class of problems unique to the IOI are *reactive tasks* which involve live input [HV02]. These interact with your program through function calls instead of data files. For example, you may be asked to explore a maze, where a function call tells you whether your next move hits the wall or not. Or you might be asked to write a game-playing program which must interact with a real opponent.

Students were offered a choice of either Linux or Windows as a programming environment at the 2002 competition. Pascal and C/C++ were possible programming languages. Students are not allowed access to any printed or online reference material.

Grading of IOI submissions is done after the end of the session, not online as in the ACM ICPC. As in typical course exams, students do not know their score until the grades are announced.

The IOI is the least corporate of the major programming contests. This lends it a more academic character according to Daniel Wright – who has reached the finals of all three contests discussed in this book. The difference shows up in the accommodations. IOI contestants stay in university dorms while ICPC/TopCoder finalists are put up in luxury hotels.

A.2.3 Preparation

United States IOI coach Rob Kolstad encourages all interested students to work hard at the training website and compete in preliminary contests before the U.S. Open. He tries to teach his students to use effective time management during the contest. Gordon Cormack, who doubles as Canada's IOI coach, encourages his students to break the "debug-until-it-sorta-works habit" and strive for correct solutions which solve all cases in the time available. He goes so far as to remove the debugger from his student's hands to help them achieve greater focus.

There is agreement that IOI problems are somewhat different than the ACM ICPC problems. According to Kolstad, IOI problems are "totally algorithmic" and are more clearly stated, avoiding "trickery or clever inputs." ACM ICPC problems have more issues with input checking and output formatting.

IOI problems "are about the same level of difficulty as the ACM problems" according to Cormack. They sometimes have shorter solutions than the ACM problems: after all, it is a single-student contest instead of a team effort. They are designed so that simple, relatively inefficient programs will solve at most a few of the inputs, but that cleverness is necessary for full credit. Past problems are available from the official IOI website, *http://olympiads.win.tue.nl/ioi/*. This site also contains pointers to two officially recommended books, Kernighan and Pike's *The Practice of Programming* [KP99] and, we are proud to say, Skiena's *The Algorithm Design Manual* [Ski97].

A strong background in mathematics seems necessary for top-flight competition. The 2001 IOI Champion, Reid Barton of the United States, also won the International Mathematics Olympiad and likely did right well when it came time for applying to college.

Participation in the IOI is good preparation for the ACM ICPC contest. There is a tremendous overlap between this year's IOI contestants and next year's ACM ICPC finalists. For example, all three members of Tsinghua's 2002 ACM ICPC team (which finished in 4th place) were drawn from the top 20 Chinese IOI 2001 candidates. Similarly, about half of the TopCoder "all-stars" were previously top performers in the IOI or ACM ICPC.

A.3 Topcoder.com

There are many good reasons for participating in programming contests. You can have fun while you improve both your programming skills and job prospects in the bargain. The programming challenge problems appearing in this book are suggestive of the interview "puzzle" problems many advanced companies give all new job applicants.

From somewhere in this vein arises TopCoder, a company which uses programming contests as a tool to identify promising potential employees and provides this information to its clients. The big draw of TopCoder contests is money. The 2002 TopCoder Collegiate Challenge was sponsored by Sun Microsystems and awarded $150,000 in prizes. Daniel Wright of Stanford University walked off with the $100,000 top prize and graciously shared his secrets with us.

TopCoder has a slick website (*www.topcoder.com*) with news articles about recent competitions which make it look almost like the sports pages. They maintain practice contests on their website to help you train for the weekly tournaments, each of which consist of three programming problems. Over 20,000 international programmers have registered as participants since the weekly tournaments started in 2001. TopCoder has paid out about $1 million in prizes to date.

The format of TopCoder contests is evolving quickly as they hunt for the most appropriate business model. Preliminary rounds are held over the web, with the final rounds of big tournaments held on site.

Each of these rounds shares the same basic format. The coders are divided into "rooms" where they compete against the other coders. Each round starts with a *coding phase* of 75–80 minutes where the contestants do their main programming. The score for each problem is a decreasing function of the time from when it was first opened to when it was submitted. There is then a 15-minute *challenge phase* where coders get to view the submissions from other contestants in their room and try to find bugs. Coders earn additional points by submitting a test case that breaks another competitor's program. There is no partial credit for incorrect solutions.

Most people seem to tackle the problems in increasing order of difficulty, although Wright likes to go for the higher-value problems if he doesn't think there will be time to solve all three. TopCoder allows resubmissions, at the cost of a time penalty, so there is some strategy in deciding when to submit and when to test. Time pressure is a critical factor in TopCoder competitions. To gain speed, Wright encourages competitors to learn to use their libraries effectively.

The coding phase of the contest is generally more important than the challenge phase, because the number of points for a challenge is not enough to make up for a difference in the number of problems solved. To plan his challenges, Wright skims through solutions to see if the algorithm makes sense. He pounces when it is an algorithm he considered but rejected as incorrect. More often he finds typos and off-by-one bugs.

A.4   Go to Graduate School!

If you find the programming challenges presented in this book interesting, you are the kind of person who should think about going to graduate school. Graduate study in computer science involves courses in advanced topics that build upon what you learned as an undergraduate; but more importantly you will be doing new and original research in the area of your choice. All reasonable American doctoral programs will pay tuition and fees for all accepted Ph.D students, plus enough of a stipend to live comfortably if not lavishly.

Making the finals of the ACM International Collegiate Programming Contest or the International Olympiad on Informatics, or even being a top finisher in a regional contest, is a tremendous achievement. It clearly suggests that you have the right stuff for advanced study. I would certainly encourage you to continue your studies, ideally by coming to work with me (Steven Skiena) at Stony Brook! My group does research in a variety of interesting topics in algorithms and discrete mathematics. Please check us out at *http://www.algorist.com/gradstudy.*

So I hope you will come to join us. By the way, official ACM ICPC rules permit each team to contain one first-year graduate student. Maybe you can help take us to the finals next year!

A.5   Problem Credits

The first name listed is the person who developed, commissioned, or curated the problem in question, and granted us permission to use it in this book. Subsequent names (if any) refer to others who wrote or worked on the problem. We thank all for their contributions to this project.

	PC ID	UVa	Title	Sponsor/Authors
1.1	110101	100	The $3n + 1$ problem	Owen Astrakan
1.2	110102	10189	Minesweeper	Pedro Demasi
1.3	110103	10137	The Trip	Gordon Cormack
1.4	110104	706	LCD Display	Miguel Revilla, Immanuel Herrman
1.5	110105	10267	Graphical Editor	Alexander Denisjuk
1.6	110106	10033	Interpreter	Gordon Cormack
1.7	110107	10196	Check the Check	Pedro Demasi
1.8	110108	10142	Australian Voting	Gordon Cormack
2.1	110201	10038	Jolly Jumpers	Gordon Cormack, Wim Nuij
2.2	110202	10315	Poker Hands	Gordon Cormack
2.3	110203	10050	Hartals	Shahriar Manzoor, Rezaul Alam Chowdhury
2.4	110204	843	Crypt Kicker	Gordon Cormack
2.5	110205	10205	Stack 'em Up	Gordon Cormack
2.6	110206	10044	Erdös Numbers	Miguel Revilla, Felix Gaertner
2.7	110207	10258	Contest Scoreboard	Gordon Cormack, Michael Van Biesbrouck
2.8	110208	10149	Yahtzee	Gordon Cormack
3.1	110301	10082	WERTYU	Gordon Cormack
3.2	110302	10010	Where's Waldorf?	Gordon Cormack
3.3	110303	10252	Common Permutation	Shahriar Manzoor
3.4	110304	850	Crypt Kicker II	Gordon Cormack
3.5	110305	10188	Automated Judge Script	Pedro Demasi
3.6	110306	10132	File Fragmentation	Gordon Cormack, Charles Clarke
3.7	110307	10150	Doublets	Gordon Cormack
3.8	110308	848	Fmt	Gordon Cormack
4.1	110401	10041	Vito's Family	Miguel Revilla, Pablo Puente
4.2	110402	120	Stacks of Flapjacks	Owen Astrakan
4.3	110403	10037	Bridge	Gordon Cormack
4.4	110404	10191	Longest Nap	Pedro Demasi
4.5	110405	10026	Shoemaker's Problem	Alex Gevak, Antonio Sánchez
4.6	110406	10138	CDVII	Gordon Cormack
4.7	110407	10152	ShellSort	Gordon Cormack, Charles Clarke
4.8	110408	10194	Football (aka Soccer)	Pedro Demasi
5.1	110501	10035	Primary Arithmetic	Gordon Cormack
5.2	110502	10018	Reverse and Add	Erick Moreno
5.3	110503	701	The Archeologist's Dilemma	Miguel Revilla
5.4	110504	10127	Ones	Gordon Cormack, Piotr Rudnicki
5.5	110505	847	A Multiplication Game	Gordon Cormack, Piotr Rudnicki
5.6	110506	10105	Polynomial Coefficients	Alexander Denisjuk
5.7	110507	10077	Stern-Brocot Number System	Shahriar Manzoor, Rezaul Alam Chowdhury
5.8	110508	10202	Pairsumonious Numbers	Gordon Cormack, Piotr Rudnicki
6.1	110601	10183	How Many Fibs?	Rujia Liu, Walter Guttmann
6.2	110602	10213	How Many Pieces of Land?	Shahriar Manzoor
6.3	110603	10198	Counting	Pedro Demasi
6.4	110604	10157	Expressions	Petko Minkov
6.5	110605	10247	Complete Tree Labeling	Shahriar Manzoor
6.6	110606	10254	The Priest Mathematician	Shahriar Manzoor, Miguel Revilla
6.7	110607	10049	Self-describing Sequence	Shahriar Manzoor, Rezaul Alam Chowdhury
6.8	110608	846	Steps	Gordon Cormack, Piotr Rudnicki
7.1	110701	10110	Light, More Light	Udvranto Patik, Sadi Khan, Suman Mahbub
7.2	110702	10006	Carmichael Numbers	Manuel Carro, César Sánchez
7.3	110703	10104	Euclid Problem	Alexander Denisjuk
7.4	110704	10139	Factovisors	Gordon Cormack
7.5	110705	10168	Summation of Four Primes	Shahriar Manzoor
7.6	110706	10042	Smith Numbers	Miguel Revilla, Felix Gaertner
7.7	110707	10090	Marbles	Shahriar Manzoor, Rezaul Alam Chowdhury
7.8	110708	10089	Repackaging	Shahriar Manzoor, Rezaul Alam Chowdhury

	PC ID	UVa	Title	Sponsor/Authors
8.1	110801	861	Little Bishops	Shahriar Manzoor, Rezaul Alam Chowdhury
8.2	110802	10181	15-Puzzle Problem	Shahriar Manzoor, Rezaul Alam Chowdhury
8.3	110803	10128	Queue	Marcin Wojciechowski
8.4	110804	10160	Servicing Stations	Petko Minkov
8.5	110805	10032	Tug of War	Gordon Cormack
8.6	110806	10001	Garden of Eden	Manuel Carro, Manuel J. Petit de Gabriel
8.7	110807	704	Color Hash	Miguel Revilla, Pablo Puente
8.8	110808	10270	Bigger Square Please...	Rujia Liu
9.1	110901	10004	Bicoloring	Manuel Carro, Álvaro Martínez Echevarría
9.2	110902	10067	Playing With Wheels	Shahriar Manzoor, Rezaul Alam Chowdhury
9.3	110903	10099	The Tourist Guide	Shahriar Manzoor, Rezaul Alam Chowdhury
9.4	110904	705	Slash Maze	Miguel Revilla, Immanuel Herrman
9.5	110905	10029	Edit Step Ladders	Gordon Cormack
9.6	110906	10051	Tower of Cubes	Shahriar Manzoor, Rezaul Alam Chowdhury
9.7	110907	10187	From Dusk Till Dawn	Rujia Liu, Ralf Engels
9.8	110908	10276	Hanoi Tower Troubles Again!	Rujia Liu
10.1	111001	10034	Freckles	Gordon Cormack
10.2	111002	10054	The Necklace	Shahriar Manzoor, Rezaul Alam Chowdhury
10.3	111003	10278	Fire Station	Gordon Cormack
10.4	111004	10039	Railroads	Miguel Revilla, Philipp Hahn
10.5	111005	10158	War	Petko Minkov
10.6	111006	10199	Tourist Guide	Pedro Demasi
10.7	111007	10249	The Grand Dinner	Shahriar Manzoor, Rezaul Alam Chowdhury
10.8	111008	10092	Problem With Problem Setter	Shahriar Manzoor, Rezaul Alam Chowdhury
11.1	111101	10131	Is Bigger Smarter?	Gordon Cormack, Charles Rackoff
11.2	111102	10069	Distinct Subsequences	Shahriar Manzoor, Rezaul Alam Chowdhury
11.3	111103	10154	Weights and Measures	Gordon Cormack
11.4	111104	116	Unidirectional TSP	Owen Astrakan
11.5	111105	10003	Cutting Sticks	Manuel Carro, Julio Mario
11.6	111106	10261	Ferry Loading	Gordon Cormack
11.7	111107	10271	Chopsticks	Rujia Liu
11.8	111108	10201	Adventures in Moving: Part IV	Gordon Cormack, Ondrej Lhotak
12.1	111201	10161	Ant on a Chessboard	Long Chong
12.2	111202	10047	The Monocycle	Shahriar Manzoor, Rezaul Alam Chowdhury
12.3	111203	10159	Star	Petko Minkov
12.4	111204	10182	Bee Maja	Rujia Liu, Ralf Engels
12.5	111205	707	Robbery	Miguel Revilla, Immanuel Herrman
12.6	111206	10177	(2/3/4)-D Sqr/Rects/Cubes?	Shahriar Manzoor
12.7	111207	10233	Dermuba Triangle	Arun Kishore
12.8	111208	10075	Airlines	Shahriar Manzoor, Rezaul Alam Chowdhury
13.1	111301	10310	Dog and Gopher	Gordon Cormack
13.2	111302	10180	Rope Crisis in Ropeland!	Shahriar Manzoor, Rezaul Alam Chowdhury
13.3	111303	10195	Knights of the Round Table	Pedro Demasi
13.4	111304	10136	Chocolate Chip Cookies	Gordon Cormack
13.5	111305	10167	Birthday Cake	Long Chong
13.6	111306	10215	The Largest/Smallest Box ...	Shahriar Manzoor
13.7	111307	10209	Is This Integration?	Shahriar Manzoor
13.8	111308	10012	How Big Is It?	Gordon Cormack
14.1	111401	10135	Herding Frosh	Gordon Cormack
14.2	111402	10245	The Closest Pair Problem	Shahriar Manzoor
14.3	111403	10043	Chainsaw Massacre	Miguel Revilla, Christoph Mueller
14.4	111404	10084	Hotter Colder	Gordon Cormack
14.5	111405	10065	Useless Tile Packers	Shahriar Manzoor, Rezaul Alam Chowdhury
14.6	111406	849	Radar Tracking	Gordon Cormack
14.7	111407	10088	Trees on My Island	Shahriar Manzoor, Rezaul Alam Chowdhury
14.8	111408	10117	Nice Milk	Rujia Liu

References

[AMO93]   R. Ahuja, T. Magnanti, and J. Orlin. *Network Flows*. Prentice Hall, Englewood Cliffs NJ, 1993.

[Ber01]   A. Bergeron. A very elementary presentation of the Hannenhalli-Pevzner theory. In *Proc. 12th Symp. Combinatorial Pattern Matching (CPM)*, volume 2089, pages 106–117. Springer-Verlag Lecture Notes in Computer Science, 2001.

[CC97]   W. Cook and W. Cunningham. *Combinatorial Optimization*. Wiley, 1997.

[COM94]   COMAP. *For All Practical Purposes*. W. H. Freeman, New York, third edition, 1994.

[dBvKOS00] M de Berg, M. van Kreveld, M. Overmars, and O. Schwarzkopf. *Computational Geometry: Algorithms and Applications*. Springer-Verlag, Berlin, second edition, 2000.

[DGK83]   P. Diaconis, R.L. Graham, and W.M. Kantor. The mathematics of perfect shuffles. *Advances in Applied Mathematics*, 4:175, 1983.

[Dij76]   E. W. Dijkstra. A discipline of programming. 1976.

[Gal01]   J. Gallian. Graph labeling: A dynamic survey. *Electronic Journal of Combinatorics*, DS6, www.combinatorics.org, 2001.

[GJ79]   M. R. Garey and D. S. Johnson. *Computers and Intractability: A guide to the theory of NP-completeness*. W. H. Freeman, San Francisco, 1979.

[GKP89]   R. Graham, D. Knuth, and O. Patashnik. *Concrete Mathematics*. Addison-Wesley, Reading MA, 1989.

[GP79]   B. Gates and C. Papadimitriou. Bounds for sorting by prefix reversals. *Discrete Mathematics*, 27:47–57, 1979.

[GS87]   D. Gries and I. Stojmenović. A note on Graham's convex hull algorithm. *Information Processing Letters*, 25(5):323–327, 10 July 1987.

[GS93]   B. Grunbaum and G. Shephard. Pick's theorem. *Amer. Math. Monthly*, 100:150–161, 1993.

[Gus97]   D. Gusfield. *Algorithms on Strings, Trees, and Sequences: Computer Science and Computational Biology*. Cambridge University Press, 1997.

[Hof99]   P. Hoffman. *The Man Who Loved Only Numbers: The Story of Paul Erdös and the Search for Mathematical Truth*. Little Brown, 1999.

[HV02]   G. Horvath and T. Verhoeff. Finding the median under IOI conditions. *Informatics in Education*, 1:73–92, also at *http://www.vtex.lt/informatics_in_education/* 2002.

[HW79]   G. H. Hardy and E. M. Wright. *An Introduction to the Theory of Numbers*. Oxford University Press, fifth edition, 1979.

[Kay00]   R. Kaye. Minesweeper is NP-complete. *Mathematical Intelligencer*, 22(2):9–15, 2000.

[Knu73a]   D. E. Knuth. *The Art of Computer Programming, Volume 1: Fundamental Algorithms*. Addison-Wesley, Reading MA, second edition, 1973.

[Knu73b]   D. E. Knuth. *The Art of Computer Programming, Volume 3: Sorting and Searching*. Addison-Wesley, Reading MA, 1973.

[Knu81]   D. E. Knuth. *The Art of Computer Programming, Volume 2: Seminumerical Algorithms*. Addison-Wesley, Reading MA, second edition, 1981.

[KP99]   B. Kernighan and R. Pike. *The Practice of Programming*. Addison Wesley, Reading MA, 1999.

[Lag85]   J. Lagarias. The $3x + 1$ problem and its generalizations. *American Mathematical Monthly*, 92:3–23, 1985.

[LR76]   E. Luczak and A. Rosenfeld. Distance on a hexagonal grid. *IEEE Transactions on Computers*, 25(5):532–533, 1976.

[Man01]   S. Manzoor. Common mistakes in online and real-time contests. ACM Crossroads Student Magazine, http://www.acm.org/crossroads/xrds7-5/contests.html, 2001.

[McD87]   W. McDaniel. The existance of infinitely many k-Smith numbers. *Fibonacci Quarterly*, 25:76–80, 1987.

[MDS01]   D. Musser, G. Derge, and A. Saini. *STL Tutorial and Reference Guide: C++ Programming with the Standard Template Library*. Addison-Wesley, Boston MA, second edition, 2001.

[Mor98]   S. Morris. *Magic Tricks, Card Shuffling, and Dynamic Computer Memories: The Mathematics of the Perfect Shuffle*. Mathematical Association of America, Washington, D.C., 1998.

[New96]   M. Newborn. *Kasparov Versus Deep Blue: Computer Chess Comes of Age*. Springer-Verlag, 1996.

[O'R00]   J. O'Rourke. *Computational Geometry in C*. Cambridge University Press, New York, second edition, 2000.

[PS03]   S. Pemmaraju and S. Skiena. *Computational Discrete Mathematics: Combinatorics and Graph Theory with Mathematica*. Cambridge University Press, New York, 2003.

[Sch94]   B. Schneier. *Applied Cryptography*. Wiley, New York, 1994.

[Sch97]   J. Schaeffer. *One Jump Ahead: Challenging Human Supremacy in Checkers.* Springer-Verlag, 1997.

[Sch00]   B. Schechter. *My Brain Is Open: The Mathematical Journeys of Paul Erdös.* Touchstone Books, 2000.

[Sed01]   R. Sedgewick. *Algorithms in C++: Graph Algorithms.* Addison-Wesley, third edition, 2001.

[Seu58]   Dr. Seuss. *Yertle the Turtle.* Random House, 1958.

[Seu63]   Dr. Seuss. *Hop on Pop.* Random House, 1963.

[Ski97]   S. Skiena. *The Algorithm Design Manual.* Springer-Verlag, New York, 1997.

[Sti02]   D. Stinson. *Cryptography: Theory and Practice.* Chapman and Hall, second edition, 2002.

[Wes00]   D. West. *Introduction to Graph Theory.* Prentice-Hall, Englewood Cliffs NJ, second edition, 2000.

[Wil82]   A. Wilansky. Smith numbers. *Two-Year College Math. J.*, 13:21, 1982.

[Wol02]   S. Wolfram. *A New Kind of Science.* Wolfram Media, 2002.

[ZMNN91]   H. Zuckerman, H. Montgomery, I. Niven, and A. Niven. *An Introduction to the Theory of Numbers.* Wiley, New York, fifth edition, 1991.

Index

TEXTS IN COMPUTER SCIENCE *(continued from page ii)*

Li and Vitányi, An Introduction to Kolmogorov Complexity
  and Its Applications, Second Edition

Merritt and Stix, Migrating from Pascal to C++

Munakata, Fundamentals of the New Artificial Intelligence

Nerode and Shore, Logic for Applications, Second Edition

Pearce, Programming and Meta-Programming in Scheme

Peled, Software Reliability Methods

Revesz, Introduction to Constraint Databases

Schneider, On Concurrent Programming

Skiena and Revilla, Programming Challenges: The Programming Contest
  Training Manual

Smith, A Recursive Introduction to the Theory of Computation

Socher-Ambrosius and Johann, Deduction Systems

Stirling, Modal and Temporal Properties of Processes

Zeigler, Objects and Systems